New Models of Be[r]
Theory and Treatm[

MW01051074

To Jack.
all y Best.
Ge[orge] Hg[man]

Honoring the centennial of Sigmund Freud's seminal paper *Mourning and Melancholia, New Models of Bereavement Theory and Treatment: New mourning* is a major contribution to our culture's changing view of bereavement and mourning, identifying flaws in old models and offering a new, valid and effective approach.

George Hagman and his fellow contributors bring together key psychoanalytic texts from the past 20 years, exploring contemporary research, clinical practice and model building relating to the problems of bereavement, mourning and grief. They propose changes to the asocial, intrapsychic nature of the standard analytic model of mourning, changes compatible with contemporary psychoanalytic theory and practice. Arguing that the most important goal of mourning is often to preserve, rather than give up the relationship to the deceased, this book provides a more positive, hopeful model. Crucially, it emphasizes the importance of mourning together, rather than alone.

New Models of Bereavement Theory and Treatment: New mourning will be the go-to resource for researchers, clinicians and interested lay people seeking a clear, accessible overview of contemporary mourning theory, useful in their daily lives and in clinical practice. It will appeal to psychoanalysts, psychotherapists and grief counsellors, as well as teachers, undergraduates and advanced students studying in the field.

George Hagman, LCSW, is a psychoanalyst and clinical social worker practicing in New York City and Stamford, Connecticut. A member of the faculty of the Training and Research Institute for Intersubjective Self Psychology, his most recent Routledge title is *Creative Analysis: Art, creativity and clinical process* (2014).

New Models of Bereavement Theory and Treatment

New mourning

Edited by George Hagman

Routledge
Taylor & Francis Group

LONDON AND NEW YORK

First published 2016
by Routledge
2 Park Square, Milton Park, Abingdon, Oxon OX14 4RN

and by Routledge
711 Third Avenue, New York, NY 10017

Routledge is an imprint of the Taylor & Francis Group, an informa business

British Library Cataloguing in Publication Data
A catalogue record for this book is available from the British
Library

Library of Congress Cataloging-in-Publication Data
Names: Hagman, George, editor.
Title: New models of bereavement theory and treatment : new
    mourning / edited by George Hagman.
Description: Abingdon, Oxon ; New York, NY : Routledge, 2016.
Identifiers: LCCN 2015039183 | ISBN 9781138809666 (hardback) |
    ISBN 9781138809673 (pbk.)
Subjects: LCSH: Bereavement. | Grief. | Grief therapy.
Classification: LCC BF575.G7 .N49 2016 | DDC 155.9/37—dc23
LC record available at http://lccn.loc.gov/2015039183

ISBN: 978-1-138-80966-6 (hbk)
ISBN: 978-1-138-80967-3 (pbk)
ISBN: 978-1-315-74989-1 (ebk)

Typeset in Times New Roman
by Apex CoVantage, LLC

Printed and bound in the United States of America by Publishers Graphics,
LLC on sustainably sourced paper.

This book is dedicated to the memories of John Alfred Hagman, Elena Davila Hagman, Jack Denham, Eleanor Denham, Mark Denham, Peter Denham, and Luke Kilroy Hagman.

Contents

Contributors

Robert Gaines, Ph.D., Supervising Analyst in Adult Psychoanalytic Program, Founding Director of the Child and Adolescent Psychotherapy Training Program, William Alanson White Institute; Faculty and Supervisor at the Child and Adolescent Psychotherapy Program, Westchester Institute for the Study of Psychoanalysis and Psychotherapy; Supervisor of the Manhattan Institute for Psychoanalysis.

George Hagman, LCSW, is a clinical social worker and psychoanalyst in private practice in New York and Stamford, Connecticut. He is on the faculty of the Training and Research Institute for Self Psychology, and the Westchester Center for the Study of Psychoanalysis and Psychotherapy. He is the author of *Aesthetic Experience: Beauty, creativity and the search for the ideal*, Rodopi (2006), *The Artist's Mind: A psychoanalytic perspective on creativity, modern art and modern artists*, Routledge (2010) and *Creative Analysis: Art, creativity and clinical process*, Routledge (2015).

Otto Kernberg, M.D., FAPA, Director of the Personality Disorders Institute at The New York–Presbyterian Hospital, Westchester Division and Professor of Psychiatry at the Weill Cornell Medical College; Training and Supervising Analyst of the Columbia University Center for Psychoanalytic Training and Research. Author of numerous books and articles.

Robert A. Neimeyer, Ph.D., is a professor in the Department of Psychology, University of Memphis, where he also maintains an active clinical practice. He has published 30 books, and serves as Editor of the journal *Death Studies*. The author of nearly 500 articles and book chapters, he is currently working to advance a more adequate theory of grieving as a meaning-making process, both in his published work and through his frequent professional workshops for national and international audiences.

Estelle Shane, Ph.D., Training Analyst at the Institute of Contemporary Psychoanalysis and the New Center for Psychoanalysis, Los Angeles. Co-author of *Intimate Attachments*, Guilford Press (1997).

Morton Shane, M.D., private practice, Los Angeles, CA; Faculty in the Department of Adult and Child Psychiatry at the University of California, Los Angeles. Co-author of *Intimate Attachments*, Guilford Press (1997).

R. Dennis Shelby, LCSW, Professor Emeritus at the Institute for Clinical Social Work, Chicago; Faculty at the Chicago Institute for Psychoanalysis; Chair of the Committee on Advocacy Relations, member of the Service Members and Veterans Initiative and Gender and Sexuality Committees of the American Psychoanalytic Association.

Joyce Slochower, Ph.D., APBB, Faculty in the New York University Postdoctoral Program. Author of many articles as well as *Holding and Psychoanalysis: A relational perspective* (1996; 2014) and *Psychoanalytic Collisions* (2006; 2014).

Preface
New mourning

It has been 100 years since Sigmund Freud published his seminal paper *Mourning and Melancholia*. In the course of the century an entire field of research and clinical practice developed out of Freud's model of mourning which became the standard for much of Western Society and Psychoanalysis in particular. Recently many researchers and clinicians have questioned Freud's assumptions and their wide-spread applications. *New Models of Bereavement Theory and Treatment: New Mourning* is a contribution to the sea change that has occurred in our culture's view of bereavement and mourning. Across disciplines, clinicians and researchers have questioned many of the assumptions that have influenced our conceptualizations about mourning over the past 80 years. Anna Aragno, Ph.D., in her chapter "Transforming Mourning: A New Psychoanalytic Perspective" (in *On Death and Endings: Psychoanalysts' Reflections on Finality, Transformations and New Beginnings*, edited by Willock, Bohm and Curtis for Routledge in 2007) refers to these developments as a "new wave" which has resulted in "key changes" in mourning theory and treatment. Given that psychoanalysis has played a central role in the development of modern mourning theory (Parkes, 1981; Jacobs, 1993; Rando, 1993), a review of the current status of bereavement research and clinical thinking in this area is called for. This book is a collection of papers written by prominent bereavement researchers and clinicians over the past 25 years. They have been selected for their relevance to psychoanalytically oriented clinicians. Several chapters were written by the volume's editor (henceforth referred to as "me," "I" or "myself") specifically for a psychoanalytic audience. We will see how some contemporary researchers and clinicians have proposed changes in the standard model of mourning that are highly compatible with contemporary psychoanalytic theory and practice. In addition, the contents of this book reflect my personal investment in the ideas and practices that they explore.

The papers in this book are both the discoveries and some of the products of my own bereavements. I read them and wrote some of my own in order to heal, to create something out of what I had endured and continue to endure to this day. The research that went into these papers helped me to articulate the unique nature of my experience of bereavement, the mourning process I engaged in, and the grief that I felt. As the reader will come to see, I have questioned the prevailing models of mourning and I argue that each of us experiences and responds to bereavement differently. I don't believe we should romanticize or standardize mourning or grief. In many cases bereavement is a cruel, senseless series of events with a horrible outcome. This isn't always true; there are instances of a "good death" (which is part of my point), but the tendency to standardize mourning, to insist that there is a normal, expectable course to the experience and that resolution and "moving on" is a normal outcome, is just not true and may often be harmful, or at least unhelpful, when used as a guide for psychotherapy.

The loss through death of an important other can be irresolvable, the suffering ineluctable and enduring. Life usually goes on, but we are never the same, and the losses that we endure leave their permanent mark. This book documents such a permanent mark for me and my effort to understand the diversity and disruptive power of my own and others' bereavements. It explores why we have come to believe what we believe about mourning and grief, and it suggests what really happens and how most people actually react.

Before proceeding further, let me clarify my use of the terms *bereavement, mourning* and *grief*. This is important given that the confusion of terms in the literature has had a significant impact on coherent dialogue. In particular, I have found that the three terms are used interchangeably, which reduces their specificity and usefulness. For my purposes I use the term *bereavement* when I am referring to the psycho-social-biological state and experience of the loss of an important other person to death. I use the term *mourning* when I am referring to the psychological response to bereavement. As you will see I understand *mourning* as a complex, evolving process that is unique to the particular nature of each bereavement. Finally, I use the term *grief* to refer to the emotional, affective component of mourning. Traditionally, grief has been associated with intense sadness, but I think we need to include all types of affective processes, sadness, humor, pride and sexual desire, even joy. In other words grief is any affective response to the experience of bereavement that a person feels during the process of mourning. Clearly, painful sadness is the most common affect but not the only one, and thus it must be understood in the context of a range of related emotional responses. Throughout the sections of this book I will use the terms as defined above. Other authors use a slightly different terminology. I will point out discrepancies if needed along the way.

At this point it would be useful to explain how I came to investigate bereavement and mourning. My story will be brief and selective, highlighting aspects of my experience as background to my later research. This is especially important in my case because a significant part of my research was my own self-exploration, conducted with the help of several therapist guides, but in the end it was my effort to understand my own experience, which led me to question many commonly held assumptions, subsequently offering a new, more open and realistic framework, a vision of a new way to understand and help bereaved and grieving people.

One day in 1964 my father noticed that he was unable to touch his pinky to his thumb. This was the inconspicuous beginning of the catastrophe that would destroy my family and disrupt the course of my life. I was 14, and he was 45 years old. Eventually he was diagnosed with Amyotrophic Lateral Sclerosis (ALS), or Lou Gehrig's disease. His muscle neurons were slowly and relentlessly weakening. Within four years he would be unable to walk, feed himself or dress. At the end, my mother, younger brother and I would have to assist him with many activities of daily living – a humiliating and depressing job for us and especially for him. A professor at Columbia University, he taught until the day he died in August 1969. At the end he used a microphone because he was unable to project his voice. Even then he was unintelligible. He came home and remarked to my mother that he never imagined his last class would have been as that one had been. That night he would die in his sleep. He was 50 years of age.

ALS is an insidious disease having a gradual and cumulative effect. Over time, the victims are subject to a cascading array of pains, humiliations and losses. The harm it causes may be unnoticeable at first, but eventually the destruction is complete. The worst part is the way it infiltrates daily life, and the patient and the family "get used to it." Eventually, as we did, you may even lose sight of the reality that there was a time before the illness. Disability and the specter of death become everyday companions, until you don't even notice their presence. You are blind to the most terrible and obvious truths.

For months after my father discovered the weakness in his hand, there was an ordeal of testing and diagnosis. At one point a doctor did surgery, rearranging tendons on his hand to restore motion to my father's thumb (the result of a misdiagnosis). Eventually, as further weakening became evident, the final diagnosis was arrived at. I don't know when this occurred. My knowledge was secondhand, I think, or overheard from my parents' discussions (and arguments). One evening my father left the house in a rage, which for some reason I knew was related to an argument about the illness. (I didn't know at the time, but my parents had been discussing a divorce prior to his illness. ALS quickly derailed whatever plans they may have made. I am sure that this fact contributed greatly to the misery that followed. My mother became trapped, caring for a dying man she no longer loved.) I remember little about those months. The way my father dealt with his illness was to stop talking about it and finally retreat into silence. In fact I don't remember ever talking together as a family about his illness. Nor did my parents ever talk to me directly, except one time. Eventually, we all became silent partners in the daily grind.

In fact there was little to no meaningful interactions between my father and me for many, many months. The single time I remember speaking with my father about his disease and eventual death was several years later. He was already very disabled and could walk only with assistance. When we visited our country cottage, he was forced to sit on the front porch because moving about the house and property was too difficult and risky. In addition, his speech had deteriorated, so he would talk less and we would often sit in silence looking at the lake. One day I ended up sitting with him for a time on the porch. As usual, we did not talk. This was when, for the first and last time, he spoke to me.

"If I had to choose," he said to me, "this would be the last way I would choose to die."

That was it. I said nothing in reply. It did not feel like an invitation to a conversation. I felt more like a witness to his statement of a fact. Even at the time, I was aware that there was something very wrong with communication in our relationship. If this was the best he could do (or I could do), it was pretty sad. We never discussed what was happening to him, or us, again, even when, eventually, towards the end, I would dress him, slipping his socks over his limp feet and helping him to the toilet. It was then especially that we never talked, never acknowledged what was going on – the mundane nightmare that we were enacting each morning. How sad and horrible those few minutes were for us.

On the other hand, my mother drank, becoming progressively chronically intoxicated. This added to our suffering. Of course the drinking did not help her. She just became sicker and sicker, until, after my father's death, she was the identified patient with emergency room visits and hospitalizations that we, her children, had to manage. Eventually my hatred for her became profound and at times unmanageable. I would rage at her for her drunkenness and pathetic state. She attacked and berated me for how I treated her. I came to hate myself as much as I hated her. I would realize much later that her alcoholism was the most destructive part of the disaster that enveloped us.

We, the children, had our roles, of course, and we were each tortured and damaged somewhat differently, but once again insidiously and in disfiguring ways. The worst part is that we were still children. The impact of illness and death on child development has been extensively studied, but to actually go through it is horrible. In our family, my older brother and sister were in college through many of those years, although I am sure even at a distance they were impacted. For the three of us who remained at home (I was the oldest with a younger brother and sister), the normal developmental challenges that we faced became skewed and disrupted by our parents' illnesses, our father's death and its aftermath.

The impact on my development was profound and enduring. Engagement in social life, academics and relationships were all negatively impacted. Normal developmental tasks were disrupted: self-development, individuation, resolution of Oedipal struggles, and attachment needs became more complex and blocked. Very troubling to me was my failure to engage fully in the social life at college, and my inability to choose a major. One striking thing (again in retrospect) was the lack of any awareness by the school that my father was terminally ill and that this might affect my schoolwork. Even though he was a professor at the university, none of my advisers or professors seemed aware of this. Of course I didn't tell them either (it didn't seem to be a significant fact to me), so as I became more preoccupied and anxious about what I wanted to do, no one put two and two together. In fact there was no need at the time for me to choose a major, one professor exasperatingly insisted. It felt essential to me, and impossible as well. When I did decide, my major (English literature) was an easy choice, so I guess that wasn't the real problem.

The full consequence for me of my father's illness and my mother's alcoholism didn't show itself until some years after his death, when my estrangement from my mother had become complete. I was 24 years old. Having taken a leave from college, my relationship with my girlfriend (one of my most important supports) had failed and we ended our relationship. Slowly I was coming apart. The most disturbing symptoms were the loss of a sense of the future, persistent depression, anxiety and self-doubt. One night I dreamed that my father and my girlfriend were in a car driving west away from me on the highway. I awoke in terror, and that day, I made my first appointment with a psychotherapist. I will not describe what was an extremely painful and wonderful relationship and therapy process. Suffice it to say, my recovery was an extraordinary struggle, but gradually over the next seven years I got better. Eventually I entered psychoanalysis and psychoanalytic training. During those years, I completed my BA degree at Columbia College as well as my master's in social work at Columbia. The illness and death of my father, and its impact and aftermath, was an important focus of both my psychotherapy and psychoanalysis. During my social work and psychoanalytic training, I had many opportunities to study the prevailing models of bereavement, mourning and grief, but it wasn't until towards the end of my seven-year psychoanalysis that I began to look at my experience and connect it to the familiar models of bereavement and mourning that I had studied.

Developments in my clinical psychotherapy practice contributed to my early research. To my surprise, I was referred a number of adult patients who shared the trauma of a parent's death during their adolescence. The death appeared to have had a similarly devastating impact on their psychological and social development (which was consistent with many papers on childhood bereavement that I had been reading). However, these patients also shared something that I was coming to view as important but often unnoticed: that is, the collapse, failure and/or absence of the surviving parent. Like myself, they had suffered a *double parent loss* as a result of the surviving parent's alcoholism, depression, withdrawal or, in one instance, incest. And in the course of their treatments (and my own analysis) I came to wonder whether the failure of the surviving parent might have been more traumatic than the other parent's death. If the surviving parent had been available to help the teenager mourn, would the death have been so damaging? Was the apparent failure to mourn a developmental issue (as some analysts claimed) or the absence of an empathic relationship to support him or her and facilitate the child's mourning? Some researchers confirmed this conjecture. "We mourn not alone but together," Erna Furman wrote. The point is that mourning depends on engagement with other survivors (most important for children, the living parent). As I will explain, this became the cornerstone of my rethinking of the entire analytic understanding of bereavement, mourning and grief. In addition, I learned that mourning was not about detaching from the dead and giving up the past, but finding a way to preserve it and make sense of it. One way we do this is by transforming and giving meaning to our relationship with the dead, perhaps even strengthening the tie, rather than decathecting from them. Bereaved children don't cling to the memory of their dead parent because they are unable to mourn; rather, it is by this means that they preserve their attachment and give it meaning. (In chapter 3, I explore in depth my findings regarding *double parent loss*.)

As I began my research in earnest, I was surprised to discover an entire literature that critiqued traditional mourning theory. Researchers like Robert Neimeyer, Ph.D., Wortman and Silver, the Strobes, etc., had in recent years not only questioned the assumptions of Western models of mourning, but had also begun to articulate new approaches.

One important discovery that I made was that Freud's description of mourning in his paper "Mourning and Melancholia" had no empirical backing. My review of earlier literature turned up little that would substantiate the assumptions that were the basis of Freud's claims. More to the point were the cultural beliefs and practices of mourning, which characterized Victorian and Edwardian periods of the nineteenth and early twentieth centuries. As you will read in chapter 1, Freud's view of mourning was composed of the common assumptions about relationships and grieving that characterized that time in the West. Extreme reactions such as he described were common during the nineteenth century when cultural leaders such as Queen Victoria promoted extreme mourning and highly visible practices expressing intense prolonged and painful grief.

In fact we are a long way from turn of the twentieth-century Vienna. Over the last century, the entire Western relationship to death, dying and bereavement has undergone profound changes. It is important to say here that Freud's model of mourning was put to use by psychoanalysis in two very different ways: (1) as a clinical model of mourning in response to bereavement, and (2) as a general psychological process which is engaged whenever a person must relinquish an important attachment, whether to an object, idea, internal representation, affect, etc. The two uses of the idea of mourning have had somewhat separate histories in psychoanalysis that I cannot get into here. The authors in this volume are primarily concerned with the first use, mourning in response to bereavement. In any case, by the 1940s and 1950s, the elaboration of a number of related models of mourning in response to bereavement models were being developed based on Freud's original article. The most important were a series of *Stage Models* that dominated the bereavement research for several decades. Researchers claimed that there was a biologically based response to bereavement that had uniform characteristics and had developed over millennia to serve important adaptive functions. It was during these years that the standard model of mourning was elaborated and promulgated across Western society and became the bedrock of modern clinical understandings and treatments of mourning. Let me briefly state the components of the Standard Model:

1   There is an identifiable, normal psychological mourning process.
2   The function of mourning is conservative and restorative, rather than transformative.

3   Mourning is a private, intrapsychic process rather than a social and relational one.
4   The affect of grief (painful sadness) arises spontaneously from within the individual, and denial and suppressions of grief lead to pathological outcomes.
5   Mourning has normal, standard characteristics, rather than being unique and personal.
6   Mourning is painful and sad, rather than involving a range of affects (including positive ones).
7   The central task of mourning is detachment (decathexis) rather than continuity.
8   The vicissitudes of psychic energy are the basis of the Standard Models; the meaning associated with the loss and recovery is not emphasized.
9   The normal mourning process leads to a point of resolution, rather than being open-ended and evolving.

As I pursued my personal analysis, worked with my bereaved patients and studied the bereavement literature, I found that the actual experience of bereavement, mourning and grief was fundamentally different from the Standard Model as described above. Each person's and/or each family's bereavement and subsequent mourning are unique, each one complex with variable, far reaching impact on the survivors' lives. Hence the mourning process itself fits no predictable or normal course or structure. Rather than conserving, bereavement disrupts life and compels people to transform their relationships and way of life. Most important, bereavement is experienced in a social context; hence the mourning process is an interpersonal, intersubjective process. The feelings evoked by loss are also highly variable and do not follow a prescribed process. Some people are distraught and sad; others are grateful and even joyful. It all depends on the specific psychology of the bereaved, his or her relationship to the deceased, the nature of the dying and death, and the larger social, cultural and historical context. The notion of the denial or pathological suppression of a normal, expectable expression of grief is not generally accurate. Mourning and grief are idiosyncratic and highly personal and may involve a range of different affects, from sadness to joy. And finally, most important, rather than giving up the dead, many bereaved people seek to elaborate and preserve the relationship with the dead and, through mourning, strengthen the meanings that the deceased had in their lives. Rather than coming to an endpoint, a resolution in which life returns to "normal," mourning and grief may be extended over time, becoming lifelong, and this may be a healthy, necessary response, enriching life even as it adds to our burden. Despite the pain, many of us come to value our losses and the meaning we find from our continuing ties with the dead.

New mourning is not just a psychoanalytic phenomenon. Over the last 20 years non-analytic bereavement research and grief therapies have changed fundamentally as well, and although psychoanalysis and bereavement studies have evolved their critiques in parallel, I believe we must ground our own analytic discoveries in the wide context of cross-disciplinary research. To this end Robert Neimeyer,

Ph.D., has graciously agreed to write an introduction to the current state of bereavement theory and clinical practice.

In chapter 1, "Mourning: A review and reconsideration," I explore the implications of the standard model of mourning for how we understand mourning and, importantly, our own bereavement experiences and mourning processes. I will review the components of the model in more detail and explore its history and why it became the dominant perspective on bereavement, mourning and grief. I will then demonstrate by means of clinical experience and research how and why the Standard Model is not accurate. I show the consequences of this misunderstanding for our treatment of bereaved people and how we help or hinder their mourning processes. Finally, I offer a way of approaching mourning from the point of view of tasks that the bereaved person must accomplish as he or she copes with the death of the other.

Chapters 2, 3 and 4 concern childhood bereavement and, in particular, the impact of parent loss. Chapter 2, "Object loss and selfobject loss" by Morton Shane and Estelle Shane, supports the notion that children are as fully capable of mourning as adults when provided with continuity, support and emotional connection. In chapter 3, "The psychoanalytic understanding and treatment of double parent loss," I look in depth at the problem of early parent loss. I argue that the failure to mourn in childhood is not linked to developmental capability but social context. Specifically, it focuses on the additional loss of the surviving parent through depression, addiction, incest, etc. In chapter 4, "Flight from the subjectivity of the other: Pathological adaptation to childhood parent loss," I examine a common clinical feature of childhood bereavement: fear of dependency and a reluctance to engage in the transference as a response to loss and abandonment. Using an in-depth clinical report, the reactivation of the motivation to engage in transference is illustrated.

Chapters 5, 6 and 7 address the social context of mourning and the role of others in facilitating or impeding mourning. In chapter 5, "Mourning theory reconsidered," R. Dennis Shelby argues that mourning involves more than the mourner and the deceased: the social context plays a crucial role in modulating the mourner's affect, subsequently assisting in the formation of the narrative and its integration into the overall structure of the self. The empathic responses of the selfobject environment also serve to orient the mourner back to the world of the living. The mourner's capacity to tolerate the affective dimension of mourning and the environmental response to the mourner's affect and situation in general are factors in the recovery process. In chapter 6, "The role of the other in mourning," I discuss the specific role that surviving others plays in facilitating mourning and how the appreciation of the role of the other in mourning impacts theory and clinical practice. In chapter 7, "Mourning and the holding function of shiva," Joyce Slochower discusses how the rituals and social interactions associated with "sitting shiva" play a part in the mourning process for Jewish individuals and families.

In chapter 8, "Self experience in mourning," I focus on the narcissistic dimension of mourning. The changing nature of the relationship to the deceased person in self experience (he or she as selfobject) and the process by which the bereaved person transforms the selfobject tie is explored. This leads to an examination of the basic function of mourning, and in particular the fate of the tie to the deceased person. In chapter 9, "Detachment and continuity," Robert Gaines discusses the question of detachment (decathexis) versus continuity. Gaines questions a basic assumption of the Standard Model – the need to give up the tie to the dead. In this lovely clinical chapter he argues that renewed attachment and the sense of relational continuity are at the heart of mourning – this paper moves us beyond decathexis towards meaning reconstruction and continuing bonds. Next, in chapter 10, "Some observations of the mourning process," Otto Kernberg supports the notion that in normal mourning there is an attempt to continue the relationship to the deceased after death, and this relationship plays an important role in the further elaboration of psychic structure, especially superego alterations.

In chapter 11, "Out of the analytic shadows: On the dynamics of commemorative ritual," Joyce Slochower extends her earlier work to consider the function of cultural rituals in facilitating the mourning process for individuals, families and larger social groups. In particular, she highlights the importance of rituals across the lifespan, serving multiple functions. She explains how mourning rituals "allow us to mark absence and create 'presence' as we access and sometimes reshape memory. Such rituals can create a sense of linkage to 'like mourners.' At their best, these acts help us deepen emotional connectedness and facilitate integrated remembering in a way that enriches and frees rather than binds."

In the final chapter 12, "New mourning," I summarize and review the past and present landscape of psychoanalytic thinking about bereavement, mourning and grief. I offer an up-to-date definition of mourning and examine the clinical implications of New Mourning Theory. Commenting on an earlier version of this chapter, Anna Aragno, Ph.D., describes it as "virtually a manifesto for a new view of mourning." The reader will find this chapter the most accessible, comprehensive and useful.

The papers that make up the chapters of this book have been previously published or presented. They have seemed to me over the years to be some of the best new mourning papers available, and as a group they constitute a comprehensive overview of New Mourning Theory and clinical practice. There are other equally important papers, which for a variety of reason I did not include in this selection. Most of these are discussed and referenced in chapter 12.

Conclusion

Psychoanalysts and psychoanalytic therapists are invariably concerned about the impact of bereavement on and the process of mourning of their patients. A number of volumes have been written on the subject, but as of yet there has been no book that can provide the analytic clinician with an accessible, useful overview of the New Mourning Theory and clinical practice. Albeit, there are several collections that reflect old beliefs; however, none have collected representative selections that reflect new findings and viewpoints. To be sure, there are non-analytic articles, manuals and self-help guides that deal with bereavement, mourning and grief. Almost invariably the perspective has been a non-psychoanalytic one, and in many instances the quality of these works is good. However, psychoanalytic therapists wishing to learn about mourning and acquire practice methods to assist bereaved patients have had to turn to these books, stepping away from psychoanalysis because there has not been a resource that is geared to their professional needs. In the present book I have tried to address this lack and provide psychoanalytically informed therapists with a clear accessible overview of contemporary mourning theory that will be of use to them in their daily practice. That being said, the authors of this volume are a diverse group. I did not evaluate the contributions based on school of thought, theoretical model, or clinical technique (as you will see in my own essays, my thinking and practice was evolving along with my observations and readings, and the models I used varied from year to year and paper to paper). The fact is, what matters about the articles in this collection is not their affiliations, but the nature of their clinical observations and the way in which even such a diverse group arrived at startlingly similar findings. Hence New Mourning Theory is not of any school or method; it is a broad set of observations that have required us to rethink some traditional assumptions. It is in that spirit that I have gathered this insightful group of analysts into one volume.

References

Jacobs, S. (1993). *Pathologic Grief: Maladaptations to Loss*. Washington, D.C.: American Psychiatric Press.
Parkes, C. (1981). *Bereavement: Studies of Grief in Adult Life*. Madison, CT: Int. U. Press.
Rando, T. (1993). *Treatment of Complicated Mourning*. Champlain, IL.: Research Press.

Acknowledgements

There is no way for me to adequately thank the people who helped me with this book. Over the years many people whom I may not even remember, and journal reviewers I never knew, have helped me. At the beginning Alan Roland conducted my analysis, which gave me the first insights into my own losses and mourning. Also, Alan encouraged me to write my first paper on Double Parent Loss and he refined the title, which had a big impact on me. Robert Friedman read the early, unwieldy manuscript and advised me to reexamine the clinical material. Finally, the fact that the American Psychoanalytic Association accepted the paper for presentation and James Herzog discussed it and liked it encouraged me to develop additional papers on mourning. As I continued to work on this subject and realized that Self Psychology was an effective explanatory model, Peter Zimmerman read several manuscripts and helped me refine my thinking from that perspective. Later, Robert Neimeyer was very supportive and eventually invited me to contribute a chapter to his book *Meaning Reconstruction and the Experience of Loss*, a modern classic. I want to thank Bob for agreeing to write the introductory essay for this book. I also want to thank Dennis Shelby, Estelle Shane, Morton Shane, Robert Gaines and Otto Kernberg for their wonderful, insightful papers. Joyce Slochower has recently been a great support, and I am lucky to have two of her excellent papers in this collection. And also, I want to thank the many people who have attended my readings and workshops on mourning over the years; your interest and support mattered, and your voices were heard. Thanks to Kate Hawes, my editor at Routledge, who encouraged me to produce this book. Finally, to my son Peter and daughter Elena, who both had to deal with death way too early. And to my wife Moira, whose companionship and love during our many losses has sustained me.

And thank you to the following publishers for granting me permission to reprint the following previously published articles:

John Wiley & Sons for chapter 1: Hagman, G. (1995), Mourning: A review and reconsideration, *International Journal of Psychoanalysis*, Vol. 76, pp. 909–925; chapter 6: Hagman, G. (1996), The role of the other in mourning, *Psychoanalitic Quarterly*, Vol. 65(2), pp. 327–352; and chapter 10: Kernberg, O. (2010), Some observations on the process of mourning, *International Journal of Psychoanalysis*, Vol. 91, pp. 601–619.

Taylor & Francis for chapter 2: Shane, M., & Shane, E. (1990), Object loss and selfobject loss: A contribution to understanding mourning and the failure to mourn, *Annual of Psychoanalysis*, Vol. 18, pp. 115–131; for chapter 4: Hagman, G. (1996), Flight from the subjectivity of the other: Pathological adaptation to early parent loss, in *Progress in Self Psychology*, Vol. 12, A. Goldberg (ed.), Hillsdale, N.J.: Analytic Press; for chapter 5: Shelby, D. (1994), Mourning theory reconsidered, in *Progress in Self Psychology: The Widening Scope of Self Psychology*, Vol. 9, A. Goldberg (ed.), pp. 169–189, Hillsdale, N.J.: Analytic Press; and chapter 7: Slochower, J. (1993), Mourning and the holding function of shiva, *Contemporary Psychoanalysis,* Vol. 29, pp. 352–367; for chapter 8: Hagman, G. (1995), Death of a selfobject: Towards a self psychology of the mourning process, in *Progress in Self Psychology*, Vol. 11, A. Goldberg (ed.), Hillsdale, N.J.: Analytic Press; for chapter 9: Gaines, R. (1997), Detachment and continuity: The two tasks of mourning, *Contemporary Psychoanalysis*, Vol. 33(4), pp. 549–571; and chapter 11: Slochower, J. (2011), Out of the analytic shadow: On the dynamics of commemorative ritual, *Psychoanalytic Dialogues*, Vol. 21(6), pp. 676–690.

The American Psychological Association for chapter 12: Hagman, G. (2001), Beyond decathexis: Towards a new psychoanalytic understanding and treatment of mourning, in *Meaning Reconstruction and the Experience of Loss*, R. Neimeyer (ed.), Washington, D.C.: American Psychological Association.

Introduction

Robert A. Neimeyer, Ph.D.,
University of Memphis, Memphis, TN

Editor's note: Dr. Robert Neimeyer is one of the foremost authorities on bereavement, mourning and grief research and clinical practices. As the author of hundreds of research papers and many volumes on contemporary grief therapies, he has had a deep and broad impact on our understanding of both normal and pathological responses to bereavement. His constructivist perspective has fundamentally altered our understanding of mourning. In particular, his concept of "meaning reconstruction" has moved us from a reductionist approach that emphasizes detachment and decathexis to a more flexible and "experience-near" perspective that appreciates the diverse and complex intrapsychic, relational and cultural processes by which we give meaning to the always stressful and often traumatic disruptions of human meaning caused by death. Although Neimeyer's influence on recent developments in psychoanalytic thinking on bereavement, mourning and grief may not always be recognized, I believe that the striking similarities in the findings of constructivist psychology and psychoanalysis are not a coincidence. As I will argue in chapter 1, there has been a revolution in our understanding of bereavement, mourning and grief that has been cross-disciplinary, with essential contributions coming from every corner of the university, clinical practice, and popular culture. Neimeyer has played an important role in the promotion and integration of these new perspectives. To this end I am very happy and grateful that he has offered to write the introduction to this volume of analytic papers. The ideas that Neimeyer shares in this chapter are at the center of contemporary research, as well as influencing broad developments in our culture's experience of bereavement, and as we delve into recent psychoanalytic findings in later chapters, we will see how psychoanalysis does not just complement the findings he discusses here, but psychoanalytic and contemporary grief therapy are fundamentally in agreement. I will elaborate on these areas of agreement in more detail in chapter 12.

This Introduction is an original contribution by Dr. Neimeyer.

Meaning in mourning: Theoretical advances in the practice of grief therapy

As a brilliant but troubled college student, Daniel had alternated between excelling in classes and succumbing to binges of drinking that challenged both his academic and social success. The decade that had followed college was similarly stormy, marked by lost jobs, a lost marriage and several rounds of treatment for substance abuse. Finally, in his early 30s, he moved back into his parents' home, stabilizing for a time before sliding back into the recurrent cycle of substance abuse.

It was in this context that Daniel arrived to his parents' home late one night, obviously inebriated, when his mother, Carol, met him. Exasperated, Carol broke off the ensuing confrontation between Daniel and his father about the son's behavior, suggesting that "they all get to bed and return to the discussion in the morning." For Daniel, however, morning never came. As Carol began to worry about him as noon approached, she opened the door of his silent bedroom to a scene of horror instantly stamped in her mind: her son, tangled in the sheets, torso off the bed, the bedding awash in a swath of blood. Rushing to him as she screamed for her husband, she attempted resuscitation as he called emergency services. Arriving to the scene within 20 minutes, the first responders rushed Daniel's unresponsive body to the hospital, where his death – apparently of drug overdose – was confirmed. Tormented by the horrific imagery of the death scene, as well as her guilt for not having recognized his condition that fateful night, Carol sought therapy with me a few months later.

After inviting Carol to share photos of her son on her iPhone and hearing stories of her pride and concern about his turbulent life, I was struck by the power of the death narrative to eclipse any sense of secure connection to her son "in spirit," though Carol was a religious person. I therefore introduced the possibility of doing a "slow motion replay" together of what she had seen, sensed, and suffered the morning she discovered her son's body, with the goal of helping her give voice to the silent story of the trauma, while being supported in managing the powerful emotions it triggered and in addressing the painful questions it posed. Bravely, Carol announced her readiness for this retelling, and I began with the events of the night before, the disturbed night of sleep for Carol that followed, and the careful unpacking in sensory detail of what unfolded as she, with increasing apprehension, opened her son's bedroom door. Braiding together the horrific images – the tangled body, the purple face, the splash of congealed red blood spilling from his mouth across the white sheets – with the associated feelings that welled up in her, we gradually walked through the experience, tracing its objective and subjective contours and the struggle to make sense of his death that ensued. Finally, as I asked what Carol would have done if she had been present at his dying, but unable to prevent it, she sobbed, "Just hold him, hold him . . . and tell him I loved him." Gently handing Carol a cushion, I watched as she spontaneously hugged it tightly to her chest and tearfully affirmed her love for her precious if imperfect child. After a few minutes, she set the pillow aside, dried her eyes, and noted how she felt "flooded with comfort" following the retelling, and less alone in a tragic story. Together, we then reflected on further healing steps that could be taken, including responsive engagement with the partly parallel, partly unique grief of her husband following a shared loss.

The death that ends the life of a loved one also punctuates, and frequently perturbs, the life stories of intimate survivors as well. When this disruption is profound and prolonged, and especially when the character of the death or the relationship with the deceased is complicated or problematic, mourners frequently seek professional therapy. Like Carol, they commonly do so hoping to find someone who can hear their accounts of love and loss without providing pabulum reassurance, and who can help them find some means of negotiating a life whose terrain has been made alien by their bereavement. Unfortunately, until recently, most therapists were equipped with only rudimentary resources for engaging these accounts, in the form of simplistic stage models of adaptation that carried few practical suggestions beyond the putative value of expressing anguished affect and "normalizing" the experience (Neimeyer, 2013). When complicated grief was addressed at all, it was commonly reduced to another diagnosable disorder such as depression or PTSD, whose treatment had at best inexact relevance to the unique separation distress at the heart of this condition, and the myriad ways in which this can find expression in the mourner's psychosocial world (Prigerson et al., 2009). Even sophisticated clinicians in the psychoanalytic tradition often remained beholden to Freud's (1917/1957) conception of grieving as a process of decathexis or withdrawal of emotional energy in the deceased in order to invest it in living relationships. In so doing, they frequently failed to integrate into their treatment of grieving patients recent advances in the psychoanalytic understanding of bereavement, mourning and grief found in contemporary ego psychology (Brenner, 1974; Furman, 1974; Kaplan, 1995), object relations (Baker, 2001; Kernberg, 2010; Volkan, 1981), self psychology (Hagman, 1995, 1996; Shane & Shane, 1990; Shelby, 1994), and interpersonal and relational psychoanalysis (Gaines, 1997; Slochower, 1996, 2011).

In the past 15 years, however, this situation has shifted substantially, as models and methods of grief therapy have proliferated and increasingly garnered research support. These developments have been truly cross-disciplinary, as evidenced by this volume of recent psychoanalytic papers, which at the very least complement many of the ideas that I will be discussing in this Introduction. Hence, my goal is to argue that these propitious developments lay the groundwork for a new psychodynamic approach to understanding and treating the bereaved; and I want to encourage psychoanalytically oriented clinicians to creatively integrate into their clinical practice models the range of newer theories, principles and procedures that address the wounds inflicted by the (sometimes traumatic) loss of key attachment relationships. To provide a context for this effort I will first sketch the outlines of a *meaning reconstruction* approach to grief and grief therapy, and then use this to organize the presentation of a handful of contemporary models of mourning, each of which suggests the relevance of specific techniques and practices. Finally, in the space available, I will offer an outline of a sample of these procedures, illustrating them with brief clinical vignettes from my practice, and pointing readers to resources for their further exploration.

Grief and the quest for meaning

Viewed in a constructivist perspective, grieving entails as a central process the *attempt to reaffirm or reconstruct a world of meaning that has been challenged by loss* (Neimeyer, 2002). That is, a fundamental feature of human functioning is to seek order, pattern and significance in the events of our lives, and in the course of doing so, to construct *a self-narrative*, defined as "an overarching cognitive-affective-behavioral structure that organizes the 'micro-narratives' of everyday life into a 'macro-narrative' that consolidates our self-understanding, establishes our characteristic range of emotions and goals, and guides our performance on the stage of the social world" (Neimeyer, 2004). Simply stated, we seek to live a life that we can make sense of, and that can make sense of us. The difficulty, of course, is that this quest for coherence poses a constantly moving target, as the conditions of impermanence and unwelcome change repeatedly unsettle our best efforts to scaffold a story with consistent themes, goals and – perhaps most importantly – intimate collaborators in the events of our lives (Neimeyer & Young-Eisendrath, 2015). The death of key attachment figures, especially under conditions that are premature, sudden, violent, or unjust, therefore can massively challenge our assumptive world and its grounding in principles of predictability, beneficence and control (Janoff-Bulman & Berger, 2000). Faced with an anguishing discrepancy between our core presuppositions and the reality of such loss, we are launched into a quest to reestablish abiding life themes or to rework them to find significance in our changed existence (Gillies, Neimeyer, & Milman, 2014; Park, 2010).

Over the past decade a good deal of evidence has accumulated to support the propositions of this meaning reconstruction model. For example an inability to make sense of the loss has been associated with more intense symptoms of prolonged grief disorder in bereaved young adults (Holland, Currier, & Neimeyer, 2006) as well as in parents who have lost children, where it accounts for as much as 15 times the variance in complicated grief symptomatology than does the passage of time (measured in weeks, months or years), the gender of the parent, or even whether the death was natural or violent (Keesee, Currier, & Neimeyer, 2008). In a cohort of older widowed persons, an unfulfilled struggle for meaning at 6 months after loss prospectively predicts higher levels of grief and depression a full 18 and 48 months later, whereas finding meaning early in bereavement predicts well-being and associated positive emotions four years after the death (Coleman & Neimeyer, 2010). Similarly, mourners who across a period of months show greater capacity to make meaning of their experience also move toward lower levels of complicated grief (Holland, Currier, Coleman, & Neimeyer, 2010), and such meaning making has "incremental validity" in predicting mental and physical health outcomes even after demographic characteristics, relationship to the deceased, manner of death and prolonged grief symptoms are taken into account (Holland, Currier, & Neimeyer, 2014). So powerful is the role of meaning making in predicting adjustment to bereavement that it accounts for essentially all of the difference between mourners who have lost loved ones to natural death and those, like Carol, who have lost them to suicide, homicide and fatal accident (Currier, Holland, & Neimeyer, 2006).

A narrative frame for pluralistic practice

Considered as complementary, rather than competitive, with psychodynamic approaches to psychotherapy, a meaning reconstruction model of bereavement offers a flexible framework for addressing the specific goals of grief therapy. Viewed through a narrative constructivist lens, the acute pursuit of meaning making in loss concentrates on (1) *processing the "event story" of the death*, and its implications for our ongoing lives, and (2) *accessing the "back story" of our lives with the deceased loved one*, in a way that restores a measure of attachment security (Neimeyer & Thompson, 2014). Each of these dialectics articulates with a range of contemporary bereavement theories and associated therapeutic practices, many of which are beginning to garner an evidence base that supports their efficacy.

Processing the event story of the loss

When mourners struggle with making sense of the death and its implications for their lives, they may contend with questions like: *What is my role or responsibility in what has come to pass? What part, if any, did human intention or inattention have in causing the death? What do my bodily and emotional feelings tell me about what I now need? How do my religious or philosophic beliefs help me accommodate this experience, and how are they changed by it in turn? Who am I in light of this loss, now and in the future? Who in my life can understand and accept what this loss means to me?* (Neimeyer & Thompson, 2014). In other words, the "effort after meaning" can unfold on any scale, from the focal (about a feature of the death itself or an internal feeling) to the global (about one's broader spiritual/existential concerns), as the mourner seeks to integrate the loss, and reconstruct his or her life. Two contemporary theories of grieving that dovetail with this perspective are Boelen et al.'s (2006) cognitive-behavioral model and Stroebe and Schut's (1999; 2010) Dual Process Model of Coping with Bereavement.

From a CBT perspective, grief becomes complicated when mourners *fail to integrate the reality of the death into their autobiographical memory*, in effect, when they are unable to update their schemas to take in the painful circumstance of their loved one's absence (Boelen, van den Hout, & van den Bout, 2006). This situation is often compounded by various forms of *experiential avoidance*, as when mourners attempt to mitigate intense grief by evading memories of the dying, or by no longer engaging in activities that were once associated strongly with the loved one. In operant conditioning terms, such constriction is positively reinforced by a reduction of distress in the moment, but only at the cost of an increasingly untenable posture of suppressing full recognition of the loss and circumscribing the survivor's life.

A second conceptualization that conjoins with a meaning reconstruction approach is the Dual Process Model (DPM), which posits two fundamental orientations in coping with bereavement (Stroebe & Schut, 1999, 2010). On the one hand, mourners engage the *loss orientation*, in which they reflect on the death, experience and try to modulate grief-related feelings, attempt to reorganize their bond to the deceased, and withdraw from the broader world to seek the support of a few trusted confidants. At other points, they engage in the *restoration orientation*, as they distract themselves from their grief by immersing themselves in work and other activities, and ultimately explore new roles and goals required by their changed lives. Thus, according to the DPM, mourners *oscillate* between these two means of coping with the loss, neither of which is viewed as dysfunctional in itself. Instead, only an inability to engage in one or the other orientation signals concern, though people differ in their degree of engagement with each as a function of personal disposition, gender and culture.

Common to these models is the view that complications in grieving arise when mourners are unable to "take in" the reality of the loss and integrate its implications for their ongoing lives. Accordingly, a number of evidence-based procedures have been developed to promote doing so, which are featured in a variety of therapies, as summarized below.

Restorative retelling of the event story of the death

Survivors of a difficult loss typically seek a context in which they can relate the story of their loved one's death, but rarely do they give voice to its most painful particulars: their mother's gasping for breath at the end of life, their own recurrent helplessness in the face of their child's advancing cancer, the picture of their partner hanging from a pipe in the basement, eyes bulging in a purple face following the suicide. Instead, these often fragmentary images live only as "silent stories" (Neimeyer, 2006) in their own thoughts and nightmares, persisting as a haunting and unspoken subtext to the highly edited stories shared with others.

In *restorative retelling*, Rynearson and his colleagues (Rynearson, 2006; Rynearson & Salloum, 2011) first establish a safe relational "container" for re-entering the detailed story of the dying, and ground the mourner in a more secure context (e.g. discussing what family members meant to one another before the loss, and what philosophic or religious beliefs they have relied on to deal with difficult times), before inviting a step-by-step recounting of the narrative of the dying as remembered or, as is commonly the case in violent death, imagined. Like Shear's protocol for *situational revisiting* of the story of the death (Shear, Boelen, & Neimeyer, 2011), Rynearson's procedure encourages the mourner to "walk through" a slow-motion replay of the events of the dying, often repeating the process on multiple occasions as the person fills in details, modulates difficult emotions with the therapist's assistance, and gradually gains greater mastery of the painful narrative. In both cases the goal is to help the mourner integrate the story of the death in the presence of a compassionate witness, ultimately being able to revisit the story with less avoidant coping, less emotional reactivity, and greater meaning. Further procedures to enhance the power of retelling are available elsewhere (Neimeyer, 2012c).

Data from an open trial on restorative retelling are encouraging in suggesting its efficacy in reducing traumatic arousal (Saindon et al., 2014), and Shear's Complicated Grief Therapy (CGT), in which revisiting the situation of the death is a cardinal procedure, has outperformed evidence-based therapy for depression in treating bereaved people in two major randomized clinical trials (Shear, Frank, Houch, & Reynolds, 2005; Shear et al., 2014). Related CBT protocols featuring prolonged exposure to difficult details associated with the loss have also garnered support in randomized clinical trials (RCTs) (Boelen, de Keijser, van den Hout, & van den Bout, 2007; Bryant et al., 2014).

An illustration of restorative retelling arose during my therapy with Luisa, who had struggled for several months to balance the needs of her two-year-old son, her demanding work as an executive, and her husband Victor's treatment-resistant depression, which grew in severity with his drinking after several years of seemingly happy marriage. One fateful morning after taking their child to day care on her way to the office, she received a series of perturbing texts from Victor that she interpreted as a veiled suicide threat. Upon receiving no reply to her panicked phone calls to him, she called the police and immediately rushed home to a silent house, the smell of gunpowder hanging in the air as she dashed through the back door. It was in the living room that Luisa discovered her husband's lifeless body slumped in his easy chair, the blood still trickling from one side of his head where the bullet had exited, with brain tissue splashed against the opposite wall. In the fog of anguish that followed, she somehow continued to function with the loving support of family and friends but found it impossible to shake the haunting imagery of her husband's dying, and the equally troubling meaning of his suicidal choice.

After spending our initial sessions shoring up her coping and appreciatively reviewing photographs of her family in better times, we turned toward a detailed retelling of the event story of the death, beginning with the texts and continuing through her discovery of Victor's body, the arrival of the police and EMTs, and finally her cleaning up after the death scene with her brother's help. In the 40 minutes allotted to the retelling, we specifically included the traumatic sensory particulars of the experience, as well as her inner landscape of emotion, and her desperate efforts to make sense of what had happened, pausing frequently to "breathe through" the most difficult parts, replaying them in her mind's eye and in her spoken narrative until she could recount them with less reactivity. In a subsequent session she brought in the sealed autopsy report from the coroner, sensing a need to review and take in its medical explanation of the context of the dying, but also terrified to do so alone. Slowly, across the course of the hour, I silently reviewed the sections of the report, described their focus, and asked Luisa if she were ready to hear what each had to contribute to the narrative of the dying. Once again breathing through the painful particulars (e.g. the path of the bullet through various centers in Victor's brain, the great volume of alcohol in his internal organs), she gradually augmented her understanding of his mental and physical status at the time of his dying. Ultimately, she was able to begin to grasp the tragedy of his dying, but also imagine chapters in her own life and that of her child that did not end with her husband's death.

Directed journaling

Written as well as spoken narratives that bear on the loss experience can promote integration and meaning making, and have the advantage of being used either as freestanding interventions or as homework to augment the effectiveness of face-to-face therapy. A good deal of evidence supports the use of emotional disclosure journaling, in which writers are encouraged to deeply immerse themselves in the emotions and thoughts connected to a traumatic event for 20–30 minutes over a series of typically three distributed writing sessions (Pennebaker, 1996). However, research has been less clear about the benefits of this emotionally immersive writing in the context of bereavement, leading clinical investigators to suggest specialized procedures for processing grief (Neimeyer, van Dyke, & Pennebaker, 2009).

Two such forms of *directed journaling* foster *sense-making* and *benefit-finding*, respectively (Lichtenthal & Neimeyer, 2012). In the former, clients who are some months or years into bereavement are encouraged to focus on questions about how and why the loss occurred, and what it portends for their lives. Prompts might include: *How did you make sense of the loss when it occurred? How do you interpret it now? How does this experience fit with your spiritual views about life, and how, if at all, have you changed those views in light of the loss? How has this loss shaped your life, and what meaning would you like it to have for you in the long run?* In contrast, benefit-finding journaling could be prompted by questions such as: *In your view, have you found any unsought gifts in grief? If so, what? How has this experience affected your sense of priorities? Your sense of yourself? What strengths in yourself or in others have you drawn on to get through this difficult transition? What lessons about living or about loving has this loss taught you? Has this experience deepened your gratitude for anything you've been given? Is there anyone to whom you would like to express this appreciation now?* A randomized controlled trial of both forms of directed journaling compared to a standard emotional disclosure paradigm and a neutral control writing condition has established its efficacy and the maintenance of improvement over a three month follow up, with the impact of such writing being particularly impressive in the benefit-finding condition (Lichtenthal & Cruess, 2010). It is likely that these variations represent only the first of several creative narrative procedures for promoting meaning making regarding loss, a field that invites greater research to document their efficacy. For example, a recent open trial of a Buddhist-inspired workshop for loss and unwelcome change integrated exercises in deep-listening, hearing one's loss story related to the group by a partner, brief interludes of mindfulness, and imaginative writing about themes of loss from a make-believe, self-distancing viewpoint to promote perspective taking (Neimeyer & Young-Eisendrath, 2015). Group participants not only reported significantly diminished grief-related suffering, but also greater integration of the loss experience on a validated measure of meaning making (Holland et al., 2010).

Journaling played an important role in the grief therapy I conducted with Gayle in the months that followed the death of her teenage son, Max, in an automobile accident. At various points our in-session work included prolonged retelling of the event story of her learning of the accident, her experiences in the critical care unit of the hospital to which he had been taken, the fateful moment of his dying, and the funeral service that memorialized his life. At other points the therapy was punctuated with imagined dialogues with Max and with discussion of Gayle's poignant struggle to make sense of her son's sudden and untimely death and her life in its aftermath. Journaling about the loss from a practical, emotional and spiritual perspective between our sessions continued and deepened the work begun together. Increasingly, it also eventuated in surprising insights and outcomes, such as her drafting a moving letter of gratitude to the hundreds of people who had attended Max's memorial service, and her drawing on her writing in the years following the loss to offer hope to other bereaved parents.

Accessing the back story of the relationship

In meaning reconstruction terms, bereaved people seek not only reaffirmation or rebuilding of a self-narrative challenged by loss, but also reconnection to the life narrative of their deceased loved one. In sharp distinction to the classical prescription to "move on" and "withdraw energy from the one who has died to invest it elsewhere," such an approach endorses the normative goal of reconstructing the bond with the deceased rather than relinquishing it (Neimeyer, 2001). When mourners seek to access the "back story" of their relationship with the loved one, they grapple with implicit questions, such as: *How can I recover or reconstruct a sustaining connection with my loved one that survives his or her death? What memories of the relationship bring pain, guilt or sadness, and require some form of redress or reprieve now? How might this forgiveness be sought or given? What memories of the relationship bring joy, security or pride, and invite celebration and commemoration? What lessons about living or loving have I learned during the course of our shared lives? What would my loved one see in me that would give him or her confidence in my ability to weather this hard transition?* (Neimeyer & Thompson, 2014). Two additional theories that subscribe to a similar view of the continuing bond as a potentially adaptive resource (Klass, Silverman, & Nickman, 1996) are narrative therapy (Hedtke & Winslade, 2004) and the Two-Track Model of Bereavement (TTMB) (Rubin, 1999).

According to a narrative therapy perspective anchored in the work of Michael White and David Epston, the dominant cultural narrative that views death only through a lens of loss and presses for "closure" and "letting go" does violence to the relational web that sustains love and community, even beyond the physical presence of the other. Thus, rather than advocating "saying goodbye" as the dominant metaphor for grief work, the goal of bereavement support becomes to "say hello again," in a sense restoring (and re-storying) a "conversation" with and about the loved one that was interrupted by death (Hedtke & Winslade, 2004). Support groups conducted along these lines therefore concentrate not solely on expressing and coping with painful grief-related affects associated with those who were lost, but instead on fostering *re-membering conversations* that celebrate the continued relevance of the relationship to the deceased in the lives of survivors (Hedtke, 2012a). From this vantage point group facilitators might well prompt members with invitations to "introduce their loved ones" to the group (Hedtke, 2012b), using questions such as *Who was _____ to you? What did knowing _____ mean to you? Do particular stories come to mind that _____ would want others to know about his life? What did _____ teach you about life, and perhaps about managing the circumstances you face currently? What difference might it make to keep her memory close to you?* From this perspective the mourner is encouraged to retain a vital connection to the loved one, carrying forward his or her symbolic and social presence in the mourner's own life story.

The Two-Track Model of Bereavement (TTMB) adopts a similar ethic but stretches it in more clinical directions. In the work of Rubin and his colleagues (Rubin, Malkinson, Koren, & Michaeli, 2009), adaptation to bereavement proceeds along two tracks simultaneously, with challenges and impediments arising on either or both. The first and more visible is the track of *biopsychosocial functioning*, which comprises much of the manifest symptomatology of grieving – depression, anxiety, changed relationships with others, a diminished sense of self, somatic concerns and impaired functioning in work and other social roles. It is problems that occur at this level that frequently draw the attention of concerned friends and family, and that constitute the most obvious targets of intervention for professionals. But it is the second track, concerned with the ongoing *relationship with the deceased*, which represents the distinctive contribution of the TTMB. Here, the focus is not merely on the historical character of the relationship with the loved one, but also on how it continues to find expression in significant affects evoked when memories are revisited or triggered, in spontaneous storytelling or ritual connection to the deceased, and on relevant strengths and conflicts in the relationship that invite attention in the course of therapy. By directing clinical assessment and intervention to both tracks of the model, the TTMB therefore extends the predominant concern with symptom management in grief therapy, offering a variety of practices for relational work between the mourner and the deceased (Rubin, Malkinson, & Witztum, 2011). A few such pluralistic procedures derived from humanistic, psychodynamic and expressive therapies illustrate this focus.

Imaginal dialogues

In a sense, grief therapy can be considered family therapy *in absentia*. Just as couples or family work typically invites both or all relevant parties into the therapy room for direct work on their relationship, so too can bereavement interventions foster direct work on the relationship of the mourner(s) with the loved one who has died. "Invoking an alliance with the deceased" in a triadic, rather than merely dyadic, relationship between therapist and client (Rynearson, 2012) can take many forms, including "corresponding" with the dead about the mourner's present state, unanswered questions, and relational needs (e.g. for forgiveness or the affirmation of love) (Neimeyer, 2012b) and guided imagery to conjure the loved one's presence (Jordan, 2012). One particularly potent intervention along these lines draws on *chair work* procedures developed within emotion-focused therapy (Greenberg, 2010), in which the client is encouraged to place the deceased symbolically in an empty chair facing the client's own, and address concerns in the relationship in a first- and second-person, present tense voice (e.g. *"I feel so lost since your death. . . . You were the only one who really understood and cared"*). In most cases the client is then encouraged to switch chairs, loan the loved one his or her own voice, and respond as the deceased might to the client's statements. The therapist choreographs the continuing exchange, prompting the client toward emotional immediacy, honesty and depth in each chair, and directing a change of positions at poignant moments in the dialogue. Detailed procedures for the presentation, performance and processing of chair work in the specific context of grief therapy are now available (Neimeyer, 2012a).

Research on empty chair monologues by bereaved spouses documents the intimate link between themes of self- and other-blame in the chairing and a variety of adverse outcomes (e.g. guilt, depression, anger) (Field & Bonanno, 2001). Moreover, Complicated Grief Therapy, which uses imaginal dialogues with the deceased as a mainstay intervention to resolve such issues, has proven more effective in the treatment of prolonged grief disorder than evidence-based therapy for depression in two randomized controlled trials (Shear et al., 2005; Shear et al., 2014).

Now in his early 40s and a successful lawyer, Rob had entered therapy to sort out his life, an effort that had in the last two years moved him to adopt a deeply Buddhist perspective on the role of loving kindness in all relationships. This was a sharp departure from the fundamental religiosity of his parents, with its strong emphasis on sin and the very real threat of eternal damnation. "Like a wild horse breaking free," Rob recalled jettisoning both his faith and family as he pursued his university and ultimately law school studies with a fierceness and "ego" that seemed the clearest alternative to the sanctimonious atmosphere of his home. Now, however, Rob realized that his detachment from family left his little brother Jimmy without a "buffer" from a deeply unhealthy and alcoholic home environment. As Jimmy slipped into an adolescence saturated in substance abuse, Rob recalled that "I judged him . . . . and he felt it." Ten years after Jimmy's ambiguous overdose, Rob now felt deep remorse but was stymied how to address it, "like an itch I can't scratch."

Having established a strong working alliance in the preceding three sessions, I asked Rob if these were things he would feel ready to address with Jimmy now, were his brother able to join us in the session, fully ready to hear what he had to say. Bravely but uncertainly, Rob nodded his head. Gesturing to the empty chair positioned opposite him, I asked him to close his eyes for a moment and envision Jimmy there, describing to me how he would be dressed (casually), seated (leaning forward, elbows on knees) and engaged (meeting Rob's gaze). I then invited him to open his eyes and using I-you language, speak to the broken heart of their relationship. Rob did so, his eyes growing moist: "I'm sorry I didn't help you. . . . As 10 years have gone by, my perspective has changed so much. I'm sorry for judging you. . . . I hope my love for you now helps carry you forward. You were always good to me, never judged me. I want to pay that forward with my own children." "Try telling him," I suggested, "I am loving my kids for you." Pausing and nodding seriously, Rob repeated this, and responded, "Yes. . . . Your memory, your essence, are still part of my family; you are forever in my life." "Try saying," I offered, "You are still my brother." Tears welling, Rob repeated this, then fell silent with private emotion.

I then gestured to Jimmy's chair, directing Rob to take his seat and respond to his older brother's honest and anguished comments, which I ventriloquized in a few phrases as a reminder. Responding as Jimmy, Rob answered lovingly, reassuringly, convincingly: "Rob, I've missed you greatly. I feel tremendous regret about my addiction. . . . I just lost the battle. Grieve me. . . . I'm happy you found beauty and purpose in your life. Love your children . . . thanks for keeping me in their minds and hearts. . . . I accept your apology."

Moving Rob to a third chair directly across from me and at right angles to the two he had used in the dialogue, I asked him from this "witness position" what he had observed about the conversation that had just taken place. Rob responded that he was struck by the "earnest sincerity in the relationship, the genuine feeling. The relationship is tremendously significant. I think I carry it with me wherever I go." As we sat with this recognition, Rob was suddenly flooded with profound emotion, and sobbing deeply, stammered out, "Of all my family, my brother loved me the best. Now I see so much of my brother in me. Jimmy never had my mean streak, my severity." Recognizing the seeds of love that his brother had planted in him, which were only now growing and bearing fruit, Rob concluded, "So now I tell my children every time I see them that I love them just the way they are." Nine months later, as our therapy drew to a close, Rob reflected on that pivotal fourth session, which seemed to resolve a longstanding sense of guilt, install more securely a brother's love, and begin to prompt greater compassion for even those wounded souls – including his parents – who remained physically present for a deeper dialogue.

Legacy work

Grief has been described as a "biographical emotion," insofar as it speaks to the near-universal human impulse to recognize and honor the life story of the deceased. In this view, anything that serves to preserve or extend that life story tends to assuage our anguish about the loss, as research on the construction of the deceased person's identity in eulogies and other forms of commemoration suggests (Neimeyer, Klass, & Dennis, 2014). In the context of grief therapy this impulse can take the form of various photographic, scrapbooking, documentary, dramaturgical and narrative methods (Neimeyer, 2012d), as well as a cornucopia of expressive arts techniques (Thompson & Neimeyer, 2014). Therapists crafting uniquely relevant *rituals of continuity* or *rituals of affirmation* can draw upon guidelines formulated to help them do so (Doka, 2012).

Among the biographical methods that can be helpful in giving meaning to the loved one's life and impact is the *legacy project*, which can serve to consolidate and communicate the story of the deceased (as in memorial blogs or biographies), or to draw upon his or her life or death to undertake some useful form of social action. In the latter case, legacy projects can be as simple as a random act of kindness in honor of the loved one, as by the bereaved mother who, sitting alone in a restaurant, discovered that the large party at the next table was celebrating a baby shower, and leaving in tears, prepaid the party's bill in honor of her child (Cacciatore, 2012). Other legacy projects can take the form of sustained social action, as by families of homicide victims taking a stand against violence through pursuing public speaking, promoting safer communities, or offering support to others suffering analogous losses (Armour, 2003). For them, such efforts reflected "a fierce commitment to their loved one. Besides being incensed by the needless loss of life, they value what his or her life stands for . . . [which] propel[s] them in directions that create meaning out of a senseless act" (pp. 531–532). Indeed, countless charitable and social justice initiatives have their origins in tragic loss, and the impulse of survivors to create a positive legacy that honors their loved one in its wake. At present a Meaning Based Grief Therapy for parents who have lost children to cancer is being refined and evaluated by Lichtenthal and her colleagues at Memorial Sloane Kettering Cancer Center in New York, with a legacy project honoring the child being a centerpiece of the therapeutic intervention (Neimeyer & Lichtenthal, 2015).

When their young adult son, Graham, died under ambiguous circumstances, Jennifer and Brian were plunged into a deep grief beyond anything they could have imagined. Grasping to articulate this ineffable desolation, Brian reflected on the "dark irony . . . that this thing that so occupies my being, unquestionably the largest, heaviest, and most omnipresent thing I have ever encountered, is . . . an absence. It is an absence that is more present than the present. . . . Our lives are divided into many spheres, but by convention, we keep these separate. Yet Graham's absence infiltrates these disparate spheres with a laughing randomness, making a mockery of convention and throwing into great relief how absurd our petty attempts to compartmentalize life are under the glare of such overwhelming loss" (quoted in Neimeyer & Lichtenthal, 2015). Brian's contribution of his poignant reflections to a book on children and death represented a means of honoring his son's life while also acknowledging his death. For her part, Jennifer organized a remarkably comprehensive, artistic and up-to-date website with informative links to scores of webpages and blogs about grief and the loss of a child, available at http://www.scoop.it/t/grief-and-loss. Unobtrusively but significantly, she saluted her son in a small script at the top of the opening page: Ave, Graham, sed non vale [Hail, Graham, but not goodbye].

Coda

In this brief Introduction I have attempted to sketch some of the principles, processes and procedures that can animate the pluralistic practice of grief therapy, which I believe can enter into fruitful dialogue with contemporary approaches to psychodynamic therapy, and perhaps even support their extension. Under the umbrella of a meaning reconstruction model of mourning, I have suggested the further relevance of the Dual Process Model and the Two-Track Model of Bereavement, as well as narrative perspectives on some of the core features of processing this event story of the loss and accessing the back story of the changed relationship. Equally, I have tried to convey some of the great variety of clinical procedures, ranging from restorative retelling and directed journaling to legacy projects and imagined conversations, which can add weight to the toolbox of practicing psychotherapists, while noting the accumulating evidence of their efficacy. I hope that this framework serves as an open invitation for psychodynamic therapists of many traditions to explore the field of grief therapy, as loss may be the one truly universal challenge that will touch the lives of every client they serve, usually repeatedly.

References

Armour, M. (2003). Meaning making in the aftermath of homicide. *Death Studies, 27*, 519–540.

Baker, J. E. (2001). Mourning and the transformation of object relationships: Evidence for the persistence of internal attachments. *Psychoanalytic Psychology, 18*, 55–73.

Boelen, P. A., de Keijser, J., van den Hout, M., & van den Bout, J. (2007). Treatment of complicated grief: A comparison between cognitive-behavioral therapy and supportive counseling. *Journal of Clinical and Consulting Psychology, 75*, 277–284.

Boelen, P. A., van den Hout, M., & van den Bout, J. (2006). A cognitive-behavioral conceptualization of complicated grief. *Clinical Psychology: Science and Practice, 13*(2), 109–128.

Brenner, C. (1974). Some observations on depression, on nosology, on affects, and on mourning. *Journal of Geriatric Psychology, 7*, 6–20.

Bryant, R., Kenny, L., Joscelyne, A., Rawson, N., Maccallum, F., Cahill, C., . . . Nickerson, A. (2014). Treating prolonged grief disorder: A randomized clinical trial. *Journal of the American Medical Association Psychiatry*. doi: 10.1001/jamapsychiatry.2014.1600

Cacciatore, J. (2012). The kindness project. In R. A. Neimeyer (Ed.), *Techniques of grief therapy: Creative practices for counseling the bereaved* (pp. 329–331). New York: Routledge.

Coleman, R. A., & Neimeyer, R. A. (2010). Measuring meaning: Searching for and making sense of spousal loss in later life. *Death Studies, 34*, 804–834.

Currier, J. M., Holland, J. M., & Neimeyer, R. A. (2006). Sense making, grief and the experience of violent loss: Toward a mediational model. *Death Studies, 30*, 403–428.

Doka, K. (2012). Therapeutic ritual. In R. A. Neimeyer (Ed.), *Techniques of grief therapy: Creative practices for counseling the bereaved* (pp. 341–343). New York: Routledge.

Field, N. P., & Bonanno, G. A. (2001). The impact of self-blame and blame toward the deceased on adaptation to conjugal bereavement: A five-year follow-up. *American Behavioral Scientist, 44*, 764–781.

Freud, S. (1917/1957). Mourning and melancholia. In J. Strachey (Ed.), *The complete psychological works of Sigmund Freud* (pp. 152–170). London, England: Hogarth.

Furman, E. (1974). *A child's parent dies: Studies in childhood bereavement.* New Haven, CT: Yale University Press.

Gaines, R. (1997). Detachment and continuity: The two tasks of mourning. *Contemporary Psychoanalysis, 33*, 549–571.

Gillies, J., Neimeyer, R. A., & Milman, E. (2014). The meaning of loss codebook: Construction of a system for analyzing meanings made in bereavement. *Death Studies, 38*, 207–216. doi: 10.1080/07481187.2013.829367

Greenberg, L. S. (2010). *Emotion focused psychotherapy.* Washington, DC: American Psychological Association.

Hagman, G. (1995). Death of a selfobject: Towards a self psychology of the mourning process. In A. Goldberg (Ed.), *Progress in self psychology, Vol. 11* (pp. 189–205). Hillsdale, NJ: Analytic Press.

Hagman, G. (1996). Flight from the subjectivity of the other: Pathological adaptation to early parent loss. In A. Goldberg (Ed.), *Progress in self psychology, Vol. 11* (pp. 207–219). Hillsdale, NJ: Analytic Press.

Hedtke, L. (2012a). *Bereavement support groups: Breathing life into stories of the dead.* Chagrin Falls, OH: Taos Institute Publications.

Hedtke, L. (2012b). Introducing the deceased. In R. A. Neimeyer (Ed.), *Techniques of grief therapy: Creative practices for counseling the bereaved* (pp. 253–255). New York: Routledge.

Hedtke, L., & Winslade, J. (2004). *Remembering lives.* Amityville, NY: Baywood.

Holland, J. M., Currier, J. M., Coleman, R. A., & Neimeyer, R. A. (2010). The integration of stressful life experiences scale (ISLES): Development and initial validation of a new measure. *International Journal of Stress Management, 17*, 325–352.

Holland, J. M., Currier, J. M., & Neimeyer, R. A. (2006). Meaning reconstruction in the first two years of bereavement: The role of sense-making and benefit-finding. *Omega, 53*, 173–191.

Holland, J. M., Currier, J. M., & Neimeyer, R. A. (2014). Validation of the integration of stressful life experiences scale – short form in a bereaved sample. *Death Studies, 38*, 234–238. doi: 10.1080/07481187.2013.829369

Janoff-Bulman, R., & Berger, A. R. (2000). The other side of trauma. In J. H. Harvey & E. D. Miller (Eds.), *Loss and trauma* (pp. 29–44). Philadelphia: Brunner Mazel.

Jordan, J. R. (2012). Guided imaginal conversations with the deceased. In R. A. Neimeyer (Ed.), *Techniques of grief therapy* (pp. 262–265). New York: Routledge.

Kaplan, L. (1995). *No voice is wholly lost.* New York: Simon and Schuster.

Keesee, N. J., Currier, J. M., & Neimeyer, R. A. (2008). Predictors of grief following the death of one's child: The contribution of finding meaning. *Journal of Clinical Psychology, 64*, 1145–1163.

Kernberg, O. (2010). Some observations on the process of mourning. *International Journal of Psychoanalysis, 91*, 601–619.

Klass, D., Silverman, P. R., & Nickman, S. (1996). *Continuing bonds: New understandings of grief*. Washington: Taylor & Francis.

Lichtenthal, W. G., & Cruess, D. G. (2010). Effects of directed written disclosure on grief and distress symptoms among bereaved individuals. *Death Studies, 34*, 475–499.

Lichtenthal, W. G., & Neimeyer, R. A. (2012). Directed journaling to facilitate meaning making. In R. A. Neimeyer (Ed.), *Techniques of grief therapy* (pp. 161–164). New York: Routledge.

Neimeyer, R. A. (2002). *Lessons of loss: A guide to coping*. Memphis, TN: Center for the Study of Loss and Transition.

Neimeyer, R. A. (2004). Fostering posttraumatic growth: A narrative contribution. *Psychological Inquiry, 15*, 53–59.

Neimeyer, R. A. (2006). Narrating the dialogical self: Toward an expanded toolbox for the counselling psychologist. *Counselling Psychology Quarterly, 19*, 105–120.

Neimeyer, R. A. (2012a). Chair work. In R. A. Neimeyer (Ed.), *Techniques of grief therapy* (pp. 266–273). New York: Routledge.

Neimeyer, R. A. (2012b). Correspondence with the deceased. In R. A. Neimeyer (Ed.), *Techniques of grief therapy* (pp. 259–261). New York: Routledge.

Neimeyer, R. A. (2012c). Retelling the narrative of the death. In R. A. Neimeyer (Ed.), *Techniques of grief therapy* (pp. 86–90). New York: Routledge.

Neimeyer, R. A. (2013). The staging of grief: Toward an active model of mourning. In S. Kreitler & H. Shanun-Klein (Eds.), *Studies in grief and bereavement* (pp. 1–18). Hauppauge, NY: Nova Science.

Neimeyer, R. A. (Ed.). (2001). *Meaning reconstruction and the experience of loss*. Washington, DC: American Psychological Association.

Neimeyer, R. A. (Ed.). (2012d). *Techniques of grief therapy: Creative practices for counseling the bereaved*. New York: Routledge.

Neimeyer, R. A., Klass, D., & Dennis, M. R. (2014). Mourning, meaning and memory: Individual, communal and cultural narration of grief. In A. Batthyany & P. Russo-Netzer (Eds.), *Meaning in existential and positive psychology* (pp. 325–346). New York: Springer.

Neimeyer, R. A., & Lichtenthal, W. G. (2015). The presence of absence: The struggle for meaning in the death of a child. In G. Cox & R. Stephenson (Eds.), *Children and death*. Amityville, NY: Baywood.

Neimeyer, R. A., & Thompson, B. E. (2014). Meaning making and the art of grief therapy. In B. E. Thompson & R. A. Neimeyer (Eds.), *Grief and the expressive arts: Practices for creating meaning* (pp. 3–13). New York: Routledge.

Neimeyer, R. A., van Dyke, J. G., & Pennebaker, J. W. (2009). Narrative medicine: Writing through bereavement. In H. Chochinov & W. Breitbart (Eds.), *Handbook of psychiatry in palliative medicine* (pp. 454–469). New York: Oxford.

Neimeyer, R. A., & Young-Eisendrath, P. (2015). Assessing a Buddhist treatment for bereavement and loss: The Mustard Seed Project. *Death Studies, 39*, 263–273. doi: 10.1080/07481187.2014.937973

Park, C. L. (2010). Making sense of the meaning literature: An integrative review of meaning making and its effects on adjustment to stressful life events. *Psychological Bulletin, 136*(2), 257–301.

Pennebaker, J. (1996). *Opening up*. New York: Guilford.

Prigerson, H. G., Horowitz, M. J., Jacobs, S. C., Parkes, C. M., Aslan, M., Goodkin, K., . . . Maciejewski, P. K. (2009). Prolonged grief disorder: Psychometric validation of criteria proposed for DSM-V and ICD-11. *PLoS Medicine, 6*(8), 1–12.

Rubin, S. S. (1999). The Two-Track Model of Bereavement: Overview, retrospect and prospect. *Death Studies, 23*, 681–714.

Rubin, S. S., Malkinson, R., Koren, D., & Michaeli, E. (2009). The Two-Track Model of Bereavement Questionnaire (TTBQ): Development and validation of a relational measure. *Death Studies, 33*, 305–333.

Rubin, S. S., Malkinson, R., & Witztum, E. (2011). *Working with the bereaved.* New York: Routledge.

Rynearson, E. K. (2012). Invoking an alliance with the deceased after violent death. In R. A. Neimeyer (Ed.), *Techniques of grief therapy* (pp. 91–94). New York: Routledge.

Rynearson, E. K. (Ed.). (2006). *Violent death.* New York: Routledge.

Rynearson, E. K., & Salloum, A. (2011). Restorative retelling: Revisiting the narrative of violent death. In R. A. Neimeyer, D. Harris, H. Winokuer & G. Thornton (Eds.), *Grief and bereavement in contemporary society: Bridging research and practice* (pp. 177–188). New York: Routledge.

Saindon, C., Rheingold, A., Baddeley, J., Wallace, M., Brown, C., & Rynearson, E. K. (2014). Restorative retelling for violent loss: An open clinical trial. *Death Studies, 38*, 251–258.

Shane, M., & Shane, E. (1990). Object loss and selfobject loss: A contribution to understanding mourning and the failure to mourn. *Annual of Psychoanalysis, 18*, 115–131.

Shear, M. K., Boelen, P., & Neimeyer, R. A. (2011). Treating complicated grief: Converging approaches. In R. A. Neimeyer, D. Harris, H. Winokuer & G. Thornton (Eds.), *Grief and bereavement in contemporary society: Bridging research and practice* (pp. 139–162). New York: Routledge.

Shear, M. K., Frank, E., Houch, P. R., & Reynolds, C. F. (2005). Treatment of complicated grief: A randomized controlled trial. *Journal of the American Medical Association, 293*, 2601–2608.

Shear, M. K., Wang, Y., Skriskaya, N., Duan, N., Mauro, C., & Ghesquiere, A. (2014). Treatment of complicated grief in elderly persons: A randomized clinical trial. *Journal of the American Medical Association Psychiatry.* doi: 10.1001/jamapsychiatry.2014.1242

Shelby, D. (1994). Mourning theory reconsidered. In A. Goldberg (Ed.), *The widening scope of self psychology: Progress in self psychology, Vol. 9* (pp. 169–189). Hillsdale, NJ: Analytic Press.

Slochower, J. A. (1996). *Holding and psychoanalysis.* Hillsdale, NJ: Analytic Press.

Slochower, J. (2011). Out of the analytic shadow: On the dynamics of commemorative ritual. *Psychoanalytic Dialogues, 21*(6), 676–690.

Stroebe, M., & Schut, H. (1999). The dual process model of coping with bereavement: Rationale and description. *Death Studies, 23*, 197–224.

Stroebe, M., & Schut, H. (2010). The dual process model of coping with bereavement: A decade on. *Omega, 61*, 273–289.

Thompson, B. E., & Neimeyer, R. A. (Eds.). (2014). *Grief and the expressive arts: Practices for creating meaning.* New York: Routledge.

Volkan, V. (1981). *Linking objects and linking phenomena.* New York: International University Press.

Chapter 1

Mourning

A review and reconsideration (1995)

George Hagman

Editor's note: I begin this selection of papers with a survey and reformulation of bereavement and mourning theory. In this paper I review the development of the standard psychoanalytic model of mourning and offer a critique from several perspectives. The psychoanalytic model of mourning, while useful in its depiction of a certain type of process, may not be valid as a general model. First, the psychoanalytic literature and data from clinical practice fails to confirm basic components of mourning theory. Second, some non-analytic research is at odds with several of the model's key assumptions, and historical studies have shown how individuals in Western culture have mourned differently over time. Finally, from a cross-cultural perspective, it is also clear that there is infinite variety in people's responses to death, in how they mourn, and in the nature of their internalization of the lost object. In closing, I propose a perspective on bereavement that, rather than being process-oriented, understands mourning to be an adaptive response to specific task demands arising from loss, which must be dealt with regardless of individual, culture or historical era.

This paper was published in 1995 by George Hagman as 'Mourning: A Review and Reconsideration' in the International Journal of Psychoanalysis, *Volume 76.*

Among the clinical constructs of psychoanalysis, few have been as influential as the 'work of mourning'. The model of mourning as a painful process of identification, decathexis and re-cathexis in reaction to the loss of a loved one is the cornerstone of the contemporary Western understanding of bereavement and has been used by psychoanalysts since 1917 (Abraham, 1927; Fenichel, 1945, p. 394; Nunberg, 1955; Pollock, 1961; Rochlin, 1965, pp. 154–5; Kohut, 1972; Greenson, 1978, p. 267; Loewald, 1980, pp. 257–76; Meissner, 1981, pp. 173–4; Volkan, 1981, pp. 67–8; Frosch, 1990, p. 369; McWilliams, 1994, pp. 109–10). This model has had a significant effect on how we view 'normal' or 'healthy' mourning, and it has defined for us when and how mourning becomes pathological. In fact in a survey of bereavement experts, 65.7 per cent claimed psychoanalytic theory to be one of the three most useful models (Middleton et al., 1991, p. 506). In recent years, a number of writers have studied mourning from historical, ethological, cultural and clinical perspectives; however, there has not been a thorough critical review of the psychoanalytic model of mourning since Siggins's contribution in 1966.

The concept of mourning has been extended to various forms of loss (Furman, 1974; Pollock, 1989). I will concentrate here on one form – bereavement, the death of a loved one. More specifically, I intend to limit our focus to the psychoanalytic model of the normal mourning process, notwithstanding that the distinction between normal and pathological mourning is often hard to make, and may be only of heuristic value. I will argue that the standard model of mourning is not a reliable or accurate model of normal mourning, and I will offer what I believe may be a more accurate way of viewing grief. Unfortunately, we will be unable to consider the extensive literature on pathological mourning, as this would divert us from our primary focus (for an excellent comprehensive review of the literature on pathological mourning see Rando, 1993).

I will embark on this critical review in full recognition of the importance of Freud's model of the intrapsychic dynamics of mourning for psychoanalytic theory – from our understanding of the development and nature of the ego to the internal world of object relations. As metapsychology *Mourning and Melancholia* is a monumental and seminal work. What I intend to question is the adoption by subsequent analysts, mental health professionals, social theorists and others of Freud's description of mourning as a general model of the normal process. In fact it is not clear whether Freud ever intended to promulgate a 'standard' model of mourning. As Furman (1974) points out, *Mourning and Melancholia* can be misleading if considered by itself:

> It was written during a period when Freud's investigative efforts focused on the understanding of narcissism and the 'critical faculty', and when he tried to clarify processes in melancholia. For this purpose he sets up a model situation for mourning (Siggins, 1966, p. 16) but does not attempt to portray actual mourning processes in their full clinical complexity and theoretical implications.
>
> (pp. 241–2)

I will begin by reviewing Freud's writings on mourning, followed by a survey of the contributions of other analysts. I will then discuss some of the relevant clinical, historical and cultural research data. In conclusion, I will reconsider our understanding of mourning in the light of this new knowledge.

Review of the psychoanalytic literature

The psychoanalytic literature on 'normal mourning' is not extensive. Nonetheless, there have been significant contributions from a variety of schools of thought. This paper will focus on those parts of the literature that have contributed to the model of mourning first delineated by Freud in his paper *Mourning and Melancholia* (1917).

Before 1917 Freud discussed mourning in several papers (Freud & Breuer, 1895; Freud, 1909, 1915). However, in these three instances he approached mourning from the perspective of psychopathology (for example, in his study of the Ratman, Freud [1909] showed the role of competitive rivalry in pathological mourning) or in primitive mental life. It was not until *Mourning and Melancholia* that Freud offered his major contribution to the study of normal mourning in a brief section that served as the introduction to his discussion of melancholia. He began with the question:

> Now in what consists the work which mourning performs? . . . The testing of reality, having shown that the loved object no longer exists, requires forthwith that the libido shall be withdrawn from its attachment to this object. Against this demand a struggle of course arises – it may be universally observed that man never willingly abandons a libido-position, not even when a substitute is already beckoning to him. . . . The normal outcome is that deference for reality gains the day. Nevertheless its behest cannot be at once obeyed. The task is carried through bit by bit, under great expense of time and cathectic energy, while all the time the existence of the lost object is continued in the mind. Each single one of the memories and hopes which bound the libido to the object is brought up and hyper-cathected, and the detachment of the libido from it is accomplished. . . . When the work of mourning is completed the ego becomes free and uninhibited again.
>
> (Freud, 1917, pp. 244–5)

Freud observed the symptoms of mourning to be similar to melancholia: (a) a profoundly painful dejection; (b) abrogation of interest in the outside world; (c) loss of the capacity to love; and (d) inhibition of all activity. Present in cases of melancholia, but absent in normal mourning, is 'lowering of the self-regarding feelings to the degree that finds utterance in self-reproaches and self-reviling' (Freud, 1917, p. 244), the difference being due to ambivalence towards the lost object on the part of the melancholic.

As to why the mourning process should be so painful, at first Freud was not sure. Later, in *Inhibitions, Symptoms and Anxiety*, he asserted that separation *should* be painful in view of 'the high and unsatisfiable cathexis of longing which is concentrated on the object by the bereaved person during the reproduction of the situations in which he must undo the ties that bind him to it' (Freud, 1926, p. 172).

As to the abrogation of interest, loss of capacity to love and general lessening of vitality, Freud saw this as an 'inhibition and circumscription of the ego' in its exclusive devotion to mourning 'which leaves nothing over for other purposes or other interests' (Freud, 1917, p. 244). This pervasive inhibition of the ego and restriction of the libido lessens as the work of mourning (the successful decathexis of the object) is accomplished and 'the ego becomes free and uninhibited again' (Freud, 1917, p. 245).

Later analysts would add identification with the lost object to Freud's model (Abraham, 1927; Fenichel, 1945). In another context, Freud himself seemed to be saying this when he stated in *The Ego and the Id*, 'It may be that this identification is the sole condition under which the Id can give up its objects' (Freud, 1923). For example, Abraham notes that the bereaved person effects 'a temporary introjection of the loved person. Its main purpose is to preserve the person's relation to the lost object' (Abraham, 1927, p. 435). Fenichel supported Abraham's point in 1945. In any case, though Freud did not specifically include identification in his original model of the mourning process, his other references to object loss and the contributions of his close supporters have led to identification being included in the standard psychoanalytic model.

In 1937 Deutsch offered an observation which has also been integrated into psychoanalytic thinking: that is, the absence of grieving is indicative and/or predictive of psychopathology. She writes:

> every unresolved grief is given expression in some form or other. . . . The process of mourning as a reaction to the real loss of a loved person must be carried to completion. As long as the early libidinal or aggressive attachment persists, the painful affect continues to flourish, and vice versa, the attachments are unresolved as long as the affective process of mourning has not been accomplished.
>
> (Deutsch, 1937, pp. 234–5)

Another feature of the psychoanalytic model of mourning is ambivalence. Freud himself introduced the notion that the essential dynamic distinction between normal mourning and melancholia is the predominance of libidinal cathexis in the former and aggression in the later. Abraham, Fenichel and Jacobson would provide support for this viewpoint. It has therefore become accepted that successful mourning can only occur when there is a predominance of feelings of love towards the lost object.

Finally, in recent years the notion of mourning as a phylogenetically based, adaptive response to loss has been put forth by Pollock (1961). Combining ethological research with observations of human bereavement, Pollock claimed that the mourning process, as we have come to know it, is biologically grounded, having developed over evolutionary time to insure optimal survival in the face of separation and loss. In many publications Pollock argued for the acceptance of the standard theory of mourning as a universal, adaptive process. Unfortunately, space will not permit a full appreciation of Pollock's rich contribution to the literature of mourning. Suffice it to say that Pollock, single-handed among analysts, wrested Freud's mourning theory from fifty years of neglect and argued for its inclusion in contemporary theory and practice.

The aforementioned psychoanalysts constructed the standard model of mourning from common sense, personal experience and through extrapolation from theories regarding the dynamics of depression. Even in *Mourning and Melancholia*

Freud offered no clinical data to support his statements regarding mourning, nor did he claim to have carried out any formal investigation of the matter. In fact Freud's only recorded clinical example was his observation (outside the consulting room) of a woman who, having suffered numerous losses, engaged in an obsessive method of disengaging from her deceased loved ones (Freud & Breuer, 1895). Freud used the example for the purpose of illustrating the occurrence of neurotic symptomatology in a case of bereavement; he did not see this woman as 'normal'. Abraham (1927) later noted the intuitive nature of Freud's findings regarding melancholia and mourning, and asserted the need for verification. Almost half a century later, Pollock would point out that 'until the early 1960s surprisingly few investigations had been made of the mourning process *per se* by psychoanalysts and others involved in psychological research' (Pollock, 1961). Even in Pollock's case, his thinking on mourning was developed, he states, from his own mourning and his observation of family members (Pollock, 1989, p. 13). Finally, as recently as 1993 Selby Jacobs continued to lament our limited understanding of normal mourning. Therefore, essentially by default, Freud's model of mourning has remained the standard one. In fact, as recently as the 1990 edition of *Psychoanalytic Terms and Concepts*, edited by Moore and Fine, the definition of the term *mourning* is a restatement of Freud's original formulation. There, mourning is defined as:

The mental process by which one's psychic equilibrium is restored following the loss of a meaningful love object . . . it is a normal response to any significant loss. The predominant mood of mourning is painful and is usually accompanied by loss of interest in the outside world, preoccupation with memories of the lost object, and diminished capacity to make new emotional investments. Uncomplicated mourning is not pathological and does not require treatment. With time the individual adapts to the loss and renews his or her capacity for pleasure in relationships. Although reality testing is preserved and confirms that the loved object no longer exists, in the internal process of mourning the aggrieved person initially is unable to withdraw attachment from the lost object. Instead the mourner turns away from reality, through denial, and clings to the mental representation of the lost object. Thus the object loss is turned into an ego loss. Through the stages of the mourning process, this ego loss is gradually healed and psychic equilibrium restored. The work of mourning includes three successive, interrelated phases; the success of each affecting the next: 1) understanding, accepting and coping with the loss and its circumstances, 2) the mourning proper, which involves withdrawal of attachment to and identification with the lost object (decathexis); and 3) resumptions of emotional life in harmony with one's level of maturity, which frequently involves establishing new relationships (recathexis).

(p. 122)

Mourning in psychoanalytic practice

Let us now look at the clinical psychoanalytic literature and see if there is support for the standard model of the mourning process. I will then discuss my own observations of bereaved patients in analytic treatment. My conclusion will be that the extreme mourning reaction described by the psychoanalytic model is just one of the many forms of mourning engaged in by bereaved people.

Mourning in the clinical psychoanalytic literature

Clinical psychoanalytic practice has rarely focused on the dynamics of normal mourning. Since Freud (1917, p. 244) advised against therapeutic interventions in normal cases of mourning (in fact, he asserted that in these cases therapy might be harmful), psychoanalysts have rarely treated people engaged in uncomplicated mourning. Brenner (1974) asserts that he has never observed a patient in his own psychoanalytic practice that exhibited mourning as Freud described it, and he warns us about the unreliability of a symptomatologically based nosology given the protean nature of the unconscious.

An exception is Abraham (1927, pp. 433–8), who discussed the analytic treatments of two patients, during which each experienced what Abraham considered normal mourning. The cases do not seem to support the standard model. In the first instance the widower does not decathect the internal image of the dead wife; rather, he introjects and psychically preserves the attachment. In the second case, after the death of his mother a son experiences not sorrow, but on the contrary, elation and bliss (a not uncommon non-pathological reaction noted by Wortman, Silver and Kessler in 1994). More recently Volkan (1981) and Viederman (1989) have discussed instances of uncomplicated grief, all of which illustrate the working through of residual neurotic elements in bereavement rather than uncomplicated mourning processes.

Once area of the clinical psychoanalytic literature where we might look for support of the standard model of the mourning process is the case histories of successful treatments of pathological mourning. My assumption is that patients who have suffered disturbances in mourning would, after an effective analysis (as a result of which neurotic conflicts and infantile attachments regarding the deceased would have been resolved), resume mourning in a normal fashion leading to resolution. After reviewing a number of these cases (Deutsch, 1937; Jacobson, 1957; Altschul, 1968; Fleming, 1972, 1974; Stolorow & Lachman, 1975; Blum, 1980, 1983, 1985; Volkan, 1981; Fleming & Altschul, 1988; Shane & Shane, 1990), I have found that none of these patients engaged in a mourning process as the psychoanalytic model describes it. If anything the cases I have reviewed support the notion that withdrawal and despondency are indications of a pathological reaction, and that the decathexis described is more in keeping with the working through of a neurosis than the resumption of healthy mourning.

An excellent example is the analysis of the patient described by Fleming and Altschul in their paper 'Activation of mourning and growth by psychoanalysis'

(1988). In the course of treatment the patient, whose maturation had been stunted as a result of the aborted mourning for her dead parents, relinquished the denial that had shielded her from acceptance of her losses. The result was both a resumption of the mourning process and emotional development. Significantly, the patient did not exhibit the symptomatology of mourning as described by the standard model. Anxiety over separation and guilt over survival were certainly evident – as was some expression of sadness. The transference intensified and the patient's investment in herself, relationships and activities increased. Her initial resistance to establishing a relationship with the analyst was not so much something related to the dynamics of normal mourning as an indication of the frozen nature of her object relationships resulting from her refusal to mourn. The resolution of her attachment to her parents largely involved the working through of neurotic conflict and gave rise not so much to decathexis as to internal object constancy through the lessening of anxiety over the destructiveness of separation. In fact the patient, as a result of treatment, was able to think about her lost parents with deep feeling and did so often, even after treatment.

Mourning in psychoanalytic practice

I have also surveyed my own practice by reviewing the treatments of two groups of patients: (1) patients in psychoanalysis where bereavement occurred in the course of treatment (six adult cases), and (2) patients who came to treatment as a direct result of pathological mourning (eight adult cases).

In non-pathologically bereaved patients, although there is generally some evidence of shock and sadness, I have rarely encountered cases of denial, despondency or withdrawal from the world. Those cases that do show such a reaction invariably have significant conflicts involving the deceased person. In most cases the patient continues to be actively engaged in analysis and there is a heightening of the transference. (My clinical impression has been that withdrawal may occur when the patient experiences a lack of support or empathy from the analyst.) Several patients have described an increased feeling of vitality and heightened perceptions that did not preclude grief but rather seemed part of their mourning. Most have found solace in their work and close relationships. Never have I encountered a patient who engaged in the type of extended memory review that Freud described.

My experience has also been that rather than decathexis, there is a permanent structuring of the relationship with the dead in the mind of the bereaved person. Rather than turning away from others and finding new objects as replacements for the deceased, the bereaved patients in my practice have continued in the relationships that sustained them throughout the period of mourning and, in those instances where there was a 'recathexis', it was not always with new objects, but with familiar ones in new roles. The following patient is a good example of the complex nature of mourning processes in an extended analysis. Her reactions to the death of her mother were distinctly different from those described by the standard model of mourning; at the same time even this patient's mourning can only be understood as determined by complex unconscious processes.

Sally, a 34-year-old woman, was in her eighth year of analysis when her mother died. Much work had been done over the course of treatment to work through Sally's fears of assertiveness and guilt over leaving home fifteen years earlier. In fact, four years before, as she worked in treatment to resolve her continuing attachment to her mother and struggled with guilt over separation, Sally did engage in a process of painful relinquishment similar to mourning. However, her sadness and despondency were more related to the emergence of aggressive wishes and guilt associated with differentiation from her mother. As Brenner (1974) suggests, in this instance Sally's overt symptoms of mourning were multidetermined compromise-formations reflecting unconscious dynamics of a neurotic nature. Eventually analysis assisted Sally in accomplishing the resolution of much of her infantile attachment and conflict regarding individuation. At the time of her mother's death Sally was married and working at a satisfying career. The mother's death was due to a lingering heart condition; nevertheless it was unexpected. Sally returned briefly to her hometown for the funeral. When she returned she described her experience to the analyst:

> When I went to see her at the funeral home with my brother I was very upset. I couldn't stop sobbing. Up to that point it had all been kind of unreal. I was sad. But I also felt happy to have Jim with me. We spent a long time talking about mom. Over the next few days we talked a lot about the old times. We all tried some things to help us remember her better. Like I say I was sad, but also I never felt so alive, close to my family, my husband and kids. And strangely, to my mom too. It felt so strong and I was so glad that a lot of the old problems between us had been resolved long ago. It was a pretty busy week. There was a lot to do. It was hard work in a way, but I was really happy that things had turned out all right for us in the end: you know everything really is all right now. I'll miss her.

Analysis revealed that Sally had long before resolved most of her infantile ties to her mother. She admitted that if the death had happened a few years earlier she would have been 'devastated'; however, she had grown to feel more independent and involved in new, adult relationships. She felt she could identify with good parts of her mother and accept the rest. Sally admitted that she felt sad, but it was also a new beginning. She felt slightly guilty about that.

Some months later I began to suspect that Sally might have shielded herself from some aspects of mourning. On or about the first anniversary of her mother's death Sally became depressed and began to reminisce, longing for her mother. We determined that some of her yearning and grief were an anniversary reaction; however, Sally had also recently been offered a much-desired promotion with added responsibility and autonomy. Analysis revealed that a large part of her despondency was defensively motivated by anxiety relating to the threatening gratification of unconscious Oedipal wishes: Sally was alive and thriving, her mother was dead. Once again the symptoms of Sally's mourning had been determined by factors beyond object loss.

The preceding case-report highlights the complexity of an analysis even of uncomplicated mourning. Sally's experience of the death of her mother, although painful, did not involve the type of extreme emotional response predicted by the standard model. In fact the analysis shows how mourning-like behaviors were related more to neurotic conflicts than to Sally's experience of loss.

Similarly, with the successful treatment of pathological mourning reactions, I have found that rather than despondency, there is a feeling of revitalization in the midst of freshly felt sadness. The patient, after years of inhibited grief, frequently revels in his or her emotionality and there is an intense engagement with others (especially the analyst) at the point of greatest sorrow. Life becomes more vivid and accessible to these patients, far from the colorless and empty world that Freud describes as the experience of reality for the bereaved. Ultimately these patients do not disengage from the deceased; rather, there is a revitalized engagement with the object internally, and also externally with transference figures, to such an extent that one can observe not decathexis but a heightened re-engagement with the dead person and eventually a transformation of memory into a permanent part of the patient's internal world.

> Sam sought analysis for relief of chronic depressions and inhibitions in his relationships and work. Over time, it was revealed that aborted mourning and dysfunctional adaptations to loss resulting from his mother's death during his adolescence were the core elements of his psychopathology. Over time, treatment led to a resolution of defenses against mourning and to the emergence of grief. These advances were accompanied by an intensification of the transference and an alleviation of depression as well as a more vital involvement in the working alliance with the analyst. In fact the symptoms of dejection, abrogation of interest in the world, incapacity to love and inhibition of activity were at no point evident during the period of acute grieving. Nor did I observe any memory review or systematic 'decathexis' of the memory of his mother. For Sam the working through of defense and the onset of full and expressive grieving was accompanied by renewed vitality, improved self-esteem and replenished libido; and these changes occurred not at the point of resolution of mourning, but rather, they seemed to be part and parcel of the mourning process itself.

Contemporary research: Clinical and longitudinal

Because the psychoanalytic model of mourning describes phenomena that are behaviorally dramatic, and since, at least to some extent, the psychological processes are conscious and, hence, communicable, it should be possible for non-analytic psychological research findings to assist us in our assessment of the model's general validity.

Reflecting on the contemporary themes and controversies of bereavement research Stroebe, Stroebe and Hansson remarked, 'One of the major themes to emerge . . . is that grief is not a simple universal process, with a progression of fixed stages, each with its own typical symptom' (1994, p. 462). In the same volume, discussing the course of normal grief, Schuchter and Zisook (1994) concur:

> Grief is such an individualized process – one that varies from person to person and moment to moment and encompasses simultaneously so many facets of the bereaved person's being – that attempts to limit its scope or demarcate its boundaries by arbitrarily defining normal grief are bound to fail.
>
> (p. 23)

In 1989 Wortman and Silver published a comprehensive review of the bereavement research literature in which they evaluated five assumptions prevalent in the psychoanalytic literature on mourning against the non-analytic research data. Importantly, Wortman and Silver *do not* find support in the research literature for these assumptions. Let us look at their findings.

I Distress or depression is inevitable

Fundamental to the psychoanalytic description of mourning is the notion that the bereaved person experiences severe emotional pain and exhibits despondency, reduced vitality and distress (Freud, 1917; Bowlby, 1980; Moore & Fine, 1990). Research has found that though distress is common in some populations it is not in others, and therefore should not be assumed to be indicative of a normal or healthy reaction to loss (Clayton et al., 1972; Vachon et al., 1982a, 1982b; Lund et al., 1985). Wortman et al. (1994) have recently found that positive affects are more common soon after loss than was once thought. Cross-cultural research has also found that there are vast differences in affect intensity and duration of grief between societies (Stroebe & Stroebe, 1994).

2 Distress is necessary and failure to experience distress is indicative of pathology

Deutsch's influential paper on 'The absence of grief' (1937) was the first to state that people who do not exhibit distress after loss are resisting the inevitable and will ultimately succumb to pathology. Subsequently, Deutsch's assertions were integrated into the psychoanalytic model of mourning. However, the bulk of available research does not support the view that those who fail to exhibit distress will experience subsequent pathology (Clayton et al., 1971; Bornstein et al., 1973; Vachon et al., 1982a, 1982b; Parkes & Weiss, 1983; Lund et al., 1985–86; Silver & Wortman, 1988). The vicissitudes of *unconscious* grief and the possibility that grieving can be engaged in without graphic display is not considered by these researchers.

3 The importance of painful working through of loss

Freud vividly describes the extraordinarily painful work of decathexis that accompanies and follows the initial distress of loss. This dramatically painful 'working through' of the loss is the cornerstone of his theory (Freud, 1917). Although Wortman and Silver admit that research in this area is sparse, that which is available indicates that yearning for the deceased or preoccupation with the lost person are not as common as has been assumed and may not be an optimally adaptive response to loss (Parkes & Weiss, 1983; Silver & Wortman, 1988). These researchers do not question that some working-through process is necessary; however, they found that the degree of despondency described by Freud presaged a psychopathological outcome rather than health. From a psychoanalytic perspective the working through of loss may indeed occur not uncommonly on an unconscious level, accessible only to analytic study.

4 Expectation of recovery

The expectation that after successful 'working through' of the loss a bereaved person should show a return to pre-loss functioning and renewed involvement in life is basic to Freud's conception of the outcome of uncomplicated bereavement. However, research cited by Wortman and Silver indicates that a significant minority of normally bereaved people experience distress related to the loss for a longer period of time than is commonly assumed to occur (Vachon et al., 1982a, 1982b; Elizur & Kaffman, 1982, 1983; Parkes & Weiss, 1983; Zisook & Schuchter, 1986; Lehman et al., 1987).

5 Reaching a state of resolution

The endpoint of mourning from the psychoanalytic perspective is resolution, i.e. acceptance of the loss, decathexis of the object and recathexis of the new object. According to Wortman and Silver, available data suggests that a state of resolution may not always be achieved. Many studies have found that normal bereavement frequently involves years of struggle with basic questions about the loss (Parkes & Weiss, 1983; Silver et al., 1983; Lehman et al., 1987; Wortman & Silver, 1987). Freud himself noted this in a letter to Binswanger: 'We know that the acute grief we feel after a loss will come to an end, but that we will remain inconsolable and will never find a substitute' (Binswanger, 1957, p. 106).

Recently evaluating the results of several major longitudinal studies of mourning, Wortman et al. (1994) found further support for their 1989 conclusions and argued for a change in theoretical framework. They claimed that the single most important factor in mourning outcome is the extent to which the meaning of the loss to the survivor conflicts with their 'world-view'. Thus some of the most current research speaks to Brenner's claim (1974, p. 14) that conflicts related to fantasy regarding loss (i.e. their unconscious meaning) rather than symptomatology should be the focus of our analyses of mourning.

Discussion

The research findings cited above are not definitive and much is still to be done. None of the references are analytically based investigations; hence, they do not address the intrapsychic processes involved. However, it seems that the process of mourning as described by Freud is not symptomatically self-evident, and that perhaps we should reconsider the psychoanalytic model, which – however valid in many instances – may not be the normal and expectable response to death that we have come to assume it is. I think that the research cited above should encourage us to look beyond our standard notion of bereavement towards a broader concep-tualization of what constitutes mourning work and its outcome.

Mourning in history and culture

The adaptive social and cultural responses to object loss are perhaps as variable as the vicissitudes of human imagination (Blum, 1985, p. 310). How can we account for the discrepancy between the observations of Freud and his contemporaries with recent research findings? Is it possible that the manner in which people mourn has changed since Freud's time? An additional hypothesis I would like to consider is the possibility that mourning is a process whose nature is structured and defined to some extent by social and historical forces. Perhaps the only way to answer this question is to explore the historical record.

In two major works Phillippe Aries investigated the evolving nature of Western cultural attitudes towards death (Aries, 1974, 1981). Aries discovered that much of what we have come to assume about our culture's attitude towards death is, from a historical perspective, relatively new. Looking back over a thousand years of cultural history, he showed how in earlier times the manner in which people died, the means by which the dead were disposed of, and the way in which people mourned were fundamentally different from today.

According to Aries, until the end of the Middle Ages the presence of death was a part of daily life. It occurred frequently and close at hand. Recognition of the inev-itability of death and the acceptance of one's own mortality was commonplace. How one handled one's death was often ritualized, as was the mourning pro-cess. Grief was generally dramatic, noisy and brief. The remains of the dead were promptly disposed of after a prescribed ceremony. Attachment to the memory of the dead was infrequent. Bereaved people remarried quickly, and there was no time or inclination for extended withdrawal and/or dysfunction. Aries called this the era of 'tamed death', when mortality was viewed as part of the natural design of life. Aries discovered, however, that with time this attitude changed. He wrote:

> In the nineteenth century . . . mourning was unfurled with an uncustomary degree of ostentation. It even claimed to have no obligation to social conven-tions and to be the most spontaneous and insurmountable expression of a very grave wound: people cried, fainted, languished, and fasted. . . . It was a

sort of return to the excessive and spontaneous demonstration – or apparently spontaneous demonstrations – of the High Middle Ages. . . . The nineteenth century is the era of mourning which the psychologists of today call hysterical mourning. . . . It means that the survivor accepted the death of another with greater difficulty than in the past.

(Aries, 1974, p. 67)

Aries believed that with the prevalence of romanticism, the dominance of 'the cult of the individual', and the restructuring of society around the nuclear family in industrialized urban communities, there arose 'a new intolerance of separation'. The fear of the loss of the other led to sorrowful outpourings of grief and anguished attempts to salvage the attachment to the dead. In agreement with Aries, Esther Schor (1994) refers to a form of 'deep mourning' common to nineteenth-century society characterized by ostentatious expression of prolonged grief. The emphasis of European society's view of mourning at that time, according to Schor, was on the 'extreme sense of the mourner's isolation' (p. 232). No longer integrated into a social network of grief, mourning had become an increasingly internal, psychological process. Since Freud's original observations and formulations regarding mourning were carried out in nineteenth-century Europe, it is possible that the prevalence of 'hysterical', 'deep' and 'isolated' mourning could account for Freud's 1917 formulation. Were cases of expressive, even hysterical, reactions to loss so common as to be assumed to be self-evident and normal? Aries and Schor would lead us to believe that this was the case. Therefore, the psychoanalytic model may have been based on this relatively new type of dramatic and passionate mourning that arose in nineteenth-century Europe.

Aries continued to study the trends in mourning practices during the twentieth century. With the medicalization of mortality, the removal of the place of death from the home to the hospital and the responsibility for the disposal of the remains from the family to the professional undertaker, death lost its grounding in the daily lives of Western men and women, eventually becoming 'invisible' (Aries, 1981, p. 560). Aries notes: 'Death, so omnipresent in the past that it was familiar, would be effaced, would disappear. It would become shameful and forbidden' (Aries, 1974, p. 85). Death replaced sex as the taboo of the mid twentieth century. Mourning rituals vanished from some Western societies. Dying became attenuated with the advance of medical care, and the 'great dramatic act of death' came to be seen as a mistake and, in some sense, a shameful failure. The sorrow of mourning was repugnant to many – a sign of loss of control, mental instability, weakness, or just bad manners. Even family members would suppress their grief out of concern for the children. 'Thus mourning is no longer a necessary period imposed by society; it has become a *morbid state* which must be treated, shortened, erased' (Aries, 1974, p. 99). Since the time of Aries's research, it appears that Western culture has entered a new phase of awareness of death and loss. Disillusionment in medical science, the ubiquity of community violence and warfare and the advent of new plagues (especially HIV) have forced a greater individual and social awareness of mortality. Changes have occurred already in our society's attitudes and behaviors. How this change has impacted the mourning of individuals and groups is still unclear.

Mourning across cultures

Additional support for this perspective comes from cross-cultural studies. Let us look briefly at how several societies deal with three issues basic to the psycho-analytic model: (1) the expression of grief, (2) the work of mourning and (3) the relationship to the deceased.

In his work on the mourning rituals of North American Indians, David Mandel-baum wrote about the Hopi tribe (1959). The Hopi prefer to keep death at a distance; it is unwelcome and causes fear. Mourners are discouraged from expressing grief and the general sentiment of the tribe is that the matter be 'quickly over and best forgotten'. Burial follows close upon the death, and there is no lingering attachment, as the deceased, through death, departs from the community forever.

Among most African societies death is 'comprehensively integrated into the totality of life' (Opoku, 1989). The dead become ancestors and there is reverence for and continuing communication with the deceased who, in spiritual form, remains a vital member of the tribe. 'The ongoing community of the living dead consists, then, of deceased ancestors who are still recalled in the minds of the living' (De Spelder & Strickland, 1992). The expression of grief is fervent at first, later becoming ritualized. The work of mourning is therefore highly structured and social. The goal of mourning is to assimilate the dead into the community of ancestors and then to re-incorporate them into living society in their new form and status (King, 1970).

Octavio Paz says that in Mexican culture, 'Death defines life. . . . Each of us dies the death he is looking for, the death he has made for himself. . . . Death like life, is not transferable' (1961). Joan Moore (1980) notes that 'uniformly, one meets the flat assertion that the funeral is the single most important family ceremony'. Death is viewed ironically, and frequently with festivities mingled with tears. Grief is accepted but restrained. The dead continue as a potent presence in the living community. Each year the famous *Day of the Dead* is a time of celebration and an occasion to pay respect to one's ancestors who are invited to return among the living.

Discussion

It seems that individual attitudes towards death and the dead are greatly influenced by the cultural life of a society. In his paper on socio-cultural considerations in the 'bereavement reaction' George Krupp states this finding quite directly:

> Bereavement practices vary as widely as other customs surrounding death. In fact, expressions of grief may often reflect society's taught responses as well as

the individual's actual feelings. . . . As normality varies from culture to culture, so healthy bereavement varies in different cultures. Each culture imposes its own cultural institutions and intentions [and] thereby prescribes the manner in which the group and individual express their emotions to the loss.

(Krupp, 1962, p. 67)

It is important to remember that the relationship between overt behaviors and unconscious processes is complex, obscure and infinitely varied. For example we cannot always assume that in societies where grief is brief that the unconscious processes are also brief, because the behavioral form that mourning takes may not accurately reflect the unconscious process. Given this fundamental psychoanalytic truth, and combining research findings with what we have learned about historical and cultural variations, I would like to offer the following reconsideration.

A reconsideration of mourning

In 1974 Brenner cautioned that

There is no more reason to expect that all patients who are sad constitute a homogenous group than to expect that all patients with fever do so. The same symptoms, even the same group of symptoms, can have different causes in different patients. . . . To make matters even worse, the same underlying cause can produce different symptoms in different patients, or different symptoms in the same patient at different times.

(p. 11)

Analysts since Freud have believed that the symptomatology of mourning was universal and that the dynamics of mourning were invariably related to object loss, decathexis and identification. On the other hand Brenner reminded us that psychoanalysis is a science of unconscious causation and that symptomatology is invariably individualized and multidetermined. Perhaps bereavement is not in and of itself pathogenic; rather, it may be the manner in which the event of death reverberates in the unconscious, becoming associated with forbidden and/or threatening fantasies (Hagman, 1996a). What must always be considered are the unconscious factors in mental life, and the complexity and mystery of individual differences. In full recognition of the truth of the above statements, I would now like to offer some observations, and propose several conclusions regarding the normal mourning process.

1   The psychological and behavioral phenomenon of mourning is far more varied and multiform than that which is described in the psychoanalytic literature and standardized in the *Glossary* definition (Moore & Fine, 1990). Many variables such as culture and historical epoch, as well as family and individual psychodynamics, influence how people mourn.

2   Mourning is a more social process than it would appear from its description in the standard psychoanalytic model (Hagman, 1996c). Freud's paradigm of the individual, closed-system psyche engaged in a solitary process of coming to terms with loss does not adequately address the role of others – lovers, family, friends, community and general cultural milieu – in the mourning process. As Furman notes, 'mourning alone is an almost impossible task' (1974, p. 114).
3   Although painful longing, sadness and grief are common characteristics of mourning, it appears that the type of dejection described by Freud and standardized in the psychoanalytic definition is not a necessary feature of normal mourning.
4   In addition, given the presence of responsive, supportive others and the relative absence of significant psychic conflict, bereaved people are not incapable of love and may continue to show an active involvement in their world. My observation from the psychoanalyses of bereaved people has been that in a setting characterized by empathy and support the patient may remain libidinally active and invested in life (Hagman, 1993, 1996b, 1996c).
5   The standard psychoanalytic model views identification as a primary means of detachment from the dead. However, it appears that there is a broad range of internalizations that characterize mourning and multiple functions are served. The bereaved's identification with attributes of the deceased is certainly common, but so are the introjection and structuring of memories, representations and imagoes that allow for a continued relationship with the lost person. As Brenner notes: 'Identification is often a consequence of object loss, but by no means invariably, and there is other unconscious motives for identification than fear of object loss' (1974, p. 17).
6   The central role of hypercathexis, memory review and decathexis in the Freudian mourning process has not held up to analytic and non-analytic observation. It seems more probable that the process of object relinquishment in mourning (when it occurs) can be engaged in unconsciously, without deliberate effort or visible distress. But even given an unconscious energic process many patients do not appear to decathect the memory of the deceased. The nature of the object relationship with the dead obviously must be transformed, but in many cases the dead continues to play a vital role in the inner world of the bereaved (Hagman, 1995).

The tasks of mourning

Pollock (1961) describes the function of mourning to be the process of adaptation to loss. This also seems to be the goal of the standard model as well as the varieties of mourning described by the research surveyed in this paper. A number of recent clinicians and researchers have argued that successful adaptation depends on the accomplishment of certain tasks (e.g. Worden, 1982; Schuchter, 1986; Weiss, 1988; Cleiren, 1993). A task perspective emphasizes that the bereaved person is an actor in the adaptation to loss, though he or she may not be conscious of the tasks engaged in (Cleiren, 1993, p. 24), and these conscious and unconscious tasks may be over determined and serve several functions. In his definitive text *Pathologic Grief* (1993) Selby Jacobs makes the assessment of an individual's successful completion of grieving tasks a central feature of his adaptive model of mourning. Cleiren (1993) argues that unlike the process model, a task model encompasses elements that are distinct but interrelated, and may be pursued simultaneously throughout the mourning process. Cleiren also stresses, correctly I feel, that the tasks of mourning are most accurately understood as *demands* with which the bereaved person must contend, rather than a set of ready-made *goals*. This also allows for a variety of ways in which the tasks may be completed – which again is in keeping with research. From this viewpoint the nature and outcome of mourning is co-determined by the specific task-demands accompanying the loss, the psychodynamics of the bereaved individual and the social context (which includes current relationships and culture). From this perspective the work of mourning includes:

1 Recognizing and understanding the reality of loss

Some writers describe instances where the initial reaction to news of death is disbelief and even denial. This may often be the case. Eventually, in normal mourning, reality testing prevails (Freud, 1917). One of the primary tasks of mourning is for the death to be recognized and its meaning elaborated; however, this frequently requires time and a degree of psychological work. The psychological impact of the death may evolve as the person begins to accept the loss and engages in the other tasks of mourning. The meanings of the death may be multiple: abandonment, rejection, punishment, revenge, wish fulfillment, curse and relief. The nature of the bereaved person's personal and cultural understanding will powerfully impact the accomplishment of the other mourning tasks. For example, the understanding of bereavement as an abandonment may intensify the aggressive components of grief, may impair one's ability to cope with changed reality, and may cripple one's capacity to restore self-esteem after loss. Wortman et al. (1994) consider this issue in their discussion of the meaning of loss for the survivor's 'worldview'.

2 Expressing, modulating and containing grief

Grief is associated with the rupture of the bond with a primary object and the experience of abandonment (Bowlby, 1980). Conscious and unconscious fantasies are structured into the expression of grief, signaling to the self and others the bereaved person's state of mourning. The manner of expressing, modulating and containing grief is determined by individual, familial, situational and cultural variables. Clinical research has shown that the normal intensity of grief is variable. Aries claims that over time Western cultural attitudes towards the expression of grief have varied from highly restrictive to overwrought and permissive. Across cultures the expression of grief is regulated by ritual and moral values. As with sexuality, the grieving of the individual will be influenced by biological, psychological and social factors. Most importantly, the bereaved person's developmental level and capacity for symbolization will determine his or her ability to integrate and structure the frequently stormy and chaotic affect states that characterize some bereavement reactions (Segal, 1952; Stolorow & Lachman, 1975; Hagman, 1995).

3 Coping with environmental and social change

Simultaneously with internal psychical demands, the bereaved person must also adapt to changes in the social and physical environment that have resulted from the loss (Pollock, 1961). If the deceased was the primary breadwinner, there are usually substantial demands placed on the surviving family members to compensate by assuming new roles. The cultural context will largely define the extent and nature of the social obligations of the bereaved. Clearly defined cultural expectations can assist with the accomplishment of this task, and in many cases the customs and rituals around bereavement also define stages of transition and the social reintegration of the survivors.

4 Transforming the psychical relationship with the lost object

Freud believed that the basic goal of mourning was for the individual to separate from the lost object and recathect new objects (Freud, 1917). However, as we discussed above, it does not seem that the attachment is so much given up as transformed internally. Therefore, I would like to suggest that there is a restructuring of the inner object relationship that allows for a range of outcomes, from complete psychological disengagement from the deceased to continued attachment despite permanent loss. The form of this structuring process will vary according to transferential factors and developmental needs, as well as societal prescriptions and restrictions. In most cases the resolution and restructuring of the relationship with the deceased is a long-term process, extending far beyond the period of mourning proper.

5 Restoring the self internally and within the social milieu

Contemporary psychoanalysis has determined that the sense of self is deeply affected by one's relationship with others. Invariably, mourning occurs when there is the death of a person who played a part in defining and sustaining important aspects of one's internal and external worlds (Klein, 1940; Grinberg, 1964; Parkes, 1981; Shane & Shane, 1990). The structure of personal experience, the bereaved person's sense of vitality and (to a degree) self-cohesion is affected by object loss (Hagman, 1995, 1996a, 1996b, 1996c). 'During the grief work', Mardi Horowitz observes, 'one reviews the relationship with the deceased in terms of all the var-ied self-concepts which have participated in working models of the attachment' (1990, p. 316). One is now a widow or widower, an orphan, a single parent, etc. For some time one's social identity and self-experience is defined by absence and lack. Aries has shown that within Western culture the vulnerability to sepa-ration and loss of the other has varied over time. Modern Western societies that are structured around small nuclear family groups have led to the individual's increased dependence on a small, quite vulnerable set of relationships. In some non-Western cultures the self may be defined more by family and tradition than by individual object relationships, in which case bereavement in these cultures may not threaten the cohesion of personal experience, yet it may in other ways have a profound impact on one's identity, social role and relationship to family. The future of the bereaved person's self-experience will therefore be determined by numerous individual, familial, situational and social factors. In regard to this area of task-demand, who one becomes is only partially under one's control; however, durable and healthy recovery depends on the bereaved person's capacity to make good personal choices, to cultivate and/or find new relationships and to reinvest his or her life with presence and fullness rather than absence and loss.

Conclusion

The resolution of bereavement will depend on the extent to which the individual is successful in accomplishing the task-demands described above. From the per-spective of a task model of mourning, the processes engaged in by the bereaved person depend on individual psychodynamics, as well as social, situational and cultural-historical factors. Pathological mourning occurs when there is psycho-logical deficit or conflict, and/or impingement or lack of support from an unem-pathic reality, to such an extent that one or more of the tasks are left uncompleted or poorly resolved. The end result of successful completion of mourning should be the maintenance or resumption of an optimal level of psychological and social functioning. The findings we have reviewed make it clear that we must be flexible and open in our assessments. A normal mourning process should be judged within a broad context that includes the multiple variables described in this paper. The psychoanalytic treatment of an individual who has suffered bereavement must take full cognizance of the unique dynamics of that person's mourning. Clearly, this makes our clinical assessments more complex and potentially difficult; how-ever, it can also make our care of this vulnerable group of patients more effective.

References

Abraham, K. (1927). A short history of the development of the libido. In *Selected Papers of Karl Abraham*. New York: Brunner Mazel.
Altschul, S. (1968). Denial and ego arrest. *J. Am. Psychoanal. Assoc.*, 16: 301–318.

Aries, P. (1974). *Western Attitudes Towards Death*. Baltimore: John Hopkins Univ. Press.

Aries, P. (1981). *The Hour of Our Death*. New York: Alfred Knopf.

Binswanger, L. (1957). *Sigmund Freud: Reminiscences of a Friendship*. New York: Grune & Stratton.

Blum, H. (1980). The value of reconstruction in adult psychoanalysis. *Int. J. Psychoanal.*, 61: 39–52.

Blum, H. (1983). The psychoanalytic process and analytic inference: A clinical study of a lie and loss. *Int. J. Psychoanal.*, 64: 17–33.

Blum, H. (1985). Splitting of the ego and its relation to parent loss. In *Defense and Resistance: Historical Perspectives and Current Concepts*, ed. H. Blum. New York: Int. Univ. Press, pp. 301–324.

Bornstein, P. E. et al. (1973). The depression of widowhood after thirteen months. *Brit. J. Community Psych.*, 122: 561–566.

Bowlby, J. (1980). *Loss: Sadness and Depression (Attachment and Loss, Vol. 3)*. New York: Basic Books.

Brenner, C. (1974). Some observations on depression, on nosology, on affects, and on mourning. *J. Geriatric Psych.*, 7: 6–20.

Clayton, P. J. et al. (1971). The bereavement of the widowed. *Diseases of Nerv. System*, 32: 597–604.

Clayton, P. J. et al. (1972). The depression of widowhood. *Brit. J. Psych.*, 120: 71–78.

Cleiren, M. (1993). *Bereavement and Adaptation: A Comparative Study of the Aftermath of Death*. Washington: Hemisphere Publishing Corp.

De Spelder, L. A. & Strickland, A. L. (1992). *The Last Dance: Encountering Death and Dying*. Mountain View, CA: Mayfield.

Deutsch, H. (1937). Absence of grief. *Psychoanal. Q.*, 6: 12–22.

Elizur, E. & Kaffman, M. (1982). Children's bereavement reactions following the death of a father: II. *J. Am. Academy Child Psychiat.*, 21: 474–480.

Elizur, E. & Kaffman, M. (1983). Factors influencing the severity of childhood bereavement reactions. *Am. J. Orthopsychiatry*, 53: 668–676.

Fenichel, O. (1945). *The Psychoanalytic Theory of Neurosis*. New York: Norton.

Fleming, J. (1972). Early object deprivation and transference phenomena: The working alliance. *Psychoanal. Q.*, 41: 23–49.

Fleming, J. (1974). The problem of diagnosis in parent loss cases. *Contemp. Psychoanal.*, 10: 439–451.

Fleming, J. & Altschul, S. (1988). Activation of mourning and growth by psychoanalysis. In *Childhood Bereavement and Its Aftermath*, ed. S. Altschul. Madison, CT: Int. Univ. Press, pp. 277–307.

Freud, S. (1909). Notes upon a case of obsessional neurosis. *Standard Edition, Vol. 10*.

Freud, S. (1915). Totem and Taboo. *Standard Edition, Vol. 13*.

Freud, S. (1917). Mourning and Melancholia. *Standard Edition, Vol. 14*.

Freud, S. (1923). The Ego and the Id. *Standard Edition, Vol. 19*.

Freud, S. (1926). Inhibitions, Symptoms and Anxiety. *Standard Edition, Vol. 20*.

Freud, S. & Breuer, J. (1895). Studies on Hysteria. *Standard Edition, Vol. 2*.

Frosch, J. (1990). *Psychodynamic Psychiatry: Theory and Practice, Vol. 2*. Madison, CT: Int. Univ. Press.

Furman, E. (1974). *A Child's Parent Dies: Studies in Childhood Bereavement*. New Haven: Yale Univ. Press.

Greenson, R. (1978). The problem of working through. In *Explorations in Psychoanalysis*, ed. R. Greenson. New York: Int. Univ. Press, pp. 225–267.

Grinberg, L. (1964). Two kinds of guilt: Their relations with normal and pathological aspects of mourning. *Int. J. Psychoanal.*, 45: 366–371.

Hagman, G. (1993). The Psychoanalytic Understanding and Treatment of Double Parent Loss. (Paper presented at the fall meeting of the American Psychoanalytic Association, New York, 1993).

Hagman, G. (1995). Death of a selfobject: Towards a self psychology of the mourning process. In *Progress in Self Psychology, Vol. 2,* ed. A. Goldberg. Hillsdale, NJ: Analytic Press, pp. 189–205.

Hagman, G. (1996a). Bereavement and neurosis. *I. Acad. Psychoanalysis*, 23(4), 635–53.

Hagman, G. (1996c). Flight from the subjectivity of the other: Pathological adaptation to early parent loss. In *Progress in Self Psychology, Vol. 12*, ed. A. Goldberg. Hillsdale, NJ: Analytic Press, pp. 207–219.

Hagman, G. (1996b). The role of the other in mourning. *Psychoanal. Q.*, 65(2): 327–352.

Horowitz, M. J. (1990). A model of mourning: Change in schemas of self and other. *J. Am. Psychoanal. Assoc.*, 38: 297–324.

Jacobs, S. (1993). *Pathologic Grief: Maladaptation to Loss*. Washington, DC: American Psychiatric Press.

Jacobson, E. (1957). On normal and pathological moods: Their nature and function. *Psychoanal. Study Child*, 12: 73–113.

King, N. (1970). *Religions of Africa: A Pilgrimage into Traditional Religions*. New York: Harper and Row.

Klein, M. (1940). Mourning and its relation to manic depressive states. *Int. J. Psychoanal.* 21: 125–153.

Kohut, H. (1972). *The Analysis of the Self*. Madison, CT: Int. Univ. Press.

Krupp, G. (1962). The bereavement reaction: A special case of separation anxiety, sociocultural considerations. *Psychoanal. Study Society*, 2: 42–74.

Lehman, D. R. et al. (1987). Long-term effects of losing a spouse or child in a motor vehicle accident. *J. Personality & Soc. Psychol.*, 52: 218–231.

Loewald, H. (1980). *Papers on Psychoanalysis*. New Haven: Yale Univ. Press.

Lund, D. A. et al. (1985). Gender differences through two years of bereavement among the elderly. *The Gerontologist*, 26: 314–319.

Lund, D. A. et al. (1985–86). Identifying elderly with coping difficulties after two years of bereavement. *Omega*, 16: 213–224.

Mandelbaum, D. (1959). Social history of funeral rites. In *The Meaning of Death*, ed. H. Feifel. New York: McGraw Hill, pp. 189–217.

McWilliams, N. (1994). *Psychoanalytic Diagnosis*. New York: Guilford Press.

Meissner, W. (1981). *Internalization in Psychoanalysis*. New York: Int. Univ. Press.

Middleton, W. et al. (1991). An international perspective on bereavement related concepts. (Paper presented to the third International Conference on Grief and Bereavement in Contemporary Society, Sydney).

Moore, B. E. & Fine, B. D. (1990). *Psychoanalytic Terms and Concepts*. New Haven: Yale Univ. Press.

Moore, J. (1980). The death culture of Mexico and Mexican Americans. In *Death And Dying: Views from Different Cultures*, ed. R. Kalish. New York: Baywood, pp. 51–61.

Nunberg, H. (1955). *Principles of Psychoanalysis*. New York: Int. Univ. Press.

Opoku, K. A. (1989). African perspectives on death and dying. In *Perspectives on Death and Dying: Cross Cultural and Multidisciplinary Viewpoint*, eds. A. Berger et al. Philadelphia: The Charles Press, pp. 14–29.

Parkes. C. (1981). *Bereavement: Studies of Grief in Adult Life*. Madison, CT: Int. Univ. Press.

Parkes, C. & Weiss, R. (1983). *Recovery from Bereavement*. New York: Basic Books.

Paz, O. (1961). *The Labyrinth of Solitude: Life and Thought in Mexico*. New York: Grove Press.

Pollock, G. (1961). Mourning and adaptation. *Int. J. Psychoanal.*, 42: 341–361.

Pollock, G. (1989). *The Mourning-Liberation Process*. Madison, CT: Int. Univ. Press.

Rando, T. A. (1993). *Treatment of Complicated Mourning*. Champaign, IL: Research Press.

Rochlin, G. (1965). *Griefs and Discontents*. Boston: Little, Brown, & Co.

Schor, E. (1994). *Bearing the Dead: The British Culture of Mourning from the Enlightenment to Victoria*. Princeton: Princeton Univ. Press.

Schuchter, S. R. (1986). *Dimensions of Grief*. San Francisco: Jossey-Bass.

Schuchter, S. R. & Zisook, S. (1994). The course of normal grief. In *Handbook of Bereavement: Theory – Research and Intervention*, eds. M. S. Stroebe et al. New York: Cambridge Univ. Press, pp. 23–43.

Segal, H. (1952). A psychoanalytic approach to aesthetics. *Int. J. Psychoanal.*, 33: 196–207.

Shane, M. & Shane, E. (1990). Object loss and selfobject loss: A contribution to understanding mourning and the failure to mourn. *Annual of Psychoanal.*, 11: 115–131.

Siggins, L. (1966). Mourning: A critical review of the literature. *Int. J. Psychoanal.*, 47: 14–25.

Silver, R. L. et al. (1983). Searching for meaning in misfortune: Making sense of incest. *J. Soc. Issues*, 39: 81–102.

Silver, R. L. & Wortman, C. B. (1988). Is processing a loss necessary for adjustment? A study of parental reactions to death of an infant. (Unpublished manuscript).

Stolorow, R. & Lachman, F. (1975). Early object loss and denial: Developmental considerations. *Psychoanal. Q.*, 44: 596–611.

Stroebe, W. & Stroebe, M. (1994). Is grief universal? Cultural variations in the emotional reaction to loss. In *Death and Identity*, eds. R. Fulton & R. Bendiksen. Philadelphia: The Charles Press, pp. 26–55.

Stroebe, W., Stroebe, M. & Hansson, R. O. (1994). Contemporary themes and controversies in bereavement research. In *Handbook of Bereavement: Theory, Research and Intervention*, eds. M. S. Stroebe, W. Stroebe, & R. O. Hansson. New York: Cambridge Univ. Press, pp. 457–490.

Vachon, M. L. et al. (1982a). Correlates of enduring stress patterns following bereavement: Social network, life situation and personality. *Psych. Med.*, 12: 783–788.

Vachon, M. L. et al. (1982b). Predictors and correlates of adaptation to conjugal bereavement. *Am. J. Psychiatry*, 139: 998–1002.

Viederman, M. (1989). Personality change through life experience III: Two creative types of response to object loss. In *The Problem of Loss and Mourning: Psychoanalytic Perspectives*, eds. D. Dietrich & D. C. Shabad. Madison, CT: Int. Univ. Press, pp. 187–209.

Volkan, V. (1981). *Linking Objects and Linking Phenomena*. Madison, CT: Int. Univ. Press.

Weiss, R. S. (1988). Loss and recovery. *J. Social Issues*, 44: 37–52.

Worden, J. W. (1982). *Grief Counseling and Grief Therapy: A Handbook for the Mental Health Practitioner*. New York: Springer.

Wortman, C. B. & Silver, R. C. (1987). Coping with irrevocable loss. In *Cataclysms, Crises and Catastrophes: Psychology in Action*, eds. G. R. Vanden-Blos & B. K. Bryant. Washington, DC: American Psychological Press, pp. 185–235.

Wortman, C. B. & Silver, R. C. (1989). The myths of coping with loss. *J. Counseling & Clin. Psychol.*, 57: 349–357.

Wortman, C. B., Silver, R. C. & Kessler, R. C. (1994). The meaning of loss and adjustment to bereavement. In *Handbook of Bereavement: Theory, Research and Intervention*, eds. M. Stroebe, W. Stroebe, & R. O. Hansson. New York: Cambridge Univ. Press, pp. 349–365.

Zisook, S. & Schuchter, S. R. (1986). The first four years of widowhood. *Psych. Annals*, 15: 288–294.

Chapter 2

Object loss and selfobject loss

A contribution to understanding mourning and the failure to mourn (1990)

Estelle Shane and Morton Shane

Editor's note: This is the earliest paper in this volume. In it, Estelle and Morton Shane discuss at length the most important discovery in recent psychoanalytic bereavement research, that rather than viewing mourning as an individual process of decathexis (disengagement) which follows its own solitary trajectory, the mourning process is highly social and is facilitated by interaction with empathic and supportive others (what Shane and Shane refer to as the "selfobject milieu"). Successful mourning depends on the availability and viability of this milieu, while the failure to mourn is often the result of the absence of this facilitating environment. This idea is central to my reconsideration of mourning and many of the other authors in this volume.

This paper was published in 1990 by Estelle Shane and Morton Shane as "Object Loss and Selfobject Loss: A Contribution to Understanding Mourning and the Failure to Mourn" in the Annual of Psychoanalysis, *Volume 18.*

The child's experience in mourning the death of a significant other has been the subject of considerable interest and debate in the psychological literature for many decades (e.g., Bowlby, 1960, 1973, 1980; Freud, 1960; Wolfenstein, 1966, 1969; Furman, 1974, 1986; Gardner, 1979; Herzog, 1980; Altschul, 1988). In this paper we are concerned with a particular facet of this topic, the role of adequate parental support in facilitating the mourning process, and with the contributions of self psychology to an understanding of this function. Therefore, the clinical material that follows, as well as our discussion of it, is restricted to that which most closely pertains to the topics of concern here, that is, the lingering effects of the child's profound response to the death of a parental figure as they are manifested in the analysis of an adult patient and the means by which those effects, if unmitigated by parental support, are defended against and disguised over the course of the person's life.

Brief vignettes from the analysis of child patients are included principally to support and illustrate this central thesis. While our review of the literature on the topic of mourning will thus be limited, we want to begin with an examination of the central question raised in that literature: At what age and to what degree can the child mourn? The questions are important because it has been felt that without the capacity to adequately mourn an overwhelming loss, the child's development is significantly impeded. It is postulated that because the child cannot mourn – that is, give up (decathect) the attachment to and investment in the representation of the lost person – or cannot preserve the relationship in the form of identification, the search goes on forever for the parent whose death is unconsciously denied and the mourner remains, in an important sense, the child at that phase or age when the loss was sustained. Thus, the fantasy that the parent still lives and can be found again precludes the possibility for true replacement, not just in childhood, but throughout life.

Some contributors have taken an extreme view in regard to the child's capacity to mourn. For example, Wolfenstein (1966) concludes that the child is developmentally incapable of decathecting lost objects until the completion of adolescence. It is only then, through object removal, that the parental object can be relinquished. Death of a parent prior to that time, Wolfenstein writes, leaves the person developmentally stunted. Even therapy for the bereaved child, or for the adult who was so traumatized, is futile in terms of completely undoing the developmental impediment.

This is indeed an extreme view. By contrast, the pioneering work of Robert Furman (1964a, 1964b) suggests that children who have attained object constancy before the death of a parent can, if deliberately aided, confront and master the loss. Others, following Furman's work, which involved the analysis of a six-year-old boy, have replicated and advanced his findings (e.g., the Cleveland group, led by Erna Furman, 1974; Lopez and Kliman, 1979; and Cohen, 1980). Further, these contributors claim that when the grown-ups in the surround are able to follow and facilitate the process, a child can mourn even without therapy. The problem lies with the bereaved parents' defenses against their own affects, their impatience with the child's attempts to grieve, or their ignorance of the significance of the loss for the child, all of which impair the child's ability to recover.

This range of responses from pessimism to guarded optimism extends to the prognosis for adults in analytic treatment who have suffered parent loss in childhood. Fleming and Altschul (1963) contend that such treatment too often presents insurmountable problems. Fleming (1972) concludes in her comprehensive paper on the topic that analysis of adults who experienced object loss in childhood reveals that these persons remain immature into adult life and that the immaturity interferes so significantly with the relationship between patient and analyst that ordinary classical analysis cannot proceed. Special technical interventions are required to understand and work with these patients. More recently, Burgner (1985) came to a similar conclusion. In a research study conducted at the Anna Freud Center on adult analysands who had suffered object loss in childhood, Burgner found that such loss before the oedipal phase results in permanent character defect; analysis can help these patients to some extent, but they still remain tied to the lost parent and unable to resolve oedipal conflicts.

It is important to note that this designation of "difficult patient" is understood as attributable to the inevitable narcissistic damage these patients, as children, suffered as a consequence of their bereavement (e.g., Rochlin, 1953; Pollock, 1978; Perman, 1979). Damaged self-esteem, devaluation of both deceased parent and self, and the threatened or real decrease in availability of and caretaking by the surviving parent and the concomitant decrease in need fulfillment describe the plight of such a child. An inability to trust or depend on the surviving parent complicates the picture.

To summarize the classical literature, then, children who suffer loss and who are denied the benefits of a sustaining environment and the opportunity to mourn are viewed as incapable of giving up the tie to the lost object. They remain forever fixated in this attachment, seeking a continuation of the old relationship in fantasy and in enactment. Psychological development is seriously impeded, with the child remaining at the level attained, regressing to earlier levels, or, at best, progressing in limited ways. These children grow up suffering from significant narcissistic injuries as well as from an unresolved bereavement over the lost parent. If they find their way into therapy, they become the difficult patients described in this literature, requiring special handling and facing a guarded or limited prognosis.

We would like to make the point that one of the difficulties these patients and their analysts have faced is that often the focus of interpretation has been on the blatant manifestations of the loss itself in terms of the person who is missed, rather than on the more silent, more subtle, but more insidious manifestations of the loss of narcissistic support from that person. For example, Fleming (1972) speaks of the patient's clamoring for a relationship in the transference with the preloss object as a significant interference with the therapeutic working alliance. She describes special techniques for dealing with this difficulty, such as confronting the patient with the reality of the parent's death, presumably to avoid isolation of affect, and directly addressing the patient's wish to experience the analyst as a new parent. It seems to us that the patient's defenses against the unbearable, inevitable permanency of the loss are thus directly assaulted. Fleming also resorts to another direct technique, advanced by Greenson (1965) and others for use with patients who require "something extra" to form an alliance: the deliberate use of "we" with the patient in referring to the therapeutic relationship. It is as if she feels the need to force an object relationship rather than address the patient's perceived lack of support in the past, in the present, and in the transference. This pessimism regarding the ameliorative effects of analysis and the consequent need for analytic measures leads us to the conviction that the classical frame of reference may be insufficient to fully meet the challenge of treating patients who have sustained parent loss in childhood. Self psychology, with its particular focus on narcissistic injury and repair, adds an essential dimension both to understanding and to working with such patients. That is, object loss, as it is conceptualized in the object concept of mainstream analysis, may not have the explanatory reach required to encompass the narcissistic damage long recognized as consequent to parent loss. Selfobject loss, as it is conceptualized in self psychology in terms of selfobject function, may provide just that needed explanatory reach. While much has been published in terms of the loss of the parent as object, that is, as the target of libidinal and aggressive drives and as provider of global narcissistic supplies, less has been written about loss of the parent in his or her selfobject function, a theoretical framework in which the required narcissistic supplies are particularized. As a theoretical addition, then, self psychology can pinpoint the specific narcissistic injury sustained by the self through such a loss and can indicate as well the remedial steps required to repair the damage.

Using this framework, we can understand that when a parent dies, a child might be threatened in any or all of the three currently acknowledged repairing, sustaining, and regulating relationships of its self. That is, the child's sense of power and importance might be compromised with the loss of a sustaining, mirroring selfobject function. His or her sense of comfort and security might be weakened, the trust and admiration in the idealized parents might be profoundly shaken, and the background of reassuring human connectedness might be disrupted. In short, such functions heretofore provided by the deceased parent would no longer be available. Were the surviving parent able to make up for this loss in a significant way, the child would, of course, be less traumatized. He or she would be able to face the impact of the loss without feeling the risk of being overwhelmed, annihilated, or fragmented. Within such a supportive milieu, compensatory self-structure would be formed not only to repair the weakened aspects of the self, but also to facilitate continued or renewed development.

In too many cases, however, the surviving parent is so adversely affected by the death that he or she is less available for support and encouragement than before. So, in effect, the child in his bereavement suffers the loss of self-regulating selfobject functions heretofore supplied by both parents. (And this double loss must be understood to be in addition to the loss of mutual affect-sharing experiences with that same deceased other, that is, the post–object constancy, oedipal and post oedipal object-centered dimension of the lost other so central to the classical literature on mourning.)

In attempting to defend against the massive loss of needed functions for the survival of the self, the bereaved child searches for substitute selfobject relationships to shore up and maintain his self-integration. In cases with pathological outcome, such relationships are either inadequate or unavailable, and the self, protected by defensive structures that merely cover over the defect, remains vulnerable.

But how is mourning itself, postulated in the classical literature to be so essential to continued healthy development, to be conceptualized in a framework expanded by self-psychological formulations?

We would like to suggest that given an adequate supportive environment to strengthen the child's total self and aid in dealing with his defensive avoidances, the child would spontaneously mourn the death of an important loved one. The pain of loss can be borne and the necessary capacity to think, talk, and reflect about it can be sustained if the child is helped to mourn rather than stifled by unempathic criticism and unrealistic standards for mourning behavior. Therefore – and this is the important point – we consider mourning in children, as it has always been seen in adults, a normal process, neither impossible nor exceptional, although the required optimal selfobject environment, more available to the adult, may be hard to provide for the child.

In addition, we would like to assert that in our experience it is not the failure to mourn per se that is primarily pathogenic, as has been suggested in the classical child analytic literature; rather, it is the absence of an empathic selfobject milieu at a time of crucial need that constitutes the chief pathogenic factor for a child who loses a parent. This is certainly not to say that the loss of a parent in itself does not constitute a major trauma having pathogenic effects. Nor are we saying that the mourning process is not important. It is well documented that if a new other is turned to without such mourning, genuine development in the capacity for relationships beyond the preloss level does not take place. The point is that in order to mourn, the child requires selfobject functions from the surround; moreover, without such selfobject functions the line of self-development, as well as the interrelated line of object relations, is impaired.

By introducing the selfobject dimension into the experience of loss and mourning a more thorough appreciation of the process and its facilitation can be achieved, as we hope the preceding remarks and the clinical material to follow demonstrate. There is another point that may be considered in this context. Because selfobject functions are experienced as a part of the self, it may be that the bereaved child can more easily replace these functions from substitute others than he can the object-centered experiences of sharing, loving and hating with a specific, unique, and distinct other. Such avenues for replacement of missing selfobject functions have been emphasized by Kohut (1977), who contends that if there is a deficiency in one or another sector of the self related to selfobject failure emanating from one parent, the child may make up for it by turning to the other parent for compensatory experiences in the same or another sector. This would seem to indicate that the self-centered (selfobject) aspects of the relationship with the lost parent are more easily replaceable and require less mourning than the object-centered aspects of the relationship. In theory, then, it follows that loss of a love object leads to identification (i.e., internalization with object tag), mourning, and turning to a new object. Loss of a selfobject leads to transmuting internalization (i.e., internalization without object tag), less mourning, and a more prompt and peremptory search for new selfobject functions.

Of more clinical importance, however, is the contention we have already made that it is the unavailability of the self-centered aspects of that lost relationship that can most crucially interfere with the mourning process itself. To repeat, children who experience traumatic failure in selfobject function sustain self pathology. They grow up narcissistically damaged. While this has been recognized in the literature, the classical frame of reference has not been adequate to address this clinical issue. Self psychology, with its focus on selfobject function, offers a means both to understand and to rectify this pathology consequent to parent loss.

Now to the clinical material. We are presenting brief vignettes of four latency-age children analyzed by us. All four were asymptomatic following the death of a parent, apparently able to accept that loss without obvious difficulty, according to the surviving parent. Three of these children were placed in treatment several years after the loss was sustained, subsequent to the development of significant symptoms. The three, all girls, lost their mothers and had fathers who responded in a less than optimal way.

Two of the fathers of these three girls actively discouraged the mourning process, conveying in more or less direct fashion their own discomfort with the topic of the mother's death and their belief that it would be better for the child "to get on with her own life." One of the two fathers said that he did not think his daughter really missed her mother and that she was just using her death as an excuse to get his attention, an effort that he felt should go unrewarded. The second reported that he had instructed his daughter to keep all reminders of her mother to herself; she was allowed to have a single envelope to contain any concrete mementos, and all pictures of her mother, including a large portrait of mother and daughter that had previously hung prominently in the house, were removed. When the father remarried, as he did within the year, the child was asked to call her stepmother "Mother" and to not talk, let alone cry, about the mother who was dead. Once a year father and daughter visited the grave site, where she could openly mourn, and that was it.

When these two girls developed symptoms, neither father could accept at first that there might be any causal connection to the mother's death. In analysis what was striking was the fact that both of these girls had understood two things: that their fathers truly loved them and that if they were to keep their fathers' love, support, and admiration, they had to stifle whatever sense of loneliness or longing they might feel for the absent mothers. Both girls guiltily reported in analysis that they had found it shamefully easy to put thoughts of their dead mothers aside and remembered enjoying whatever exclusive attention they were able to get from their fathers, but these issues of conflicts over aggression and oedipal victory were not as crucial to the resultant pathology as the literature appears to suggest.

In contrast to the fathers of these two, the father of the third girl did his best to encourage expression of her grief. He himself was devastated by the loss and openly mourned his wife's death. He was able to understand his daughter's feelings and did not disapprove of her for them. However, the child revealed to her analyst that she remembered being hindered by her father's open distress and feeling, despite his efforts to encourage her to mourn, that it was her responsibility to be supportive of him and to stifle her own neediness. Nevertheless, there is no question that the third father was the most able to provide selfobject functions for his daughter, with the result that she was more able than the other two girls to overcome the effects of the mother's death. While the first two girls suffered pathology that could not be ignored by even the most insensitive of fathers, the third's difficulties were subtler, and it was a mark of the father's empathy that she entered therapy at all.

We want to make the point that in all three cases there was no question that the fathers, as well as the stepmothers, were intelligent people who loved their daughters, felt kindly toward them, and wanted the best for them. What we are talking about is a capacity in the parent to serve for the child as a needed selfobject, that is, a capacity to appreciate the inner world of the child and to respond appropriately in a way that supports the child's self. These selfobject functions are difficult for even the most empathic of surviving parents to supply when there is death in the family. Our contention is that the pathology in the child is more than the object loss and is consequent to, and proportionate to, the loss of selfobject function.

The fourth child in this series is included to serve as a contrast to the previous three. Scott, who was eight when he lost his father, was also asymptomatic and apparently accepting immediately following his bereavement. Nevertheless, Scott's mother, herself in analysis when her husband died, felt that her son should be helped to deal with his father's death through an analytic experience. In analysis, as in his life in general, Scott defended himself against feelings or preoccupations concerning his father, though their subtle expression could be discerned. For example, in a maze game played repeatedly and with increasingly difficult mazes that he himself had constructed, Scott traced out the path from start, which he invariably labeled "S," to finish, which he labeled "F." It was clear to the analyst that the intense affective striving Scott exerted to connect all the "S's" to all the "F's" was a repeated effort to reconnect Scott to his father, but the analyst said nothing. Finally, in one analytic hour the maze itself was unconsciously designed by Scott in the unmistakable shape of the two initials of his father's name, in addition to including the usual "S" and "F" for start and finish or, as the analyst surmised, Scott and Father. The connection was finally made for him, and it was a moving experience for both patient and analyst to see how strongly Scott missed his father.

Months later, Scott drew a picture of himself and his analyst camping together under the stars. When the stars of one of the constellations were connected, a big "F" appeared. Scott was then able to describe the affect-laden fantasy that his father was not really dead but there, in heaven, from which place he continued his relationship with Scott. Becoming conscious of this fantasy increased Scott's awareness of his loss. While these indications of missing his father were uncovered in the office, in the world outside, Scott continued to function without difficulty, as if there were no loss at all. A follow-up of this patient 15 years later, when he was in his 20s, revealed a healthy, enthusiastic, vigorously masculine person who cared about others. Arrests in development at the preloss level, which one might have expected, were nowhere in evidence, the result, we believe, of his mother's sensitive support and her provision of auxiliary support through the relationship with an analyst at a time of great selfobject need. We speculate that this child's development was not impeded because he had been allowed to mourn and because missing selfobject functions were supplied in the process. In the following exposition of an adult case analyzed by E.S., we will attempt to demonstrate that the early loss of a parental object in the context of an inadequate selfobject milieu leads to the classical picture of an individual arrested at the preloss level. The patient, Mr. W, lost a parental surrogate at age three, after the establishment of object constancy. On the face of it, he should not have suffered to the degree he did, inasmuch as his mother and father remained physically available to him.

But neither parent was able to understand or respond to the narcissistic lack the parental surrogate's absence entailed for him. Selfobject functions were compromised and, unfortunately, were not supplied by his parents. Had they been, this patient would not have had to wait until he was in analysis to be allowed to mourn. He would not have had to turn to medication to soothe himself nor to repeat endlessly the search for a lost idyllic relationship.

Mr. W, a 42-year-old trial lawyer, entered analysis because of lifelong feelings of anxiety, depression, and low self-esteem, which he attempted to control through the use of tranquilizers and recreational drugs. These dysphoric affects centered mainly on an inability to commit himself either in love relationships or professionally. He described himself in his relationships with women as being intensely infatuated almost upon meeting the woman and consumed with a desire to win and possess her; then, having reached his goal, he found himself, for inexplicable reasons, having to get away. In analysis, details emerged of this configuration, which he had heretofore kept himself unaware of despite several episodes of therapy in the past. We came to recognize that the process always followed the same pattern. The feelings and fantasies of love would give way to a sense of disappointment, disillusionment, feelings of being trapped and suffocated, and then intense anger and determination to escape. At first an impassioned and effective lover, he would lose interest and, in fact, become impotent, that state serving as a barometer of the fact that it was time to pull out of the relationship. He would then extricate himself with more or less difficulty, and feel an immediate sense of relief and pleasure; then the inevitable feeling of remorse would set in. He would find himself reliving romantic moments with the woman, dream of having found her again, and then awaken weeping when he rediscovered his loss. He would call out to her in his imagination to please come back. The period of truncated mourning would run its course and he would begin to feel both loneliness and aloneness (Adler, 1985). There followed a sense of despair, sometimes with suicidal ideation, extending to fleeting experiences of depersonalization and derealization. These states would prove so unbearable that he was driven to seek out a new relationship, not a difficult undertaking, given his good looks, engaging personality, and intense romantic inclinations. Each new relationship would begin with profound optimism and a sense of great well being, only to retrace the same course from seeking, to winning, to wanting out, to relief, to regret, and to loneliness and despair. These experiences with women had begun in adolescence when he started dating. He had had many such relationships, some lasting a week, others lasting longer, the longest being for a two-year period. With each affair the anger with the particular woman and the regrets over losing her did not go away; instead of establishing a partnership, or at least the mixed pleasure of bittersweet memories, all he had to show for his efforts was an ever-growing mountain of regret and an ever-renewed reservoir of anger. Finally, 18 months into the analysis, after the pattern itself had become clear to both analyst and patient, it became possible to point out to him during the infatuation phase of one such affair that he didn't even know the woman, that she was, in effect, no more than a fantasy, and yet, as usual, he was planning a life with her that included marriage. He was truly surprised and so impressed that this elaborate pattern was not repeated. Despite this helpful insight, however, and the fact that he was able to cease the actual behavior with women, the underlying sense of loss remained strong with him, along with the anger and regret.

The analysis began with links to the past that demonstrated the oedipal connection to these difficulties with love (and with work as well). Mr. W, an only child, was an infant when World War II ended. His father left for the service just after his birth, returning when he was three. He remembers his father descending upon his intense relationship with his mother and disrupting it. His father, who seemed harsh and cold and displeased with him, threw himself into the task of returning to civilian life. He worked hard to make money and was rarely with the family. The experience of sudden disruption of the close relationship with his mother was repeated at age six, when his sister was born, and at age eight, with the birth of his younger brother.

In the transference the oedipal issues were handled by displacement, with Mr. W finding girlfriends who had physical characteristics similar to mine even though, as he stated with some embarrassment, I was definitely not his type. In one particular dream, which he had after some romantic experience with a dark-haired woman, a hot dog in the refrigerator appeared split in two, and he awoke in terror. The castration anxiety was easily interpreted and accepted by him. On another occasion, when he found himself having a sexual fantasy about me, he had a sudden image of razor blades inside a vagina. He connected me with his mother, who appeared in dreams as a woman who frowned at him, expressing, he felt, her depressive and undependable nature. He feared that I was similarly unreliable, susceptible to moods, and likely to disapprove of him, reject him, and, most terrifying of all, simply pull away from him and disappear, leaving him bereft and unsteady in his bearings. At such moments the old depersonalization and derealization returned, indicating an anxiety far in excess of what could be characterized as castration anxiety and closer to what Kohut (1977) and others (e.g., Freud, 1960) have termed annihilation anxiety.

It was through this transference elaboration of the character of his mother that an understanding of the deeper nature of his problems evolved. I came to see that beneath the Oedipus complex lay something even more profound. The slow discovery of these deeper problems was made in the context of an emerging, predominantly idealizing selfobject transference, which eventually supplanted the positive oedipal transference that had preceded it. Months of experiencing me as one who could be relied on to be there, as steady, predictable, and dependable, indicated the flowering of this new transference constellation. He was reassured and calmed by my presence and by the perception that I was listening and attempting to understand what he was feeling. He came to see me as perfectly attuned to him, and he began to feel very strong and self-contained. In time he was able to give up relying on the various drugs and medications he customarily took to modulate and control his affect states. Only then, in the security established by the smoothly evolving selfobject transference, embedded as it was in the real relationship, could the full story of his early years emerge into consciousness.

The veil of repression was lifted through a dream. The setting in the dream is a courtroom. There is a cage in which a small, deformed creature lies, more dead than alive. The prosecutor points to the figure with a long stick and pokes at it, attempting to get it to move. He turns accusingly to Mr. W. The patient knows he is guilty of doing harm to this creature and feels that all those present know he is guilty as well, but he cannot for the life of him understand what he has done. In associating to the dream, Mr. W first talked about his mother, about whom he has always felt guilty. When she was in a bad mood, he assumed it was due to something he had done. His mother had had the habit of going to her own room and not speaking to anyone for days. He remembered how surprised he was to discover, just a couple of years earlier, that it was not he whom she was mad at, but his father. Mr. W then went on to wonder about the creature in the dream, all shriveled up, more dead than alive. He suddenly recalled, for the first time as an adult, that he and his mother had not lived alone together during the first three years of his life when his father had been away. They had gone to live with his maternal grandmother during that period, and his grandmother had died around the time that his father had come home. He slowly came to the conviction that the small figure in his dream was his grandmother.

The dream, as well as Mr. W's surprising associations to it, was the beginning of an emotion-laden uncovering of the powerful but forgotten relationship between his grandmother and himself and of its tragic end. With lengthy discussions with his mother along the way, the patient dedicated himself to a voyage of discovery about his origins that included trips back home, visits to the graveyard, explorations of the family Bible, and, most importantly, a study of his old baby book. In the sessions that followed, his affect changed from a limited range, which was guarded, flat, and depressed on one end and hostile and angry on the other, to a more authentic and much-expanded range of emotion, best described as buoyant, excited, and lively on the one end and tearful and sad on the other. The patient experienced a change in his sense of himself, which he naively but aptly described as a change from a false self to a real self. The facts that emerged over this time, one year into the analysis, were the following: Mr. W was born one year after the marriage of his teenage mother, at which time several events converged to shape his mother's, and concomitantly his own, experience. First, her husband left for the army; she was shaky and uncertain in her new role as mother and returned to her own mother's home and the support her mother could offer for the duration of her husband's absence. Second, her brother, her mother's favorite, was reported missing in action, presumably dead. At first devastated and inconsolable, the grandmother ultimately responded to these events by regarding the new baby as her dead son restored to her by God, and, sweeping aside her daughter, assumed the full role of mother to the infant. This state of affairs continued for two years until the grandmother became ill and slowly died. His mother told Mr. W that because she herself had been so upset, she had given him no explanation during the time his grandmother was dying or at any time thereafter, though the patient was three years old by the time his grandmother died. From the mother's point of view at the time, the little boy did not notice the loss. She had written in his baby book, "Poor child; his real mother has died. Luckily he shows no signs of missing her," revealing that she had not understood what he was going through or how a child defends himself against painful affect. She now recalls that after his grandmother's death, the patient alternated between refusing to have anything to do with her, and clinging to her, refusing to let her out of his sight. We can assume that Mr. W knew some of this story before his analysis, but all of it was either suppressed or repressed when he started and for the first year thereafter. We can speculate that it was only in the context of a solidly established and developmentally facilitating selfobject transference that Mr. W could allow himself to face the full impact of the loss of his grandmother and work through in that transference the double loss of her selfobject sustenance and her love-object presence. Working through is often likened to the process of mourning; in this part of the analysis of the case, it was identical to it. Furthermore, it became possible with Mr. W via the quality of the transference that evolved to arrive at the idealizing selfobject nature of the relationship he had had with his grandmother, whom he had apparently experienced as available to him in a kind of asexual, egocentric paradise. But the full sense of what it must have been like for him to lose that idyllic relationship only emerged through an incident in the analysis in which he experienced a profound disruption of the empathy and trust that had been built up between us. That is, the smoothly functioning selfobject matrix, so helpful to the recovery of this patient's early and profound parental object loss, was disrupted by an unempathic response on my part that, I realize in retrospect, expressed my effort to join the patient's derogation of me. When he was exploring his roots in order to understand his connection with his grandmother, Mr. W was simultaneously researching the popular psychological literature in order to understand his connection to me. One day he announced that analysis, according to his reading in Alice Miller, is heavily concerned with empathic understanding as a part of the therapeutic process. He added most sincerely and gratefully that he had always been impressed with my ability to be understanding of him. Then, suddenly, in what appeared to be a humorous mood, he said with a laugh, "Do you really understand me, or are you just bullshitting me?" Joining in what I took to be his joke, I spontaneously laughed. To my chagrin, he was deeply incensed, with the result that I had burst in an instant the sense of well being and trust in me that had been developing over the previous six months.

There are many ways in which this rupture might be understood. It might be seen as a defensive effort on his part to break the idealizing tie, a tie that threatened a traumatic repetition of the disappointment and disillusionment experienced with his grandmother. But the analyst cannot be left out of the picture. Mr. W's nervous laughter, which was mistaken for humor, was, I realize in retrospect, a defensive distancing that perhaps should have been discerned. Instead, I sided with it for unconscious reasons, no small part of which was relief from the strain and responsibility of being so heavily idealized. In any case, many months after this momentary and seemingly slight breach in empathy, Mr. W sadly recalled the ambience in the analysis prior to it as his long-lost Eden wherein trust, hope, and confidence had been restored, only to be lost again forever. He continued to struggle in the analysis over restoration and loss of that idyllic state, the transference meaning of which became increasingly clear to him. That is, Mr. W came to understand that he had sought all his life for a restoration of the ideal relationship he had experienced with his grandmother but had never been able to allow one to stabilize because he feared that if he dropped his guard, he would suddenly and traumatically be deserted, which is how he experienced both the grandmother's death and his analyst's empathic failure. This fear of traumatic loss had led him from one aborted relationship to another. It was only in the selfobject transference that this repetition could be understood, interpreted, and worked through. To illustrate Mr. W's struggle to defend himself against a recurrence of this trauma, let us present a vignette of a session that occurred during this period of the analysis.

The session takes place on a Friday before a two-week vacation. All week Mr. W described himself as feeling somewhat depressed although, as he told me, work was going very well and he actually should be feeling good. He knows after much experience with me that I will suggest that the depression might have to do with the upcoming separation, but he doesn't accept that. Yesterday, he noted that he could never admit to anyone that he longed for him or her while he was currently in a relationship. He could only admit to himself his deep need for someone after he had lost that person. He imagined that while I was on vacation, he would think of me as helpful and would miss seeing me, but he was not currently having any of these feelings. He was angry with Sarah (the woman he had lived with for two years) and wished death and destruction on her for marrying someone else; he believed she could not be happily married. He wondered then if I was thinking he was really talking about my husband and me.

Today, a Friday hour, Mr. W comes in struggling again with his low-key mood, which he relates on an intellectual level to my upcoming vacation, of which he again assures me he can feel nothing. He says he only feels numb, a hated feeling that he associates with the way he used to feel all of the time. He would like to say to me, "Don't leave me. What will I do without you?" But he honestly does not feel that; he only thinks that. When I comment that he seems to still find these feelings difficult to bear, he becomes hurt and very irritated with me. It makes him feel condescended to, as if I am treating him like a small child; he knows he acts like one sometimes, but he doesn't want to be treated like one.

He then pauses nervously and says that a conversation he had last night keeps coming to his mind but that it seems totally off the subject and of no interest or value for discussion. Yet it keeps coming back; he wonders, why is that? He wants to go on, but I bring him back to the recurrent thought. He reluctantly begins to tell me about a conversation he had over dinner with a new friend. His friend described the situation with his own therapist, who makes suggestions to him about what he should do. His friend doesn't follow these suggestions and then feels guilty. Mr. W told his friend that his analyst never tells him what to do. She only listens patiently to what he has to say, makes a few connections, and asks a few questions, and somehow things evolve. Even more hesitantly, Mr. W tells me that he told his friend that he is deeply impressed with all he has learned about himself in analysis and that he admires my dedication and patience very much. He imagines, he tells me, that his dead grandmother must have been like that. He pauses and then says that he guesses he has a hard time telling me that he is grateful to me for what I have done, and continue to do, for him and that he thinks I am really a good analyst, despite all the criticism he directs toward me. He pauses again and says suddenly, in earnest, "Do you plan to give up your practice soon? Are you tired of what you are doing?" He himself, in his law practice, likes to see a client, figure out the legal problem quickly, come to a decision, and then show the client out. He says he couldn't stand to do the work I do; it is too demanding. He wonders, anticipating me, why this comes to his mind now. I tell him that we can understand why he finds it so difficult to admire me or pay me a compliment and that I agree it is hard for him to talk directly about any of his feelings. I tell him that I think it is particularly hard for him to talk about any good feelings he has about me, because he fears not only that that makes him weak and me powerful, but also, more importantly, that I might respond as he tends to when someone expresses a need for him: that is, he wants to run away, to get out of the relationship forever. He is afraid that if he shows me that he depends on me, I will respond by wanting to get away from him, by giving up my practice; he fears I have as much trouble committing myself to him and to my work as he does to others and to his work. He responds, as the hour ends, by saying, "Let's get off this topic; it's getting too heavy."

Recapitulation and Summary

In summary, Mr. W, who had repressed the loss of his parent-surrogate at age three, was able to revive in analysis both the memory and the affective experience of the death. While the analysis began in a positive oedipal transference, it was only in the context of the full flowering of an idealizing selfobject transference that this patient was able to face the task of mourning. Ramifications of his view of the death of the parent-surrogate, including his own feeling of responsibility for it, were explored. A lifelong unconscious character pattern was understood as a defense against intense emotional involvement with women, an involvement that would have recapitulated the early trauma of his parent-surrogate's death. By turning passive into active behavior, the patient abandoned any and all women who threatened to become close to him before they had too much power or could abandon him. In a repeatedly failed effort to master this trauma, he demonstrated the pre-loss fixation on the lost object. The establishment of a selfobject transference that most likely repeated the supportive experiences with the parent-surrogate, but unfortunately was not available with his parents, occurred in the context of the analysis.

In analysis the mourning process was engaged, and signs of the resumption of development became evident. The patient's self-structure was much strengthened through this experience, as evidenced by his increased sense of authenticity, inner harmony, the absence of derealization and depersonalization, and, most impressive to him, his ability to regulate his affect states without medication or recreational drugs.

Here, then, we have attempted to add a self-psychological vantage point to the topic of parent loss. The contentions that mourning in childhood requires adequate selfobject support and that with this support mourning is a more or less spontaneous, effective process are illustrated with both child and adult case material. While we have alluded briefly to the general nature of the selfobject functions required to sustain mourning in childhood, additional work in self psychology is required to particularize these important functions.

References

Adler, G. (1985). *Borderline Psychopathology and Its Treatment*. New York, London: Aronson.

Altschul, S. (1988). *Childhood Bereavement and Its Aftermath*. Madison, CT: International Universities Press.

Bowlby, J. (1960). Grief and Mourning in Infancy and Early Childhood. *Psychoanal. Study Child* 15: 9–52.

Bowlby, J. (1973). *Attachment and Loss – Separation*. New York: Basic Books.

Bowlby, J. (1980). *Attachment and Loss – Loss*. New York: Basic Books.

Burgner, M. (1985). The Oedipal Experience: Effects on Development of an Absent Father. *Int. J. Psycho-Anal*. 66: 311–320.

Cohen, D. J. (1980). Constructive and Reconstructive Activities in the Analysis of a Depressed Child. *Psychoanal. Study Child* 35: 237–266.

Fleming, J. (1972). Early Object Deprivation and Transference Phenomena: The Working Alliance. *Psychoanal Q*. 41: 23–49.

Fleming, J. and Altschul, S. (1963). Activation of Mourning and Growth by Psychoanalysis. *Int. J. Psycho-Anal*. 44: 419–431.

Freud, A. (1960). Discussion of Dr. John Bowlby's Paper. *Psychoanal. Study Child* 15: 53–56.

Furman, E. (1974). *A Child's Parent Dies*. New Haven, CT: Yale University Press.

Furman, E. (1986). On Trauma: When Is the Death of a Parent Traumatic? *Psychoanal. Study Child* 41: 191–208.

Furman, R. A. (1964a). Death and the Young Child: Some Preliminary Considerations. *Psychoanal. Study Child* 19: 321–333.

Furman, R. A. (1964b). Death of a Six-Year-Old's Mother During His Analysis. *Psychoanal. Study Child* 19: 377–397.

Gardner, R. A. (1979). Death of a parent. In: *Basic Handbook of Child Psychiatry, Vol. 2*, eds. J. Call & R. L. Cohen. New York: Basic Books, pp. 270–282.

Greenson, R. R. (1965). The Working Alliance and the Transference Neurosis. *Psychoanal Q*. 34: 155–181.

Herzog, J. M. (1980). Sleep Disturbance and Father Hunger in 18- to 28-Month-Old Boys: The Erlkönig Syndrome. *Psychoanal. Study Child* 35: 219–233.

Kohut, H. (1977). *The Restoration of the Self*. New York: International Universities Press.

Lopez, T. and Kliman, G. W. (1979). Memory, Reconstruction, and Mourning in the Analysis of a 4-Year-Old Child: Maternal Bereavement in the Second Year of Life. *Psychoanal. Study Child* 34: 235–271.

Perman, J. M. (1979). The Search for the Mother: Narcissistic Regression as a Pathway of Mourning in Childhood. *Psychoanal Q.* 48: 448–464.

Pollock, G. H. (1978). Process and Affect: Mourning and Grief. *Int. J. Psycho-Anal.* 59: 255–276.

Rochlin, G. (1953). Loss and Restitution. *Psychoanal. Study Child* 8: 288–309.

Wolfenstein, M. (1966). How is Mourning Possible? *Psychoanal. Study Child* 21: 93–123.

Wolfenstein, M. (1969). Loss, Rage, and Repetition. *Psychoanal. Study Child* 24: 432–460.

Chapter 3

The psychoanalytic understanding and treatment of double parent loss (1993)

George Hagman

Editor's note: This was my first paper on bereavement and mourning. It was the result of both my own psychoanalytic treatment as well as the analysis of several patients of mine who suffered parent loss in adolescence. The most important finding was that the failure to mourn a parent was often due to the loss of the surviving parent due to illness, depression, addiction, etc. Although I had yet to read the paper by Shane and Shane, many of my observations and conclusions echo their findings. "We mourn not alone, but together," as Erna Furman noted.

This paper was presented in 1993 by George Hagman as "The Psychoanalytic Understanding and Treatment of Double Parent Loss" at the winter meeting of the American Psychoanalytic Association in New York City.

The impact of childhood bereavement on personality development has been extensively discussed in the psychoanalytic literature (Wolfenstein, 1966; Nagera, 1967; Furman, 1974 and 1986; Bowlby, 1980). In addition, several authors have examined the implications of parent loss for the psychoanalysis of adults (Fleming and Altschul, 1962; Altschul, 1968 and 1988; Fleming, 1972; Blum, 1980). Nevertheless, I believe that a central factor in our understanding and treatment of adults with problems due to parent loss has been underemphasized. It has been my observation, from the psychotherapy of adults who have lost a parent by death in childhood, that, in many cases, psychopathology results when there is a double parent loss. That is, the death of one parent is accompanied, or followed, by the loss of the surviving parent through dysfunction or emotional withdrawal. Regarding children, Bowlby and Furman have made the same point previously (Furman, 1974 and 1986; Bowlby, 1980). Additionally, data from childhood bereavement research indicates that consistent parenting may be the single most important variable in a child's adaptation to loss (Krupnick, 1984); however, the relevance of this finding for our understanding and treatment of adults has rarely been addressed.

Therefore, this paper will focus on the impact of double parent loss on personality development (specifically, the accomplishment of adolescent developmental tasks), and its significance for the psychoanalytic treatment of adults. My thesis will be that a stable, healthy and intact family provides assistance in accomplishing the various tasks of this demanding life passage. Inevitably, the death of a parent damages the family structure, impacting development. In addition, frequently, the death of one spouse leads to impairments in the functioning of the survivor, or highlights a previous lack of availability or disability with negative implications for the relationship with their children. Hence, the child suffers *double* parent loss. Given this, we see in our clinical work that, though the loss of a parent damages the context which sustains development, the added loss of the surviving parent is especially traumatic (see also Blum, 1985, p. 307). As a consequence, not only does the mourning process often cease, but there may also be a skewing of normal development, as emergency adaptations are initiated to cope with possible, or actual, family collapse. The resulting psychopathology can be significant, chronic and resistant to change.

Though the subject of this paper is parent loss through death, I believe my thesis may have broader implications for work with patients suffering from the sequelae of divorce and severe and disabling mental and physical illness in parents. Unfortunately, consideration of these conditions is beyond the scope of this paper.

After a brief literature review, we will discuss the psychoanalyses of three adult patients who suffered double parent loss during adolescence. The clinical sequelae of loss will be highlighted through consideration of several major developmental tasks that the adolescent must resolve: a) oedipal resolution, b) separation/individuation, and c) character consolidation. We will then review the role of the family in adolescent development and the importance of interpersonal processes in the facilitation (or obstruction) of the mourning process.

A review of the literature

Unfortunately, space will not permit a full discussion of the literature related to mourning, childhood bereavement and the treatment of adult survivors of early parent loss. Excellent reviews are available on all these subjects (Pollock, 1961 and 1989; Fleming, 1963; Siggins, 1966; Miller, 1971; Furman, 1974; Krupnick, 1984). For our purposes I will discuss the literature which bears directly on our subject: the psychoanalytic understanding and treatment of adults who suffered double parent loss in childhood.

Child psychoanalysts have noted the importance of surviving objects in the resolution of childhood bereavement. Most prominently it has been noted that the successful adaptation to loss depends on the continued availability of parental (or substitute) supports (Krupnick, 1984). Erna Furman provides the most extensive discussion of this viewpoint; she writes: "Our experience shows that the surviving love objects play a crucial part in the life of the bereaved person and contribute much to the manner in which he deals with his loss" (Furman, 1974, p. 109). In the assessment of bereaved children Furman states: "We have to take into account the interaction of two variables, the developmental status of the child's personality and the nature and availability of the auxiliary ego of the mothering person" (Furman, 1986, p. 203). The surviving love objects offer security and need fulfillment in the midst of loss and love, which involves empathy and the acceptance of feelings. "Help with mourning is the essence of the surviving love object's role. . . . Mourning alone is an almost impossible task even for a mature adult" (Furman, 1974, p. 114). One crucial area of help is in the expression and regulation of grief; Furman writes: "Sometimes . . . the difficulty in affective expression stems simply from not having anyone who shares feelings or towards whom they can be expressed" (p. 261). In her review of the clinical literature of childhood bereavement Furman noted the almost complete neglect of the role of others in bereavement (p. 285–286). Later, Harold Blum would add support to Furman's claim; he wrote:

> The older emphasis in the literature . . . did not give sufficient attention to the parallel identification with the surviving objects. The child's further personality development is crucially dependent on the availability of the surviving parent; the continuity and consistency of care; the quality of empathy, sensitivity, and concern; and the parent's understanding and capacity to bear with the child, their own, and the child's anxiety, depression, and guilt concerning the loss.
>
> (Blum, 1985, p. 311)

As to the treatment of adults, in the 1950s, the Chicago Institute of Psychoanalysis began a study of adult patients in psychoanalysis who had lost a parent by death in childhood (Fleming and Altschul, 1962; Fleming, 1963 and 1972; Altschul, 1968 and 1988). The primary observation of the Parent-Loss Project was that adult psychopathology could result when there is "an adaptation to loss of a significant object prior to maturity when the structure of the personality is more vulnerable to deprivation of an object needed to supply experiences essential for normal growth and development" (Fleming and Altschul, 1962, p. 278). This may lead to an arrest at the phase of development when the loss occurred. These patients typically experience distress as adults when "life forces urged adult sexuality and career roles on them and adaptations to stresses of adolescence and to the trauma of parental loss broke down" (p. 301). The clinical task is to break through the defensive denial of loss and resume the work of mourning, so as to facilitate the emergence of an analyzable transference neurosis. Effective treatment is possible only when the analyst becomes a transference object and a "new object, useful for new integrations" (p. 280). In a review of the findings of the Parent-Loss Project, Joan Fleming asserted that "the detrimental effects of parent loss depend very much on the age at which the loss occurs, on the character of the pre-loss relationship, on the availability of a good substitute, and on the type of relationship maintained with the surviving parent" (Fleming, 1972, p. 35). Unfortunately, the Project failed to elaborate on the role of the substitutes and/or the surviving parent in facilitating, or impeding, the child's adaptation to loss, nor did they include this area in their psychoanalytic research with adult survivors. In this regard, I am in agreement with Bowlby (1980) who asserted that most disorders of mourning in childhood result from the failure of the surviving parent, or substitute, to provide assistance with the child's reactions to the loss. It is his belief that virtually all children (regardless of developmental level) have the capacity to mourn the loss of a parent and to fully adapt through attachment to a new object when they are provided with adequate support, empathy and active involvement from an available parenting figure. In a recent contribution, Sol Altschul reaffirmed key aspects of this viewpoint (Altschul, 1988). On the other hand, Furman (1986) cautions that though the physical and emotional availability of a parenting figure greatly facilitates the mourning of bereaved children, the opposite is true as well – the absent or unempathic parent may impede the recuperative process. Echoing Furman in a paper accompanying Altschul's, Hummer and Samuels explore the impact of the recent death of a spouse on the functioning of the surviving parent (Hummer and Samuels, 1988, pp. 37–64):

> The death becomes an organizer of the parent's character and defensive structure, providing the child with a maladaptive model . . . contributing to major developmental interferences, skewing development and diminishing the quality of the child's life.
>
> (p. 59)

> The child more or less suffers a double loss.
>
> (p. 51)

Clinical examples

In the following case reports, I intend to show how the nature of the patient's relationship with the surviving parent takes on significance for our understanding of the transference relationship in adult psychoanalysis, not just as to how the parent obstructed the mourning process, but also as to how they failed to provide adequate parenting, hence provoking developmental conflicts which contributed to the consolidation of neurosis. To this end, following each report, I will highlight for discussion a specific developmental disturbance, illustrated by the clinical data, for the purpose of exploring the significance of double parent loss for the understanding and treatment of adult psychopathology. Obviously, in focusing on a single developmental task, I do not mean to deny that there are multiple dynamic factors and developmental issues which play a crucial part in each case.

Susan

Susan, a 21-year-old woman, had recently moved to the city from her hometown. She was finding the transition difficult. Depressed and anxious, she feared that she would be unsuccessful in her new life, as she simultaneously risked abandonment by her family. Overweight, with an attractive, engaging smile, she believed herself to be physically undesirable and "doomed." Having become convinced that she would never find a man, she was, she concluded, fated to be alone.

I soon learned that Susan's father died of a heart attack when she was fourteen. She believed his death to be, at least in part, the result of an argument that they had shortly before his death. Afterward, her mother became depressed, withdrawing to her bed for several months. When recovered, the mother continued to be emotionally distant, and the father's death remained undiscussed in the home. "I lost my mother too – which made me miss my father even more. I felt I had to try to take care of things – of her – like my father did." Susan did not remember being depressed herself and, beyond some initial sadness, she did not mourn. Since that time, however, she had held (as if preserved in mind) remembrances of her father, nurturing them as inner, mental objects that linked her with the vanished past. To me in sessions, she described him as a good but fragile man with whom she frequently fought and of whom she had been critical. In her current dream-life, he would appear as an idealized figure: "the man of my dreams."

After her mother remarried, Susan was forced to live alone. She felt abandoned. Nonetheless, because Susan's earlier development had been good, she was able to cope, maintain relationships and eventually enter college. After graduation, she decided to move away from home.

Once in the city, Susan sought out analytic treatment. During our early sessions, she spoke in a pressured, "rapid-fire" manner leaving little room for me to participate. She seemed to live at a high pitch of anxiety and dread, complaining of confusion and depression. Her fear of treatment seemed equally intense and persistent. She focused on the vicissitudes of her ambivalently platonic relationship with her roommate, Paul, to whom, at times, she would cling with a barely contained hunger, while, at other times, she would reject him as unreliable and selfish. Paul remained, during those first months of treatment, her single source of solace and companionship in a strange, new world. Susan's reports to me of the angst and turmoil of her relationship with Paul seemed to express through displacement the potential experience of the transference.

Throughout the first year, Susan was avoidant and reluctant to engage with me in the analysis. Use of the couch provoked in her fears of the emergence of memories of her dead father. She seemed to dread being entrapped by treatment, dependent on me and unable to "fix things" on her own. For months, she fought off regression, refusing to reflect on her inner life, focusing on situational problems and anxiously "reporting" the events of the week. In fact during the first year, she shared many rich and interesting dreams, all of which, she claimed, were just silly and meaningless disturbances. My attempts to interpret these dreams resulted in silence, simple denial or missed sessions. I noted her apparent fear of looking closely at herself and her feelings. Repeatedly, over time, I suggested that she seemed to be intentionally keeping a distance from me so as to protect herself from something.

Gradually, I began to understand that Susan's initial resistance to treatment resulted from anxieties exacerbated by her recent separation from her family. Intrapsychic conflicts related to her wish to establish her own life, which involved the pursuit of professional ambitions and the search for a sexual partner, were coupled with longings for an archaic form of merger with a parental object. The work of treatment involved the analysis of Susan's prematurely consolidated pseudo-individuation and its function in defending her against the experience of grief, panic and fantasies of engulfment by a depressed mother. Because of this, Susan resisted the emergence of transference wishes which she feared would involve both the experience of merger fantasies as well as the activation of mourning processes specific to separation from and loss of her parents and childhood family life.

For example, after a vacation break, during the second year of analysis, Susan talked about how she had missed me and had looked forward to my return. She told me that she could not accept these feelings. She should be independent and take care of things, she asserted. I interpreted her fear of being dependent on me: "By refusing to engage in a relationship with me in treatment, you are trying to protect yourself from your fears of needing me, and the danger which you feel about possibly losing once again someone you have come to depend on. Because of this, you have tried to keep one foot out the door, but you hunger for protection and security, which was lost with the death of your father, and then the collapse of your mother." In response, Susan said that she felt as if there was a darkness surrounding her and she feared being smothered in blackness. Then, she began to talk about her chronic depressions and feelings of hopelessness. She spontaneously recalled a single image, as if from a dream; she said: "There is a small figure standing alone, sort of hunched over, afraid; because, hovering above the figure, as if about to eat them, is an enormous mouth, like a fish's, ready to gobble the little person up." Her associations to this image were:

> I'm afraid if I'm not careful, something horrible will happen, again. The fish mouth – it's like the badness, maybe inside me. And my mother, her depression. I have always tried to fight that in myself, to not let her get to me. I am angry with her because she's not different. I feel alone, like that little person, and unprotected. I guess that's why I dream about my father coming back, as if he just went away somewhere. After he died, I lost everything, including my mother.

Susan's resistances to analysis were motivated by her investment in a state of pseudo-individuation that protected her against the threat of the regressive experience of transference. To depend on me as "her" analyst would be to risk the experience of longed-for merger, as well as reawakened grief at the full acceptance of her father's death (an internal, psychic attachment she nurtured in fantasy) and the possible reenactment of her tragic, emotional abandonment by her mother (whose love she still longed for). It would also mean an increasing commitment to true separation/individuation with the threat of the loss of internal, infantile representations of her parents, and the potential loss of her relationship with the surviving family. (Guilt over her sexual and aggressive striving compounded these resistances.) In other words, she had to finally engage in the painful process of object removal: the mournful decathexis of primary childhood objects.

Lyn

Lyn, a 31-year-old woman, came to analytic treatment after experiencing problems in her relationship with a man named Bill. She complained to me about
fluctuations in her mood, which she felt to be as a result of Bill's treatment of her.
When she found him to be emotionally attuned and securely available, she was
elated, passionate and confident about the relationship. If he was late for a date
with her, or seemed in other ways uncaring, she despaired, feeling hopeless and
abandoned. At times she complained of sexual enslavement, experiencing heightened erotic pleasure when she fantasized herself to be under his control during
intercourse. She saw this as unusual for her; in the past she would resist her lovers,
so as to assert her independence and control.

Her mother died after a six-year struggle with cancer when Lyn was twelve
years old. She reported that, toward the end, her mother insisted that she take
over for her after she died. Lyn remembered how she tried to learn to care for the
home, her four siblings and, she thought, her father. He had done poorly during
the mother's illness, and even before the death was withdrawn and emotionally
unavailable. As Lyn saw it, her father prevented her from taking on the mother's
role, as she had hoped to do and thought had been expected of her. She recalled
feeling disappointed and confused by him. In time, her father became increasingly
depressed and emotionally withdrawn from his children. She remembered him
coming home from work and, after dinner, sitting by himself far into the evening
while she and the other children retreated to their separate bedrooms. When the
father remarried, Lyn felt excluded and unwanted. She recalled waiting impa-
tiently for her chance to leave home, and finally, when she was seventeen, she
ran off with an older man, whom she says "kidnapped" her. This was the first in a
series of relationships characterized by initial, passionate attachment and eventual
abandonment.

At the beginning of each session, as she lay back on the couch, Lyn felt enveloped by despair. Not seeing my face made me a stranger to her, she claimed.
She imagined herself as lying alone in her childhood bedroom, initially with her
mother ill and in pain downstairs, and then, later, with her father, solitary and
morose in the years after the death. When I interpreted these depressions as possible reenactments through identification of her mother's illness, Lyn would feel
reawakened, invigorated by my "analysis." As the treatment progressed, Lyn realized that, though she had for many years mourned her mother, she continued to
feel hurt by and resentful toward her father, viewing him as she had as a teenager. Eventually, we began to understand how her depression on the couch, her
repeated experience of abandonment by men, and her father's withdrawal after
the mother's death were all of one piece; having never mourned the loss of the
living father, she repeated in numerous areas of her life the experience of that loss.
And now, in the treatment, there was the enactment of the fantasy of a longed-for
return of the object, followed, once more, by its loss and eventual recovery, in a
seemingly endless cycle. Lyn's depression was also motivated by her desire to

avoid full involvement with me as her analyst. Her reassurance, when she could see me, arose, not just from knowing I was there, but also from being able to "keep an eye" on me. Her desire to be paternally (and sexually) cared for provoked a powerful urge to retreat and decathect the loving, transference derived projection of the father; she said:

> Lying here, I feel the depression all through me, like a sickness. I remember my poor mother lying at night on the living room couch, banging on the wall to wake my father. I'd crawl out of bed to get him for her. He was not aware. He would have left her alone, if not for me. Now, here I am. Why? What's the point? I need so much, from Bill . . . from analysis. No, I think I want you . . . I mean I want Bill to stop being selfish. And he should want to be with me . . . What's the use? I should just give up.

Lyn admitted that she felt about me exactly as she had about her father: that I was self-centered, unaware of her, and would abandon her. In despair, she dreamed of running away, escaping from treatment. These fantasies would always end in loneliness and hopeless longing. When I "reached out" through my interpretations, she would feel "found" again, elated and at one with me – an experience of solace, which, she admitted, she had longed for with her father.

Eventually, the analysis revealed how the reality of replacing her mother (and the wish to) had to be denied by both her and her father. The repression of the incestuous wish, partly accomplished through a process of painful and extended alienation between father and daughter, led to chronic feelings of loneliness, guilt, poor self-esteem and a mournful attachment to the inner representation of the mother. This maternal attachment also served to defend against incestuous yearnings intensified by the preoedipal wish to merge with the father (who, on an unconscious level, had displaced the dead mother). The exploration of oedipal fantasies led to the recall of earlier, loving interactions with the father prior to the time of the mother's illness, thus facilitating the process of oedipal resolution. A lessening of depressive regression on the couch accompanied this work, as increasingly overt sexual fantasies entered the transference.

Chris

Chris, a 32-year-old man, entered psychoanalysis several months after his father's death from a heart attack. He reported to me how, after the death, he had withdrawn emotionally from his girlfriend, who strongly recommended that he seek treatment. He said that he had been frequently depressed over the past few years. Unable to complete projects, his apartment was cluttered with unfinished papers, and his work on his doctoral thesis had now extended into its fifth year – with no end in sight. He felt unsupported by his supervisors and unable to ask for help from peers. He saw himself as a "loner," but always felt lonely and angry that no one wanted to help him.

Chris's approach to treatment was a highly intellectual one. Issues in his life were, he believed, to be logically considered and solved. He saw himself as a scientist, admitting that he was "a slave to logic," seeking to submit everything (inner and outer) to rational inquiry and "analysis." However, in sessions with me, science failed him as he discussed his mother's death fourteen years earlier. She had been diagnosed with breast cancer when Chris was twelve. After numerous treatments and surgeries, she died, physically shrunken and in great pain, seven years later. She never spoke of her illness to Chris. His father, a controlled, disgruntled and distant man, cooperated with the mother in maintaining silence about her disease. As the family members took over the mother's responsibilities in the home, their grief became increasingly submerged and isolated, even as the mother's approaching death became the central, determining reality of the family's life.

Chris described his adolescent years as a type of emotional and psychological wall. He remembered himself as spiritually numb, walking through life, accepting what was happening to his mother and family without question – "just the way it was, I guess. I didn't think about it." He recalled losing a sense of connection to the past and ceased to plan for the future. Rather than taking steps away from the family, with the goal of establishing a gratifying, autonomous life for himself, Chris felt trapped in the present, increasingly focused on his mother, and marshaling all his psychological resources to cope.

He told me how he prepared for every session, deciding on the most pressing issue of the day. He admitted he was fearful of free association. He felt that, by revealing himself, he risked losing a secure, valued way of understanding and managing his world.

Chris began one session by noting that he did not know what to talk about. Trouble with the train had led to his arrival five minutes before session – rather than the twenty minutes that he preferred. He had not had time to prepare himself. "It's actually to protect myself, sort of. I feel like I need to be careful what I say – not really what I say, I guess, but how I say it. It is very important that I say what I mean clearly. I'm afraid of being misunderstood."

"And if I misunderstand you?"

"I don't know. My experience is of not being understood, and of being judged harshly, not being taken seriously – as a person." This led to a memory:

> When my mother was sick. I guess I was fourteen, or so. She had just come out of the hospital. It was bad, she was really sick. I think it was the first time I really felt it. That she might die. My father and I were arguing, about something. I usually didn't lose my temper. I don't remember anything like this happening before or after, but I started to demand that he say something – I'm not sure what. We just stood facing each other – he didn't answer me – he didn't say anything. He just turned and walked away. I think I wanted to know about my mother. I was holding him responsible. But he didn't want to hear it . . . I guess.

Since that time, Chris felt he could never be open or assertive with those he perceived as authorities. Expression of emotion, self-assertion, had to be avoided. Personally valued ideas and feelings had to be carefully controlled and clearly expressed to avoid the "misunderstandings" he feared. This fear, he pointed out, influenced his perception of me, hence the need for preparation before session. However, the more he felt that his ideas were understood and valued by me, the more he was able to explore the psychological function of his logic and the protective motives for his self-imposed isolation. I repeatedly addressed the defensive nature of his obsessive-compulsive character style and its role in suppressing feeling and adapting to what he perceived as a dangerous reality. His internal world was no less threatening to him; for this reason he had repressed strong sexual desire, sadness and competitive wishes. Over time in treatment, Chris began to recall progressively detailed memories of his early relationship with his loving, admiring mother. As an adolescent faced with the loss of her excited, invigorating involvement, he became increasingly despairing and depleted of self-esteem. His father (in earlier years remembered as a formidable man) retreated from the oedipal battlefield at the vaguest hint of Chris's assertiveness and demand for involvement.

As he began to experience me as safe and non-judgmental, there was a gradual loosening of his rigid character defenses and an increasing expression of longing for the admiration and support of paternal figures (his advisers and therapist) who, previously, were perceived as hopelessly self-interested and rejecting. His competitive and ambitious wishes, which had remained repressed, were gradually recognized and integrated into his professional life, leading to his effective collaboration with his dissertation committee. After years of stalemate, he became able to compromise on several iconoclastic sections of his dissertation, settling on a document which he felt could be successfully defended, and of which he could be proud. Eventually, a full expression and working through of the mourning process occurred, as did a vigorous involvement in productive oedipal competition. These psychic advances were marked by Chris's marriage and successful defense of his doctoral thesis.

Discussion: The impact of double parent loss on adolescent developmental tasks

Separation/individuation

Regression in drive and ego, resulting in psychical disequilibrium and anxiety, characterize the adolescent state of conflict (Blos, 1979). There is a recathexis of pregenital and preoedipal positions, which are, so to speak, revisited and lived through again. Progression in the areas of internal restructuring and differentiation from infantile object imagoes is part of the normal developmental tasks. The adolescent resists the appeal of the regressive use of the parents, seeking out the protection, gratification and solace provided by peers and other extra-familial relationships. The intact adolescent ego responds to temporary regressive states through internal reorganization and structuralization. This "second individuation process" (Blos, 1979) results in the formation of a more cohesive and stable internal world, which is increasingly differentiated from the societal and familial context, the end result being the formation of an autonomous adult character.

The continuity of the relationship with the actual parents is often sorely tested as the adolescent seeks to individuate from infantile parental representations. The confusion of archaic imagoes with the current experience of the parents must be sorted out for the adolescent to progress beyond regressive attachments toward the establishment of adult relationships, including the consolidation of a mature inner object world. As with Susan, the death of a parent and the unavailability of the survivor have a complicating impact on the accomplishment of this developmental task.

Confronted with her mother's depression, after the death of her father, Susan became the family caretaker. Enraged by the traumatic disillusionment of her childhood idealizations, she was impatient and provocative with her mother. She continued to harbor enormous guilt about the circumstances of her father's death, and an enduring longing for his return. Paradoxically, when she left home for the city, she experienced another abandonment, which intensified her wish for her father's return. For the first three years of analysis, she remained preoccupied with her ambivalence about leaving home, and the resurgence of childlike longings for protection and comfort. Her resistance to the experience of these archaic longings in the transference was the focus of the analysis during the early years of Susan's treatment.

Oedipal resolution

Puberty breaks down the repressions of latency as sexual wishes are experienced in increasingly mature fantasies, desires and behaviors. Extra-familial objects are sought out for sexual purposes. At the same time, the disengagement from infantile objects increases anxiety, ego weakness and regressive longings. The incest taboo demands that the newly intensified desires should not be experienced within the family. Both the adolescent and parents, with varying degrees of success, resort to powerful defenses. A mature resolution of the oedipal complex depends on a delicate balance between sexual expression and defense. The continuing presence of the parents as both a sexual couple and a source of security, authority and control is important. The adolescent can turn with more confidence to extra-familial relationships if they know that the parents accept their sexuality, while at the same time requiring adherence to cultural norms. In addition, the parents' survival in the face of adolescent aggression also leads to increasing assurance that oedipal wishes can be managed and defensively channeled. The renunciation of ties to the parents (object removal) results in adolescent mourning. The need for support and drive satisfaction leads to new object choices.

Double parent loss can make this already difficult process become badly distorted, if not impossible to complete. For example, in the case of the loss of the oedipal rival, the child may feel that the death of the parent is the result of his or her own aggressive fantasies and incestuous desires. As we saw with Lyn, the realization of the disastrous consequences of oedipal wishes may lead to defense and re-repression. The subsequent collapse or withdrawal of the surviving love object may be felt to be (and may be in actuality) a rejection in response to a frightening oedipal victory. As a result the work of oedipal resolution is foreclosed with disastrous consequences for super-ego and ego-ideal consolidation.

> *As she lay dying, Lyn's mother told her daughter that she would have to take over after her death as the mother of the family. Later, when Lyn tried to perform some of her mother's functions, her father refused to let her, and he withdrew into a morose state of prolonged mourning. Lyn rebelled, and for the next four years, she and her father were locked in painful conflict, which only came to an end when she ran away with a much older man, a gambler and alcoholic. During several years of her analysis, Lyn would alternately establish an intense, productive transference and then drop out of treatment for several months, due to financial problems. This mirrored her passionate, unstable relationship with Bill, whom she inevitably and repeatedly "lost," only to be found by him again. In time, the analysis revealed a rejection of her desire to be sexually possessed by a man, and therefore she had a recurrent need to "lose" the man, whom it was not safe to allow herself to be had by. In addition, the mother of two children, she at times repudiated her self-image as a mother, following a bohemian life-style, while, at the same time, she longed for a stable family life. She struggled with authority, often believed herself to be a victim, and suffered from depression and guilt. The analysis of her guilt for surviving and replacing her mother, and being spurned, she believed, by her father, led to a gradual lessening of self-hatred and an increasing acceptance of her mature sexual role and identity.*

Character development

Trauma is a universal human condition during childhood, leaving a residue, which must be assimilated through the formation of stable character structure (Blos, 1979). The healthy adolescent will typically re-experience, through memory and repetition, the once forgotten trauma and dread state of helplessness. "Patterned responses to these prototypic danger situations or signal anxiety" are the stuff of adolescent character formation. "Character is identical with the conquest of residual trauma: not with its disappearance, nor with its avoidance, but with its continuance within an adaptive formation" (Blos, 1979, p. 183). Failure to internalize the danger situation through its transformation into character structure results in an inability to come to terms with trauma. As with Chris, fears of helplessness, disabling regression, and victimization may persist, leading to continued vigilance, premature closure and rigidity. In this case, character is less "the internalization of a stable, protective environment" (p. 190), and more the fortification of a vulnerable self against the dangers of both inner and outer worlds. Obviously, when trauma is not residual but ongoing, throughout the adolescent period (as it is in the case of double parent loss), premature character consolidation can occur as a result of structuralization of defensive and reactive (albeit adaptive) character traits. The adolescent's defensive response to the trauma of a collapsing social structure precludes an open and flexible character organization.

Chris was faced with a frightening terminal illness in his mother combined with the absence of support and emotional involvement from his father. The development of a highly intellectual, rational and schizoid character style allowed him to repress disturbing affects such as grief, rage and panic. Everything could be submitted to logical analysis and thereby "solved." Rationality became a means to maintain a feeling of control over both reality and emotional life, and may have been his sole area of communication with his father. It was the experience of the father's rejection of his healthy expressiveness and self-assertion during adolescence that had led to the consolidation of his obsessive-compulsive defenses. In sessions he could talk about what happened to his parents, but he could not remember feeling anything. Adaptively he found a career where the intellect was valued and there were others with similar character defenses. However, gradually, in treatment, his character style failed him as memories of his mother's cancer, and his father's intolerance and emotional abandonment, were experienced transferentially, thereby becoming subject to analysis.

Adolescence, parent loss and the family

> A firm social structure is a necessary condition for adolescent personality formation to evolve.
>
> (Blos, 1979, p. 161)

The adolescent passage occurs within the context of the family, which has a decisive and often determining impact on the unfolding of the developmental process. The relationship with the actual parents will profoundly influence the four areas of adolescent development, which we have discussed in the preceding clinical reports. For example, the resurgence of oedipal and preoedipal fantasy life as a result of drive and ego regression affects the experience of the actual parents, who become confused in the adolescent's mind with the highly charged infantile imagoes, returned from the repressed. The management by the parents of these projections, *as they are enacted* in regressive and defensive behaviors (so typical of adolescence), will decisively influence the adolescent's inner task of conflict resolution, decathexis and eventual object removal. When the parent's own psychopathology mirrors, or otherwise confirms, the regressive nature of the adolescent's projections, conflict will result. Optimal attunement to the inner state of their child, combined with the maintenance of essential parenting functions, is necessary if the facilitation of adolescent development is to occur.

Double parent loss damages crucial family functions. As an environment, the family may be unable to provide for its members' needs as usual. Basic security is called into question. The family is radically altered, and its supportive function undermined. For the adolescent confronted by the collapse of the family as a source of security, a developmental moratorium may occur. The family is also a system of relationships, which is normally structured to provide for the open and flexible expression of affect and conflict resolution. The family supports, nurtures and facilitates the maturation and development of its members, especially the children. The death of a parent frequently results in closure of the family system (Bowen, 1985): interpersonal boundaries either break down or become attenuated; affect expression is discouraged or unregulated; extra-familial social contacts are reduced; and conflict within the family is either suppressed or becomes chronic. The family system's functions are greatly impaired, with devastating consequences for the adolescent.

In terms of the family as a set of object relations, double parent loss has a dramatic impact. For example, the adolescent as the horrific enactment of fantasy life may experience the actual death of the oedipal rival, or love object. Frequently, subsequent to the death, and often in response to the needs of the surviving parent, the adolescent becomes more involved in the family and, at times, any attempt at separation is actively interfered with, and the urge to differentiate becomes a source of guilt. In any case, the developmentally appropriate drive to individuate may be frustrated or blocked as a result of double parent loss. The intensification of the attachment to primary objects can then lead to additional problems in decathexis, internalization and the establishment of a mature inner object world. Given this, we commonly find that the adolescent, who might normally have been given a second chance to re-experience and work through earlier areas of fixation, repressed conflict or character deficits within the context of a good enough family milieu, encounters trauma, death and family collapse. With this in mind, when we factor in significant disturbances of the mourning process as an additional consequence of family collapse, the disruption of adolescent development appears inevitable.

I have attempted to show, through discussion of double parent loss, how the classical psychoanalytic theory of mourning may at times prove to be inadequate when we are confronted with the complex clinical problems, which can result from the death of a love object. Most importantly, I believe that we mourn not alone but with others, and that the dynamics of the surviving relationships frequently determine the process and outcomes of our bereavements. This is most clearly seen in cases of loss in childhood but remains, I believe, true throughout life. As we have seen, psychoanalysis can provide the interpersonal context and the opportunity to readapt to past losses and resume the work of mourning.

However, successful analysis requires not only the resolution of aborted or established mourning, but, in addition, the alteration of maladaptations, and the resumption of a healthy developmental process. Unlike authors who advise that a period of "re-grief work" occur prior to the initiation of analytic treatment (Volkan, 1981), my finding has been that, for patients who have suffered double parent loss, the genetics of the adult neurosis (and an enduring determinant of its course and structure) are inseparably tied to the nature of the relationship with the surviving parent, the aborted mourning process, the adaptations resorted to in response to illness, death and environmental collapse, and the phase-specific impact of parent loss on development tasks. The work of mourning must be an ongoing process in the analyses of these patients, as fixations to specific self and object constellations and protective/defensive strategies are analyzed and given up.

   In closing, it is important to note that, for these patients, the mourning process may extend over years of treatment. The loss of life and sustaining relationships will never be forgotten, and may remain the central focus of treatment. Eventually, *all* will come to grieve the destruction of their child-self, and the loss of an entire epoch of life (in Susan and Lyn's cases, their adolescence), which, rather than being a period of hope, excitement and expanding horizons, was a time of personal tragedy and loss.

References

ALTSCHUL, S. (1968). Denial and ego arrest. *J. Am. Psychoanal. Assn.*, 16:301–318.

ALTSCHUL, S. (Ed.) (1988). *Childhood Bereavement and Its Aftermath.* Madison, CT: International Universities Press.

BLOS, P. (1979). *The Adolescent Passage.* New York: International Universities Press.

BLUM, H. (1980). The value of reconstruction in adult psychoanalysis. *Int. J. Psychoanal.*, 61:39–52.

BLUM, H. (1985). Splitting of the ego and its relation to parent loss. In *Defence and Resistance: Historical Perspectives and Current Concepts.* Edited by Blum, H. New York: Int. Univ. Press, pp. 301–324.

BOWEN, M. (1985). *Family Therapy and Clinical Practice.* Northvale, NJ: Aronson.

BOWLBY, J. (1980). *Attachment and Loss. Vol. 3, Loss.* New York: Basic Books.

FLEMING, J. (1963). The evolution of a research project in psychoanalysis. In *Counterpoint, Libidinal Object and Subject: A Tribute to Rene Spitz on His 75th Birthday.* Edited by Gaskill, H. New York: International Universities Press, pp. 75–105.

FLEMING, J. (1972). Early object deprivation and the working alliance. *Psychoanal. Q.*, 41:23–29.

FLEMING, J. & ALTSCHUL, S. (1962). Activation of mourning and growth by psychoanalysis. In *Childhood Bereavement and Its Aftermath.* Edited by Altschul, S. Madison, CT: International Universities Press, 1988, pp. 277–307.

FURMAN, E. (1974). *A Child's Parent Dies: Studies in Childhood Bereavement.* New Haven, CT: Yale University Press.

FURMAN, E. (1986). On trauma: When is the death of a parent traumatic? *Psychoanal. Study Child*, 41:191–208.

HUMMER, K. M. & SAMUELS, A. (1988). The influence of the recent death of a spouse on the parenting function of the surviving parent. In *Childhood Bereavement and Its Aftermath*. Edited by Altschul, S. Madison, CT: International Universities Press, pp. 37–64.

KRUPNICK, J. (1984). Bereavement during childhood and adolescence. In *Bereavement: Reactions, Consequences and Care*. Edited by Osterweis, M. & Green, M. Washington, DC: Nat. Academy Press, pp. 99–141.

MILLER, J. (1971). Children's reactions to the death of a parent: A review of the psychoanalytic literature. *J. Am. Psychoanal. Assn.*, 19:697–719.

NAGERA, H. (1967). Children's reactions to the death of important objects: A developmental approach. *Psychoanal. Study Child*, 25:360–401.

POLLOCK, G. (1961). Mourning and adaptation. *Internal. J. Psycho-Anal.*, 42:341–361.

POLLOCK, G. (1989). *The Mourning-Liberation Process*. Madison, CT: International Universities Press.

SIGGINS, L. (1966). Mourning: A critical review of the literature. *Int. J. Psycho-Anal.*, 47:14–25.

VOLKAN, V. (1981). *Linking Objects and Linking Phenomena*. New York: International Universities Press.

WOLFENSTEIN, M. (1966). How is mourning possible? *Psychoanalytic Study of the Child*, 21:93–122.

Chapter 4

Flight from the subjectivity of the other

Pathological adaptation to childhood parent loss (1996)

George Hagman

Editor's note: One consequence of double parent loss is the defensively motivated reluctance to engage in later relationships, which might risk a repetition of the earlier abandonment. Clinically, the failure of these patients to engage with the analyst in the transference has been noted by earlier researchers and therapists. I also experienced this resistance to the transference with some parent loss patients, and in this paper I attempt to offer an explanation based on the failure of the self-object milieu and the fear of engagement with an other along with the risk of loss.

This paper was published in 1996 by George Hagman as "Flight from the Subjectivity of the Other: Pathological Adaptation to Early Parent Loss" in Basic Ideas Reconsidered: Progress in Self, *Volume 12, edited by Arnold Goldberg, released by the Analytic Press, a Taylor & Francis imprint, New York and London.*

Frequently psychoanalysts and other psychotherapists encounter patients who suffered parent loss during childhood. Over time a small but significant literature has developed that focuses on the special clinical problems of this population (Freud, 1927; Deutsch, 1937; Lewin, 1937; Fleming and Altschul, 1962; Jacobson, 1965; Altschul, 1968; Fleming, 1972, 1974; Stolorow, Atwood, and Lachmann, 1975; Blum, 1980, 1983, 1984; Shane and Shane, 1990a, 1990b). A frequent observation of these analysts has been that many analysands who have experienced parent loss avoid engagement in and experience of the transference, and it has been agreed that the analyst's ability to understand and analyze this complex transference response is essential to successful treatment outcome. To this end, I intend to explore a key motivation of the transference in these patients.

My observation has been that a certain group of these patients withdraw psychologically and emotionally from others as a result of the childhood loss of a sustaining intersubjective context of mutual relatedness that was lost with the death of a parent. More specifically, the resistance to the experience of the transference and the engagement in a "new relationship" with the analyst arises from anxieties regarding the recognition of the analyst's subjectivity (the experience of his or her "otherness" [Shane and Shane, 1990b]), which is associated by the patient with vulnerability to traumatic loss. Because of this the patient resists, often for some time, the experience of the analyst as a separate and distinct other, thus turning the analytic situation into a one-person process with the primary, dynamic tie being to the internal representation of the lost parent. This state of flight from the other's subjectivity results in chronic pathology of the self. An associated finding is that the recognition of otherness (the *experience* of intersubjectivity [Benjamin, 1991]) is essential to satisfactory, mature self-selfobject relationships and thus the full vitality and cohesion of the self.

I will begin with a brief review of the parent loss literature that highlights the clinical observations and theoretical formulations regarding the transference resistance of these patients. I will also discuss recent concepts from self psychology, intersubjectivity theory, and developmental psychology. I will then reinterpret the transference resistance in light of my notion of a flight from the subjectivity of the other. A case illustration will follow, and the chapter will close with a discussion.

A review of parent loss literature

In this section I will briefly highlight several major findings in the parent loss literature. I will break down the discussion into three areas: 1) the unconscious attachment to the lost parent, 2) issues of defense and deficit, and 3) the problem of the transference.

The unconscious attachment to the lost parent

Freud (1927) observed that some patients who had suffered the death of a parent in childhood continued to deny the reality of the loss into adulthood. In the cases he discussed he noted a "split" in the patient's mental life: one current fitting in with reality, the other current continuing to deny the fact of the parent's death. This early observation of Freud's has been validated time and again by subsequent analysts (Deutsch, 1937; Lewin, 1937; Fleming and Altschul, 1962; Jacobson, 1965; Blum, 1984). These authors found that, though the clinical manifestations of the "split" between acceptance and denial can take many forms, all of their patients remained attached to the memory of the lost parent.

Defense and deficit

Freud (1927) asserted that the motivation for the "split" was to defend against the recognition of a traumatic and unacceptable reality. Trauma arises owing to the immaturity of the child at the time of the loss; children in this situation are incapable of realistic understanding and are victimized by their own primitive fantasy life and cognitive limitations. Virtually all the parent loss authors agree that the defenses erected in response to loss can interfere with the developmental process, and that some level of arrest is common. Hence, the adult patient may show a range of problems involving deficits and conflicts. Most of the parent loss analysts make note of the obvious psychological immaturity of their patients, who continue to struggle with early developmental challenges well into adulthood.

Transference issues

Fleming and Altschul (1962) were the first to emphasize the importance of transference resistance in these patients. Most of the other authors agree that there is a
defense against regression and fears regarding attachment to the analyst as a "new
object." Belief in the dead parent's survival may remain the central organizing
principle in the patient's life, and the patient will resist anyone or anything that
might threaten recognition of the loss. These patients seek treatment during periods when this fantasy attachment is threatened by current separations, transitions,
or actual losses. Therefore, there is a window of opportunity in which the analyst
is able to analyze the core issues of the patient's conflict. The resulting emotional
investment in the analyst, combined with the analyst's survival and continuing
availability, provide the security necessary to complete the work of mourning.

In summary, the classical literature of parent loss stresses several points: 1) these
patients remain preoccupied with the internal attachment to the dead parent,
2) they attempt to reenact the relationship with the lost parent in the transference,
3) they fear the experience of the analysis as a "new relationship," 4) to a greater
or lesser degree they suffer from developmental arrest, and 5) they resist engagement in the work of mourning.

The impact of parent loss is influenced by many variables, most importantly
the developmental level at which the loss occurred and the presence or absence
of preexistent psychopathology. In the specific instances that we will be discussing, the loss of the parent occurred late in a relatively healthy childhood after the
consolidation of the self, but before full maturity. Typically, development had
been arrested at the level concurrent with the parent's death. As an adult, the
patient remains tied to an unconscious fantasy of the lost parent that continues
to serve selfobject functions. The analyst as a potential source of new selfobject
experiences is feared, both in terms of the threat of the loss of a new object and the
even more fearful loss of the tie to the inner representation of the dead parent. In
support of my thesis I will briefly discuss the problem of recognition of the other,
selfobject functions, intersubjectivity, and loss.

The otherness of the selfobject

A number of analysts (Winnicott, 1965, 1971; Modell, 1984; Stern, 1985; Benjamin, 1988, 1991; Stolorow and Atwood, 1992) have argued that the experience
of the self is inseparable from intersubjective relatedness. Stolorow and Atwood
(1992) in particular believe that the "myth" of the isolated, intrapsychic mind
does not accurately portray the reality of human psychological experience, which
is profoundly interrelational and intersubjective. They state: "The concept of an
intersubjective system brings into focus *both* the individual's world of inner experience *and* its embeddedness with such worlds in a continual flow of reciprocal
mutual influence. In this vision, the gap between the intrapsychic and interpersonal realms is closed, and, indeed, the old dichotomy between them is rendered

obsolete" (p. 18). However, the fact that persons are indissolubly linked does not tell us about how intersubjectivity is experienced by the coparticipants; most importantly, by emphasizing intersubjectivity in a *general* sense (i.e., as an essential dimension of all levels of human relatedness), Stolorow and Atwood do not consider the specific area of *recognition* of the other by one or both subjects (intersubjectivity in the *specific* sense), which I believe comprises the dynamic tension of the interpersonal field.

Jessica Benjamin (1991), in agreement with Stolorow and Atwood, stated: "The human mind is interactive rather than monadic, and the psychoanalytic process should be understood as occurring between subjects rather than within the individual" (p. 43). However, she continued: "A theory in which the individual subject no longer reigns absolute must confront the difficulty that each subject has in recognizing the other as an equivalent center of experience" (p. 43). It is the vicissitudes of recognition of subjectivity that Benjamin placed at the center of her developmental model: "The other must be recognized as another subject in order for the self to fully experience his or her subjectivity in the other's presence. This means, first, that we have a need for recognition and second, a capacity to recognize others in return, mutual recognition. But recognition is a capacity of individual development that is only unevenly realized" (p. 45). Utilizing Winnicott's theory of the use of the object, Benjamin described a dialectical process of negation and recognition through which the developing child finds pleasure in the experience of the mother as a subject. Benjamin stated: "The capacity to recognize the mother as a subject is an important part of early development" (p. 46).

Daniel Stern's research (1985) confirmed the fact that by the ninth month infants exhibit a capacity to recognize the mother as a subject distinct from himself or herself. Stem stated: "Infants gradually come upon the momentous realization that inner subjective experiences, the 'subject matter' of the mind, are potentially sharable with someone else" (p. 124). From that point a central feature of the infant's reality is the perception of the mother as *subject*. In fact Stern described how the recognition of *inter*-subjectivity develops along with the awareness of the self's own subjectivity. For Stern the pleasure of intersubjectivity unfolds spontaneously as an inherent part of the infant's experience of the world. Affective attunement and empathy are other forms of intersubjective sharing – the core experiences that contribute to the crystallization of a cohesive self, an earlier form being "core relatedness" and a later form being "verbal relatedness" (Stern, 1985).

Although an archaic experience of "being-at-one-with" an idealized or mirroring other has been found to be essential to the establishment of a cohesive and vital self, the creative elaboration of mature selfhood throughout the lifespan depends on the capacity to recognize the *inter*-subjectivity of the selfobject bond; it is through this creative *tension* (Benjamin, 1988) between recognizing the other and asserting the self that self-experience is elaborated and continually renewed. Kohut (1984) distinguishes the undifferentiated nature of archaic selfobjects from the recognition of separateness that characterizes *mature* self – selfobject relations. See also Ornstein (1991) for a discussion of the "intertwining" of selfobject and object experiences in maturity. In the absence of these renewing experiences development ceases, resulting in arrest, fixation, and stasis.

Winnicott (1971) argues powerfully that the recognition of otherness is essential for useful engagement in the social world (which includes psychoanalysis). He writes: "A world of shared reality is created which the subject can use and which can feed back other-than-me substances into the subject" (p. 94). It is through this process, according to Benjamin, that the ability to love, empathize, and be an other to the other arises (see also Shane and Shane, 1990a, on the capacity to be an "other"). These forms of subjective-selfobject relating, felt to be simultaneously part of and separate from the self, are essentially mature selfobject experiences; they reflect a developmental advance beyond the self-consolidating experiences of archaic merger toward a lifelong elaboration of the vital and creative self (Kohut, 1984).

But the recognition of the other and the experience of that other's unique subjectivity leaves one vulnerable to irreplaceable loss. Benjamin (1988) considered this possibility: "When the other does not survive . . . it becomes almost exclusively intrapsychic." A defensive process of internalization takes place when "mutual recognition is not restored. When shared reality does not survive destruction, complementary structures and 'relating' to the inner object predominates" (p. 54). Stern (1985) described a similar process in the child's response to the massive misattunement of the parent: the infant learns that there is a "danger in permitting the intersubjective sharing of experience, namely that intersubjective sharing can result in loss" (p. 214). (This process must be distinguished from transmuting internalization, which occurs in the context of the survival or restoration of the selfobject tie.) In other words, when the subjective other is traumatically lost (as in death and bereavement, or more commonly in empathic failure) there may as a result be a flight from other-recognition and subjective relating, and a defensive retreat into an inner fantasy life.

Flight from the subjectivity of the other

The loss through death of a parent, whom one has experienced as a distinct, delimited center of subjectivity and with whom one has shared a crucial, mutually regulating selfobject bond is traumatic. The self has developed, has been sustained, and has continued to be elaborated with the support of the unique selfobject functions provided by the essential other – the parent. The child experiences the core danger as follows: "I have invested my self innocently in the unique, irreplaceable existence of another; my own subjectivity has been inextricably bound to their special nature, and now they are gone from me forever. How can I possibly give them up; and how can I dare to risk another such loss?" In response to this experience of danger to the self, the child seeks refuge by means of a retreat to forms of schizoid relating; this primarily takes the form of the reactivation of the selfobject functions of the internal fantasy tie to the lost parent accompanied by a flight from the recognition of others. Lacking the vital, protean nature of "a true other," the memory of the parent joins the traumatized self in a frozen state of internal exile. The bereaved's connection to vibrant, unpredictable, and ultimately creative involvement with other persons becomes attenuated, or perhaps even severed.

Essentially, I am describing a process similar to that identified by Kohut (1984) as the reactivation of archaic selfobject relating in reaction to the loss of more mature selfobject experience. More specifically in the cases we are discussing, the patient retreats from involvement with significant objects and reactivates the archaic, fantasy selfobject tie with the memory of the dead parent; hence, these patients fear and avoid the experience of the transference. Therefore, as we will see later, it is important for the analyst not to simply facilitate the spontaneous unfolding of the selfobject transference (the development of which the patient *resists*), but more importantly, to do so through the interpretation of defenses *against* selfobject relating in the treatment relationship.

Clinically, we observe this conflict most clearly during the first weeks of treatment when the patient's reliance on long-term, defensive strategies are threatened or fail in their functions in sustaining self-experience (owing to transition, new losses, increased intimacy, etc.) and the person enters a state of self-crisis that may be manifested by acute anxiety, depression, work inhibitions, and most commonly, complex difficulties experienced in engaging in and sustaining intimate relationships. Characteristically with this patient, the most striking feature of the beginning phase of treatment (often continuing to some degree into the middle phase) is an avoidant, even evasive, attitude toward the analyst. In severe cases it is as if the patient is alone in the room engaged in a self-analysis.

His flight from recognition of the subjectivity of the analyst results in one of the most characteristic features of the treatment relationship during its early phases. That feature is the absence of a feeling of mutual responsiveness and affective interplay between the analyst and patient – a lack of *the empathic resonance*, which Kohut (1984) identified as the hallmark of mature selfobject relating. This leads to a quality of emotional deadening, and experiences of isolation and self-attenuation in the analyst. It is this sense of affective estrangement that I will describe in the following case.

Patricia, a 24-year-old woman, had lost her father when she was 14 years old. She had moved to the city 6 months before entering treatment to pursue a career in publishing. She complained of depression and loneliness, and was preoccupied with her involvement in an emotionally highly wrought, sexually charged "platonic" relationship with her male roommate. Intense unconscious longings for him, coupled by conscious denial of her sexual needs, made their friendship stormy at best. Patricia claimed to be desperate.

She was white, middle class, and from a large rural town. She did not describe significant early pathology in herself or her family until her father's death. As she reported it, she had been arguing with her father, refusing to help him shovel the snow from the front walk. He had gone out to do the job himself while she remained in the house with her brother. Sometime later, they found their father lying unconscious on the snow. They were unable to revive him and he was dead upon arrival at the hospital.

Patricia did not remember grieving. She vividly recalled her mother's subsequent depression. Withdrawing to her bed, the mother became physically and emotionally incapacitated. By Patricia's account, the social context that might have supported her involvement in mourning collapsed. Her relationship with her mother became strained, and later, after the mother recovered, they fought frequently and for a time were estranged. Patricia's adolescent character was one of self-sufficiency, coupled with care taking for others. She did well in college, after which (as noted previously) she left her hometown to pursue a new life in the city.

Patricia dominated our sessions with her frantic, rapid-fire speech and relentless, fruitless groping for the "answers" to her problems. She was preoccupied with trying to control the convoluted and conflicted nature of her relationship with her roommate. She was afraid of being left alone, unable to return home and incapable of finding a place for herself in the city.

My initial assessment was that Patricia might have been suffering from a severe character disorder; however, the lack of childhood family pathology and the evidence that she presently functioned at a high level, handled complex interpersonal work situations well, and had maintained healthy long-term relationships with childhood friends seemed to counter indicate a diagnosis of severe psychopathology.

Over the first 3 months I went from being an eager and curious "potential" analyst to a frustrated and ineffectual witness to her solitary search for answers. It was as if there was a one-way mirror between us – I felt blocked, anonymous, and unrecognized. This feeling persisted for the first 6 months of treatment. Nevertheless, the treatment appeared to be helpful to Patricia, lending her support as her troubled friendship "self-destructed" several months later. Subsequently she became more relaxed in session, more reflective. Given this, 3 months into the treatment, I proposed analysis. "Funny," she noted in response, "I haven't even noticed the couch until now." It was as if entire aspects of the treatment situation had gone unrecognized by her – the large blue couch . . . myself.

She said that she feared the return of memories of her father. In fact, soon after the beginning of the analysis she shared dreams of his return, as if from a trip, healthy and intact, his disappearance unexplained. The first analytic month coincided with the anniversary of her father's death. That day she spent alone waiting for a call from her family that never came. "There is a wall," she said. "I am on one side, everyone else is on the other. I have been behind the wall for years. But I sense it most now. They don't feel anything. Do they even remember my father?"

Despite Patricia's increasing openness about her isolation the wall loomed large in sessions. But what I came to experience most acutely was the absence of physical interaction. Most of my patients respond to me physically as they enter the room, as they settle in, and even while they lie on the couch. It was this subtle, usually subliminal, "background" quality to the interaction that I experienced as absent with Patricia. She would pass me on the way to the couch with little or no acknowledgment of my presence. It wasn't that she ignored me; in fact I spoke often to her and she responded, often thoughtfully, to my interventions. However, I felt unrecognized as a distinct person, as someone physically, emotionally, and psychologically relating to her, person to person. I felt like a shadow, a ghost.

But it is not as simple as saying she related to me as if I were her dead father. More to the point, it was her fear of my "coming to life" for her, that she might become involved with a "flesh and blood" *other* who might draw her out of her self-sufficient, mournful inner world of memory and self-protection. Nevertheless, she reported a dream with a new figure, "the man of my dreams," she noted, who would take her away and care for her.

However, for a time, even my queries about the meanings of her often dramatic and emotionally vivid dreams met with shrugs and denials of meaning – "just silly and useless," she would say of them, as if to suggest that hidden meaning would court discovery and disaster.

I began to interpret to her my experience of her fear of me, of her need to protect her self-sufficiency, her fears of revealing the unresolved grief and feelings of abandonment and loss. For a while there seemed to be no effect. She would be silent. I would continue to feel as if I were talking to myself.

But during the next summer, after I returned from a short vacation, she reluctantly admitted that she missed me. "I don't feel comfortable with that . . . missing you. I don't want to feel this way. What if you leave, or something else?"

"What if I died?"

"Yeah. Died or left the city, or something. You can't say . . . I can't control you, or what might happen."

"As you couldn't when your father died . . . and then you were alone with nobody."

"Nobody. . . . Even my mother was no good for me. I took care of her, and then when I still needed her she threw me out. I'm better if I take care of things alone."

It was after this that I felt a change in my experience of Patricia. One day I went out to the waiting room to invite her into a session. She walked toward me down the narrow hallway, and I felt a sudden attraction to her, not powerful or compelling by any means, but a sexual response that was quite unusual. Thinking about it later, I realized that she had subtly responded to me as she approached, glancing at me and reacting to my welcome with a slight nod and shrug. She responded to me as she hadn't before – not seductively (or rather, not purely so) so much as a normal, expectable relating. Soon after that she called me for the first time by name. These developments by no means led to a flowering of the transference, but I had a growing, cumulative experience of being recognized by her. This feeling deepened over time as the analysis ventured into unresolved areas of her bereavement and current struggles around her work ambitions, self-image, and sexuality. But the primary feeling I had was of eventually being related to as a subjectively recognized other with whom she was willing to engage in a mutual process of exploration and change.

Discussion

This short case report is not intended to convey the full complexity of Patricia's five-year treatment. Rather, what I have tried to do is sketch the development of a type of transference encountered in work with some adults who suffered parent loss in later childhood. The following is a summary of the analysis of Patricia's flight from recognition of my subjectivity.

The experience of her father's death was sudden and traumatic. The additional loss of her mother to depression and the eventual collapse of their relationship, and thus the last vestiges of parental support, led to the crystallization of Patricia's pseudo individuation and defensive self-sufficiency. Unconsciously she remained preoccupied with her father and nurtured a continuing fantasy attachment to him. Countertransferentially this was reflected in my sensation of "being like" the dead father. But more important, on a deeper level, she feared recognizing me as "someone new" with my own unique identity, sense of self, and distinct perspective on life. To risk recognizing me would mean moving away from her father toward an "other" man and engagement in a new relationship that could be lost just as suddenly, and perhaps irrevocably, as was her father. Patricia's flight from relating to others resulted in a broad developmental arrest in mid adolescence and a retreat from the work of mourning.

This became evident to me through my understanding of the estrangement that dominated my experience of our relationship. This lack of relatedness is consistent with Benjamin's viewpoint referred to previously: flight from the subjectivity of the other means a retreat to more schizoid forms of relating, often with adaptive results; however, reliance on internal "objects" (as opposed to subjectively experienced others) impacts negatively on the person's capacity for mutual recognition, psychological development, and self-elaboration. The parent loss analysts noted the clinical manifestations of this retreat from other-relating in their patient's transference resistances, states of developmental arrest, and obsessive engagement in repetitive and generally self-defeating relationships. Optimally the development of the self involves a movement over time from the need for self-consolidating, repairing, and self-sustaining merger experiences toward more differentiated, creative, and mature ones (Kohut, 1984). Flight from the subjectivity of the other is a retreat from these developmentally advanced selfobject experiences. In the best of cases, such as with Patricia, the person attempts to maintain, through the continuing fantasy tie to the lost parent, a cohesive and vital sense of self. However, it is eventually revealed that engagement in new forms of truly creative and mature forms of relating has been defensively foreclosed. To that end, what I have encountered in cases such as Patricia's is a retreat from engagement with subjectively recognized others as mature selfobjects in favor of a reliance on a moribund selfobject tie lacking in the perishable qualities of subjectivity.

Technically the treatment of Patricia illustrates a three-step sequence involved in the resolution of the transference resistance frequently encountered in parent loss cases: 1) the facilitation of the emergence of defenses against selfobject relating in the treatment situation, 2) the exploration of the function of the inner tie to the lost parent, and 3) the interpretation of defenses and underlying anxieties related to engaging in developmentally more advanced levels of self-experience involving recognition of the selfobject's perishability. With the provision of continuity, security, and the growing experience of empathic resonance in the analytic situation, Patricia began to risk the recognition of, and engagement with, me as an other. It was through this process that a mature selfobject tie was restored and the previously arrested self-elaboration processes resumed. Over time, I found myself experiencing a growing excitement and investment in the treatment. The transference grew richer and more varied. She accepted my interpretations and valued them for their freshness, their potential for surprise and usefulness. Patricia and I shared the experience of a working alliance. It was during that period of the analysis when the full creative capacities of the treatment were realized.

Conclusion

The idea of a flight from subjectivity in response to the experience of selfobject failure has potentially broad applications. This chapter focuses on childhood bereavement, but loss later in life may result in similar reactions. Winnicott's (1971) notion of the use of the object involved not just the recognition of the existence of the other as outside the range of one's omnipotence, but extended the idea to explain broad areas of culture and creativity. In 1984, Modell saw the retreat from relating to and communicating with others as one of the fundamental defenses of the narcissistic disorders. Stern (1985) believed that a typical response of children to empathic failure and misattunement is withdrawal from involvement with the subjectivity of the other. Benjamin (1988) argued powerfully that the failure to recognize the subjectivity of the mother, and women in general, is the basis of male sexual tyranny in western culture. Given this, the fate of our capacities to recognize other selves as distinct and unique while at the same time similar to ourselves may be a core issue in human relatedness in general and psychopathology in particular. This viewpoint may broaden the traditional concepts of the object and selfobject to include areas of human relating that have so far remained undeveloped.

References

Altschul, S. (1968). Denial and ego arrest. *J. Am. Psychoanal. Assn.*, 16: 301–318.
Benjamin, J. (1988). *The Bonds of Love*. New York: Pantheon Books.
Benjamin, J. (1991). Recognition and destruction: An outline of intersubjectivity. In: *Relational Perspectives in Psychoanalysis*, eds. N. Skolnick & S. Warshaw. Hillsdale, NJ: The Analytic Press, pp. 43–60.
Blum, H. (1980). The value of reconstruction in adult psychoanalysis. *Int. J. Psycho-Anal.*, 61: 39–52.
Blum, H. (1983). The psychoanalytic process and analytic inference: A clinical study of a lie and loss. *Int. J. Psycho-Anal.*, 64: 17–33.

Blum, H. (1984). Splitting of the ego and its relation to parent loss. In: *Defense and Resistance: Historical Perspectives and Current Concepts*, ed. H. Blum. New York: International Universities Press, pp. 301–324.

Deutsch, H. (1937). Absence of grief. *Psychoanal. Q.*, 6: 12–22.

Fleming, J. (1972). Early object deprivation and transference phenomena: The working alliance. *Psychoanal. Q.*, 41: 23–49.

Fleming, J. (1974). The problem of diagnosis in parent loss cases. *Contemp. Psychoanal.*, 10: 439–451.

Fleming, J. & Altschul, S. (1962). Activation of mourning and growth by psychoanalysis. In: *Childhood Bereavement and Its Aftermath*, ed. S. Altschul. Madison, CT: International Universities Press, 1988, pp. 277–307.

Freud, S. (1927). Fetishism. *Standard Edition, Vol. 21*. London: Hogarth Press, 1961, pp. 235–239.

Jacobson, E. (1965). The return of the lost parent. In: *Drive, Affects, Behavior, Vol. 2*, ed. M. Shur. New York: International Universities Press.

Kohut, H. (1984). *How Does Analysis Cure?* eds. A. Goldberg & P. Stepansky. Chicago: University of Chicago Press.

Lewin, B. (1937). A type of neurotic hypomanic reaction. *Arch. Neural. & Psychiat.*, 37: 868–873.

Modell, A. (1984). *Psychoanalysis in a New Context*. New York: International Universities Press.

Ornstein, P. (1991). Why self psychology is not an object relations theory: Clinical and theoretical considerations. In: *The Evolution of Self Psychology Progr. Self Psychol., Vol. 7*, ed. A. Goldberg. Hillsdale, NJ: The Analytic Press, pp. 17–30.

Shane, E. & Shane, M. (1990a). Object loss and selfobject loss: A consideration of self psychology's contribution to understanding mourning and the failure to mourn. *Annul. Psychoanal.*, 18: 115–131.

Shane, M. & Shane, E. (1990b). The struggle for otherhood: Implications for development in adulthood of the capacity to be a good-enough object for another. In: *New Developments in Adult Development*, eds. R. Nemiroff & C. Colorosso. New York: Basic Books, pp. 487–498.

Stern, D. (1985). *The Interpersonal World of the Infant*. New York: Basic Books.

Stolorow, R. & Atwood, G. (1992). *Contexts of Being: The Intersubjective Foundations of Psychological Life*. Hillsdale, NJ: The Analytic Press.

Stolorow, R., Atwood, G. & Lachmann, F. (1975). Early object loss and denial: Developmental considerations. *Psychoanal. Q.*, 44: 596–611.

Winnicott, D. W. (1965). *The Maturational Processes and the Facilitating Environment*. New York: International Universities Press.

Winnicott, D. W. (1971). The use of an object and relating through identifications. In: *Playing and Reality*. London: Tavistock, pp. 86–94.

Chapter 5

Mourning theory reconsidered (1994)

R. Dennis Shelby

Editor's note: In his work with seropositive men and their partners, R. Dennis Shelby observed the mourning process frequently and firsthand. This paper describes his observation that the facilitative environment was crucial to the successful coping with illness and death, as well as the psychological processing of the affects of grief.

This paper was published in 1994 by R. Dennis Shelby as "Mourning Theory Reconsidered" in The Widening Scope of Self Psychology: Progress in Self Psychology, *Volume 9, published by the Analytic Press, a Taylor & Francis imprint, New York and London.*

The inspiration for the beginning reformulation of mourning theory presented in this chapter came from two sources. The first was a research endeavor designed to reconstruct the experiences of gay men whose long-term partners contracted and died from acquired immunodeficiency syndrome (Shelby, 1992). The second was the considerable reformulation of clinical theory: the psychology of the self and long-overdue efforts to reexamine analytic theory in light of cognitive and linguistic theories.

The study design consisted of a series of open-ended interviews with well partners, ill partners, and surviving partners in long-term relationships impacted by AIDS. Individuals and couples were interviewed over a 9- to-12-month period. The interviews were then coded and analyzed according to the grounded theory method of Glaser and Strauss (1967) and Glaser (1975). This relatively open-ended interview approach, in which the study participants were asked to tell me what was going on in their lives versus answering my questions about their experience, yielded data not previously elucidated in the analytic literature on mourning. The first topic is the integral role other people play in facilitating the survivors' mourning process; the second concerns the impact on the mourning process of a surviving partner when he too is infected with the same agent that resulted in his partner's death.

Clinical theory has evolved considerably since the work of Pollock (1961), in which mourning was conceptualized as a realignment and modification of the self-representation and object representation. Self psychology has gained an ever-increasing influence; analytic theorists such as Basch, Goldberg, and Palombo, in addition to their many contributions, have begun to reconsider analytic theory in light of cognitive and linguistic theories. Stern, drawing on infant research studies, has also challenged many of our long-held assumptions about the human mind and its development.

The results of the study and advances in clinical theory indicated that a beginning reformulation of our theory of mourning is in order, if not long overdue. The data also demand that attempts be made to give a theoretical accounting for the observed differences in the mourning experiences of seropositive and seronegative men. Though discussed in the context of a population of gay men whose lives have been irrevocably changed by the HIV virus, the theoretical formulations are applicable to mourning theory in general and offer a framework for understanding not only the experience of mourning per se but phenomena both environmental and intrapsychic that can interfere with the process.

To develop the framework I will discuss the development of psychoanalytic mourning theory, including the problems with the theory in general and for the understanding of gay men in particular; offer a more elaborated self-psychological model; and present two cases of surviving partners who were experiencing a complicated mourning process. One case involves a man who was seronegative for the HIV virus, the other a man who was seropositive. Hopefully, the cases and the discussion will illustrate the process of mourning and the complications in the mourning process often observed in seropositive surviving partners.

The development of mourning theory

The basic formulation regarding the nature of the mourning process that has guided our theoretical and clinical understanding for more than 70 years can be found in Freud's (1912–1913) work "Totem and Taboo": "Mourning has a quite specific task to perform: its function is to detach the survivor's memories and hopes from the dead. When this has been achieved the pain grows less, and with it the remorse and self reproach" (pp. 65–66). The two interrelated and enduring elements are the following: (1) mourning concerns two central figures, the mourner and the deceased, or, more specifically, their memories, hopes, and affects. That is, mourning essentially concerns the meaning of the particular relationship and its loss. (2) Mourning is a process that, in an undistorted form, consists of a reorganization of the ego of the mourner. Essentially, the loss of a central person and the accompanying psychological manifestations of loss gradually move from a central, painful, and often overwhelming aspect of the survivor's experience to a less central affectively charged position. When this reorganization has been achieved, the survivor is able to again feel a part of the world of the living and has the psychological resources to actively participate in new love attachments.

With the publication of "Mourning and Melancholia" Freud (1917) laid out a theory of relationships, including their loss and subsequent role in the structuralization of the mind. The process consists of a libidinal cathexis to another person. With the loss of the person, the libidinal energy must be withdrawn. The ego initially protests and resists as this represents the abandonment of a libidinal position. In successful mourning the object is eventually preserved in the form of identification, and libidinal energy is available for new attachments. In pathological mourning, or melancholia, the object is not decathected owing to unresolvable ambivalence; rather, the libido is withdrawn into the ego and the ambivalence toward the lost object becomes an aspect of the ego's structure.

Pollock (1961), using the framework of analytic ego psychology, describes the mourning process as a gradual realignment of the self-representation and the object representation, which are intrapsychic counterpoints to the individual's experience of the world. Object representations consist of the images and experiences with individuals to whom the person has formed an attachment, while self-representations consist of images and experiences the person has of himself. Over the course of the life cycle, reality calls for modifications in both self and object representations. In the case of mourning, the process consists of integrating the reality of the loss. The object representation is decathected, giving rise to the pain associated with the loss of an attachment. As part of the process, the mourner experiences a gradually shifting series of identifications with the deceased. Eventually the self-representation is modified and "reshaped," partially in the image of the dead individual. Two potential pathological outcomes to the process are (1) an excessive identification with the lost individual, in which the object representation becomes incorporated into the self-representation, and (2) an inability to tolerate the process of mourning with the result that the object representation remains intact and the fantasy evolves that the person never died. Crucial to the mourning process is the ability to work through ambivalent feelings toward the deceased. As the ambivalence toward the deceased is resolved, the object representation is transformed into a set of memories, cathexis is withdrawn, and the individual is available for new attachments.

The emphasis on the ability to work through ambivalent feelings toward the deceased indicates the extent to which traditional analytic theory is based on the concept of drives, with their organization or psychic structures being the primary determinants of behavior; consequently drives are key determinants in the ability of the individual to mourn. The ability to resolve ambivalence is contingent on the resolution of the oedipal phase and the consequent laying down of the repression barrier. A reflection of the importance of ambivalence resolution is seen in the debate concerning what age and level of intrapsychic structure a child must theoretically obtain in order to be able to mourn (see Shane and Shane, 1990, and Palombo, 1981, for more thorough reviews of this literature). This connection between ambivalence resolution and resolution of the oedipal phase is the very problem that makes traditional analytic theories problematic in understanding the mourning process of gay men; in the traditional analytic framework, homosexual men and women have not reached the oedipal level of drive organization (Lewes, 1988). Consequently, children and homosexuals are considered to be infantile in terms of psychic structure and hence, theoretically, unable to mourn.

The theoretical consequences of an unmourned loss in an individual incapable of mourning are considerable. Shane and Shane (1990) observe:

> . . . it has been felt that without the capacity to adequately mourn an overwhelming loss, the child's development is significantly impeded. It is postulated that because the child cannot mourn – that is, give up (decathect) the attachment to an investment in the representation of the lost person – or cannot preserve the relationship in the form of an identification, the search goes on forever for the parent whose death is unconsciously denied, and the person remains, in an important sense, the child at that phase or age when the loss was sustained. Thus, the fantasy that the parent still lives and can be found again precludes the possibility for true replacement, not just in childhood, but also throughout life.
>
> (pp. 115–116)

Clinical theory and homosexuality

The relationship between mourning, ambivalence, and homosexuality is but one of the many theoretical problems one encounters when addressing psychological phenomena in a homosexual population. Friedman (1988) states: "Concepts about male homosexuality, of undeniable importance in their own right, are also an organic part of the larger issues in the history of psychoanalytic ideas" (p. 269). Given this centrality, a brief discussion of homosexuality is in order.

Clinicians who strive to practice from a depth psychology model with gay men or lesbian women face a central theoretical problem. Until fairly recently, all of our depth, or analytic, psychological models were rooted in libidinal drive theory. The self psychology framework helps us avoid the multiple theoretical problems one encounters with libidinal and ego-analytic theories, which ultimately rely heavily on the cornerstone of Oedipus and the heterosexual functioning that successful resolution represents (see Lewes, 1988, and Friedman, 1988, for more thorough discussions of the multiple theoretical problems). Isay (1989) has attempted to describe clinical intervention with gay men within a drive-theory-based theoretical framework. However, his selective inattention to key aspects of the theory – especially the resolution of the oedipal conflict and the formation of the superego, the laying down of the repression barrier, and the difference between homosexuality and neurosis – essentially leaves him operating from an atheoretical position.

The basic issue comes down to the role of sexuality in the development or organization of the mind. Does the development of sexual or libidinal drives shape the mind, or does the self's organization and coherence influence the experience of sexuality and the ability to form relationships that are mutually enhancing? Clearly, the general direction in which analytic theory is currently moving indicates that the latter provides a broader explanation of the phenomena than the former.

In clinical work with gay men "the issue is not what caused the patients' homosexuality, it is the meaning that being homosexual has for the particular person"

(Shelby, 1989). In the course of development, homosexual children live in the context of a selfobject environment (both parental and the larger environment) that is culturally phobic, if not outright hostile, toward homosexuality and its sexual expression. Consequently, the developing self often experiences numerous selfobject failures and outright narcissistic assaults.

The shared sense of sexuality or masculine competence is an important element in the mirroring and alter ego components of the father–son dialogue and often dramatically affects the idealizing sphere as well. Temperamental differences that are often read and responded to along gender lines, as well as the basic lack of a shared sexual orientation, often result in distortions in the relationship with the same-sex parent. Subsequently, the homosexual child does not experience selfobject functions that pertain to the realm of gender in an uncomplicated manner, and the self-organization begins to include the experience of being different and incompetent. If the child's temperamental and/or orientation differences are experienced by the parent as a narcissistic injury, the child may be subjected to narcissistic assaults. The implication of this perspective is that there is a normative developmental process observed in homosexual children and that the pathogenic process often centers around the lack of environmental sustaining and modulating of the child's evolving self in the areas of gender and sexual orientation.

A series of meanings often becomes structured around these frequently painful experiences, and a gap often develops in the father–son dialogue that is difficult to mediate. These early experiences become the organizers through which messages from the larger homophobic environment are understood and become the basis for the self-experience that Maylon (1982) has referred to as "internalized homophobia." In the course of the mourning process these experiences and meanings are often reawakened. If the environmental response is nonsupportive or attacking, they may take on a central significance.

Mourning and self psychology

Palombo (1981, 1982) points out "in the self-psychological model, the loss [of a significant relationship due to death] is viewed as the loss of a selfobject relationship, which brings about an imbalance in self-esteem." In many cases the imbalance in self-esteem is more accurately described as a massive disorganization of the self and a shattering of self-esteem. Relationships vary in the degree to which individuals rely on one another for specific selfobject experiences; hence, each relationship varies in terms of the meaning of the loss and, consequently, in the psychological impact on the mourner.

Shane and Shane (1990) extend formulations of mourning theory within a self psychology framework. Though they focus on children, they assert that it is not the degree of psychic structure that enables the child to mourn but, rather, the presence and ability of the surviving parent or other adult to tolerate, mirror, sustain, and share the range of the child's affects regarding the lost parent, essentially the ability of that adult to provide "compensatory self-structure . . . to repair the

weakened aspects of the self, but facilitate continued or renewed development"
(p. 199).

In the face of the massive loss of selfobject functions of the deceased parent,
the surviving parent (when not overly compromised by his or her own grief)
serves as a selfobject that facilitates the mourning process. When this supportive
environment is available, the child is able "to face the impact of the loss without
feeling the risk of being overwhelmed, annihilated, or fragmented. . . . The pain
of the loss can be borne and the necessary capacity to think, talk, and reflect about
it can be sustained if the child is helped to mourn" (pp. 118–119). The Shanes
postulate that for many children the surviving parent's inability to perform these
functions results in a double loss for the child and accounts for the considerable pathology observed later in life. The loss of the parent is complicated when
the surviving parent is so compromised by his or her own grief as to be unable
to provide the sustaining selfobject environment to support the child's mourning process. Hence, in the face of an overwhelming loss the child is once again
abandoned.

It is reasonable to assert that adults as well as children require selfobject experiences to facilitate the varying degrees of self-reorganization that mourning
involves. While Shane and Shane (1990) indicate that the presence of a required
"optimal selfobject environment [is] more available to the adult" (p. 119), they do
not elaborate on the nature of the role of the selfobject matrix in adult mourning.
The results of the study on which this chapter is based illustrate the central role
that selfobject encounters with those individuals who exhibit their understanding
and tolerance of the mourners' affects, concerns, and general psychological state
play in facilitating the reorganization of the self that mourning involves.

At this point in time an elaborated theory of mourning in a self-psychological
framework has not been posited. The basic elements exist in the literature: Kohut's
(1977) assertion that there is "no mature love in which the love object is not also a
selfobject, or, to put this depth psychological formulation into a psychosocial context, there is no love relationship without mutual self-esteem enhancing, mirroring
and idealization" (p. 141); Palombo's 1981 statement that "the loss must also be
viewed as the loss of a selfobject relationship which brings about an imbalance in
self-esteem"; and the Shanes' 1990 statement that there exists a "required optimal
selfobject environment" for the mourning process. The results of the present study
and recent advances in clinical theory enable us to make a beginning in the formulation of a theory of mourning within a self-psychological framework.

In recent years many theorists have worked toward integrating linguistic and/
or cognitive theories into psychoanalytic theory. As Krystal (1990) points out,
analytic theory since the time of Freud has tended to develop in a context of its
own, generally ignoring advances in cognitive and linguistic theories. This reex-
amination of psychoanalysis in the context of theories of other parameters so basic
to human experience – cognition, language, and development – has resulted in a
necessary revision of the philosophical underpinnings of clinical theory, including issues such as how the mind develops and is organized and, perhaps most

importantly, the nature of the therapeutic process itself (e.g., Stern, 1985; Saari, 1986; Basch, 1988; Goldberg, 1990; Palombo, 1991).

Palombo (1991) presents an integration of numerous theorists into a cohesive theory of the nature of meaning, of the processes by which it is organized into the structure we refer to as the self, and of the process we call psychotherapy. The central stance concerns the innate aspect of being human, namely, that from birth onward, humans strive to organize or give meaning to their experience. "Meanings are initially constituted by the sense a person makes of his or her lived experiences as filtered through his or her own peculiar environment. These meanings are residues from these experiences that are retained by the person but they go beyond the facts of the experience itself. They initially are the definitions a person uses to organize and integrate experiences" (p. 181). Central to the organization of meanings is the role of others in the environment: "They [meanings] evolve out of the early affective states which in infancy occur in interaction with a caregiver who attempts to give significance to the affective states, to modify them, and to share in them. Meanings then, whether personal or shared, are embedded within a matrix of affectivity and cognition" (p. 181–182). The interplay between affect and the role of other individuals in the formation of meaning is a key component: "The integration of affect serves to organize experience. Affects constitute a signaling system which when joined with cognitive faculties and a caregiver's responses result in a residue of comprehension of the experience by the child" (p. 182). This is the process by which the self-narrative, the individual's account of his own experience, is formed. Palombo defines narrative as "the means by which we organize and integrate our experiences. They make our experiences coherent by integrating them into each other" (personal communication, May 12, 1992).

Language plays a central role in the development and organization of the mind. For Palombo (1991), "language. . . is a medium through which meanings become encoded and are capable of being recalled and of being communicated to others" (p. 183). Thus, language is the central tool by which we encode personal meaning and participate in the larger world. Palombo states that language mediates "experience." In a similar vein, Goldberg (1990) states: "Language as a link to other people produces a different kind of orientation that says that the signifiers allow for a developmental process to take place, which process allows for the completion of a configuration, in this case a configuration called the self, one that was not completed during development" (p. 111).

The nature of the mind or the self is defined by Palombo (1991) as a "hierarchy of meanings"; thus "psychic structure may be defined as a set of symbols that remain stable over time" (p. 178). "Eventually the hierarchies of the meaning systems acquire a coherence that defines the personality. This coherence is experienced as a sense of cohesion . . . the sum of these coherent systems may be said to constitute a person narrative" (p. 184). While there is a considerable degree of stability to the self's organization, elements are subject to change and reorganization: "Experiences and events may not retain their original meanings but are constantly re-interpreted" (p. 184).

While the basis of these theories is the development of meaning in the context of childhood development, they include models that can be thought of as part of a dynamic process that extends throughout the life span. As human beings living in the context of the larger world, we are exposed to events and experiences that tax our psychic resources, reactivate old meanings, and challenge us to form new meanings and engage in relationships that often serve a central role in the process.

Thus, while psychic structure is reasonably stable over time, elements of our personal narratives are subject to change and revision. In defining the therapeutic process Palombo quotes Saari (1986) as saying that it "involves the organizing of old meanings into newly constructed consciousness. What is curative is not so much the recovery of deeply rooted repressed material, but the reordering of structures that underlie personal meaning and the symbolic capacities of the individual so the new meanings can be differentiated, constructed or abstracted" (p. 27).

The process of mourning and the role of the selfobject matrix

Drawing on current clinical thinking, I am proposing the following definition of mourning: a process that involves a reorganization of central aspects of the self, of major affect states, and, consequently, of the meaning of the loss into a narrative that can be integrated into the overall structure of the self. Mourning begins with a state of acute disorganization of the self, with a resultant lack of coherence and disequilibrium in self-esteem, brought about by the loss of a relationship in an individuals' life. Central to the disorganization and self-esteem difficulties are the massive loss of selfobject functions that the survivor experienced within the context of the relationship, the loss of the shared experience or dialogue that occurs within a relationship, and any specific meaning that the loss entails (in the case of an AIDS-related death, the potential that the survivor may also die of the same disease).

Mourning as a process involves a gradual and often painful reorganization of the affects secondary to the loss and an integration of the meaning of the loss into the self. The degree of disorganization and intensity of the affects involved depends on the centrality of the relationship and the degree to which the individual relied on the deceased person to complete his own experience of self. Initially, the self is in a deficient state; the person has lost a sense of coherence because it is impossible to integrate the meaning of the loss of a central person in his life, the selfobject dimensions of the relationship, and the intense affects associated with the loss. Initially in the mourning process the emphasis is on the missing of the lost individual and the desire for the experience of the relationship. Cherishing the belongings of the deceased, holding personal "conversations" with the deceased, and visiting the gravesite offer the mourner a sense of continuing the relationship with the lost individual.

This is a crucial distinction: The mourner is not missing, yearning, or searching for a lost figure, "object," or representation thereof; rather, what is absent is his

particular unique experience of that individual and the shared experience, the dialogue, that an intimate relationship entails. Goldberg (1990), using cognitive and
linguistic theories, presents a thorough and convincing argument for essentially
dispensing with the concept and theory of representations. He argues that analytic
theories of representations are not consistent with the findings of cognitive and
linguistic science, namely, that the mind is not structured or "mapped" by a series
of object representations. There are no "objects" in our minds, only the subject –
ourselves. For Goldberg, "the Kohutian analyst is not concerned with the hidden
representation of the object as with the representation of the deficient self" (p. 110).

If mourning does not center on the preservation of the object in the form of identifications or realignment of self and object representations, then just what does the
process entail? The process is the reorganization of affects and the construction of
a new or modified narrative: an account of the meaning of the death that can then
be integrated into the self-organization. The person who has become increasingly
accustomed to an intimate, ongoing dialogue, the bedrock of shared experience
with another, must now integrate the experience of being alone. In this disorganized
and vulnerable state, affects are intense and volatile and self-esteem is diminished
and unstable; consequently, the environment feels very unsafe and unfamiliar. The
work of mourning concerns the gradual reorganization of the affect states and integration into the experience of the self. As the affects become less intense, a narrative can be formed; the mourner makes meaning out of his loss. Language and the
narrative gradually supplant shifting affect states. As this is achieved, the narrative can be integrated into the overall self-organization. The experience of the loss
comes to be viewed as a complicated and painful event in a larger life experience.

The central figures are not so much the mourner and the deceased as the mourner
and the selfobject environment. By responding to the mourner's affect states and
the meaning or centrality of the loss, the environment assists in the organization
of affect and, consequently, in the construction and integration of the narrative.
Stolorow, Brandchaft, and Atwood (1987) state that "selfobject functions pertain
fundamentally to the integration of affect into the evolving organization of self
experience" (p. 86). Hence, selfobject encounters help modulate and regulate the
intensity of affects, which enables the individual to integrate the meaning of his
experiences. Socarides and Stolorow (1984/1985) assert that "what is crucial to
the child's (or patient's) growing capacity to integrate his sadness and his painful
disappointments in himself and others is the reliable presence of a calming, containing, empathic selfobject, irrespective of the 'amount' or intensity of the affects
involved" (p. 113). Ultimately, the result of the mourner's encounters with the
responsive selfobject environment is the transformation of the experience from
one of massive selfobject loss, with its attendant fragmentation states and loss of
coherence, into a very sad and painful life event, one that has been lived through
and overcome, the process often stimulating renewed growth.

Affects are soothed and organized, and the narrative is formed through the
mourner's personal and public activities and selfobject relationships. The mourner's cherishing of, and interactions with, symbols of the relationship and his

shared experience with the deceased complete the configuration that represents the deficient self in a personal manner. The empathic response of the selfobject environment to the mourner's missing of the individual, the associated affects, and the general psychological state complete the configuration in a shared experience with living people.

Public encounters serve to orient the self toward the world of the living and rekindle the hope that the self can become enriched through participating in ongoing shared experiences with the living, rather than by attempting to find meaning and solace by recreating the shared experience with the deceased. Ultimately, these experiences often result in the formation of idealizing relationships with living people, which can spur further growth, enabling the person to take on new challenges in his career and form relationships that reflect a higher level of self-organization.

I am proposing that the mourning process consists of three distinct but interrelated elements: The first is the cherishing of the deceased's possessions and of photographs and memories of the relationship, "conversations" with the deceased, and rituals such as visits to the gravesite and acknowledging anniversaries. All these acts reflect not identification with the deceased but, rather, attempts to complete the familiar configuration of the relationship, which ultimately serves to soothe and modulate affect. The second element concerns the response of the selfobject environment to affects associated with the loss. Mourners often turn to others whom they experience as sharing the meaning of the loss – relatives or close friends of the deceased – during times of acute loneliness, which holidays and anniversaries tend to represent. Mourners consider the sharing of mutual affects regarding the loss as deeply meaningful and helpful, and a greater degree of coherence is often evident. This represents the completion of the configuration of the deficient self in a public way with living people. The third element of the mourning process is the gradual formation and integration of the narrative of the loss in the mourner's overall life experience.

Case illustrations

An important finding of Shelby's study (Shelby, 1992) concerned the differences in the mourning process of seropositive and seronegative surviving partners. Essentially, seropositive partners tended to be in a more protracted mourning process and were not able to reengage with the world in the same manner as seronegative survivors. As I turn to clinical application of the framework, I will present two cases: The first is of a man who was seronegative; the second is of a man who was seropositive. Both men had encountered difficulty in their mourning process, and both were significantly depressed upon entering treatment. However, there were significant differences between the two cases; hopefully, these important differences will come through as I recount aspects of the clinical process. The cases are presented in a way that emphasizes the process of mourning and intervention aimed at reestablishing the process. The area of pre-existing self pathology and its role in complicated mourning is another topic entirely.

Case I: The seronegative survivor

Mr. B was a 35-year-old professional man who sought treatment at the insistence of his physician. His partner had died approximately five months earlier. He had gone to his physician with a long list of somatic complaints and preoccupations, including lack of energy, chest pains, and headaches. His physician had worked him up and could find nothing amiss. His assessment was that Mr. B was severely depressed, and he prescribed Prozac on the condition that Mr. B seeks psycho-therapy. Mr. B was rather chagrined by this assessment but dutifully followed through with the firm recommendation. Further questioning revealed that Mr. B was sleeping 14 to 16 hours a day; he would come home from work at lunchtime and sleep and would go to bed shortly after he returned home in the evening.

Mr. B was very reluctant to enter treatment. Although his affect was excruciat-ingly depressed, he was very resistant, maintaining that he was only interested in short-term intervention and had come at the insistence of his physician. I had worked with his partner and, periodically, with his partner's family for over two years during a long, complicated illness. Mr. B sought me out, he said, because I knew his partner and, therefore, he would not have to explain everything to me the way he would to someone else.

Mr. B related that immediately following his partner's death, the family began harassing him by demanding things that went against the spirit and specifica-tions of the will. They had also begun a lawsuit challenging the document even though they had been handsomely provided for. As Mr. B had been given power of attorney, they demanded a thorough accounting of the money spent during his partner's illness, outrightly accusing him of embezzlement. The first two months after his partner's death were spent attempting to account for every penny spent, an exhausting and complicated task since Mr. B often contributed his own money to pay the expenses even though his partner had ample resources. Although he came up with an accounting, the family went ahead with their lawsuits. Several of his partner's cousins, whom Mr. B had become quite close to, stopped returning his calls, which enraged and devastated him. He felt all-alone, with sharks circling about him.

As we explored this, Mr. B came to realize that his desperate attempts to account for the finances were also an attempt to convince his partner's mother that he was not a bad person, which, of course, was futile. He related that he had come to question himself, at times believing he was the awful, vile embezzler of a helpless, dying man's estate that his partner's mother said he was.

As I listened to Mr. B I sensed no mourning process and heard mention of none of the activities, concerns, and rituals that mourners often engage in; instead, I heard depression and a questioning of his own integrity. Mr. B also reflected on this, pointing out that he did not find himself missing his partner or feeling grief stricken. At times he felt the lawsuits were not worth the hassle of fighting them; he was not actively cooperating with his lawyers and had begun to consider just turning over his partner's entire estate to his parents. Shortly after he realized that he was engaged in a desperate, futile effort to prove his integrity to his partner's mother, he became less resistant and more engaged with me and began to actively work with his attorney.

During the next session Mr. B obliquely hinted at regrets in his associations. I asked him what regrets he had. He began to cry. He related that he had fallen in love with his partner all over again during the last few months of the illness and that he was devastated that his partner had died during the night, by himself in his sleep, when neither he nor the family were present. Mr. B also admitted that this was the first time he had cried since his partner's death.

Following that session I began to hear evidence of a mourning process. Mr. B flew to one of the places where his partner's ashes had been dispersed. He began to seek out contact with his partner's best friend, someone also deeply affected by the loss, and they would spend a great deal of time reminiscing. He also began to reminisce with me and to try and sort out several old and often painful conflicts between himself and his partner. Mr. B also became determined to do his best in defending himself and the will, especially, because it was what his partner had wanted. Needless to say, his depression was lifting considerably. Although he had been dreading his partner's approaching birthday, he went alone on that day to a restaurant the two of them had gone to practically every Sunday they were together. Mr. B related that this visit was "sad and bittersweet, but it felt good, it felt right." He then began planning a panel for the AIDS Quilt and invited a group of his partner's close friends to participate in making it and to make their own contributions to the memorial.

Though the lawsuits continued to be quite taxing and a nuisance, Mr. B did not become overwhelmed by them as readily as before. Concurrently, his sleeping pattern returned to normal, and he became more actively engaged socially and at work, even earning a promotion. Approximately six months after beginning treatment he went off Prozac, his affect held, and he continued his process of mourning and engagement. Nevertheless, he also became preoccupied with his antibody status and became convinced that he was seropositive. Though he had consistently tested negative prior to his partner's death and had had no sexual contact since, he became convinced that he too was positive. He eventually was tested and was again negative.

Discussion of Case I

The case of Mr. B illustrates a number of important aspects of working with people who are having difficulty in the mourning process. The first concerns the delicate balance between depression and mourning. When the mourning process is thwarted in adults, one often sees depression. Mourning does involve a great deal of sad affect, but if a process of integrating the experience is occurring one also hears of efforts to soothe the affect through rituals and by engaging with others who are also deeply affected by the loss. In theoretical terms, efforts to complete the now-missing configuration of the dialogue are made. When the process essentially stops, depression and/or anxiety often comes to dominate. If a person is too depressed he cannot sustain or soothe the sad affect and is overcome by it. Clearly, Mr. B was in the midst of a major depressive episode by the time he came to me. When this is the case, the use of antidepressant medication, in conjunction with individual therapy, is often necessary to essentially reestablish the process of mourning and to return the patient to a more reasonable level of functioning.

Mr. B's selfobject environment was not supportive of him and his efforts to mourn. The challenging of a will interjects chaos, uncertainty, and, often, a profound sense of betrayal when the mourner is in such a highly vulnerable state. Family members were attacking and abandoning Mr. B, rather than engaging with him in a mutual process of mourning their loss. Relatives with whom Mr. B might have shared his grief cut off contact with him. In his disappointment he failed to engage with people who were available for mutual reminiscing and the sharing of affect regarding the loss.

The clinician's role becomes one of helping the patient reestablish the mourning process. In this case it was necessary to first help Mr. B sort out his suspicions regarding himself so that he could then relate to me and the memory of his partner without the fear of his being found out to actually be an evil person. Survivors often experience ruminations of guilt. Many times this feeling of guilt can be traced to the survivor's perceived or actual empathic breaks with the deceased. However, if the ruminations are too intense or are seemingly confirmed by an angry family, the survivor may come to believe them as facts. He may become reluctant to relate them to others for fear they will be found to be true, a reluctance that deprives him of the possibility of an environment that can respond to and modulate his painful self-doubts.

As the treatment relationship evolves, the therapist should express his interest in the mourned relationship and its history and validate the rituals that the survivor engages in. The personal "conversations" with the deceased often provide important data for understanding the selfobject dimensions of the relationship, dimensions that can be used by the clinician in helping the patient understand the many aspects of the meaning of the loss. The therapist's interest in the relationship and his encouragement of the mourner to relate its history, including the good times and the bad, enhances the process of reflection and reminiscing while establishing the clinician as an active participant in the mourning process.

Like many men who have lost partners to AIDS, Mr. B became preoccupied with his antibody status, convincing himself he was positive, despite previous testing. This behavior was consistent with the study's findings in that participants tended to become preoccupied with their antibody status (regardless of prior test results) during the middle phase of mourning, when they were beginning to feel more alive and more engaged with the world. When survivors test negative, one often sees renewed efforts at self-redefinition as a single person and in engagement with the world; when they test positive (or already know they are positive), one often sees the mourning process slow down, if not stop.

Case II: The seropositive survivor

One often finds a complicated and protracted mourning process in seropositive surviving partners. In keeping with the theoretical framework I propose,
the problem becomes the continued shared experience with the deceased partner
that seropositivity represents. These men are infected with the same virus that
killed their partner, the implication being that they will follow in their partner's
footsteps. Even as these men attempt to integrate the death of their partner from
AIDS, they are faced with their own infection and their own potential death. At
this point the mourning process often slows down, if not stops, and depression
and anxiety come to dominate their experience. Dynamically, one often observes
the combination of a strong continued idealization of the deceased partner and
an "identification" of the survivor's infection with the partner's death. Though
they may be medically stable, these men's experience of self may nevertheless
become organized around impending death. Consequently their self-esteem is
diminished and their affects are unstable. Although they feel painfully isolated,
these men have considerable trouble feeling engaged with the world and being
part of it.

Mr. T was a 41-year-old white male whose partner of ten years had died
approximately one and a half years earlier. He had known that he was seropositive a number of years before his partner's death. His chief complaint upon
entering treatment was expressed as follows: "Something is wrong. I am not
excited about anything. I have this new job with great opportunities. I should be
excited, but I am not." The clinical interview revealed several other problems: a
significant level of depression and periodic acute anxiety. Although his T-cells
were in the 500 range and had been for several years, Mr. T was convinced he was
dying, and his self was organized around the assumption of impending death. He
had developed a reputation in his seropositive support group as a rebel, actively
challenging the leader's "recipes" for seropositive people to remain that way and
not contract AIDS. He would often angrily point out that even though his lover
had been a vegetarian, had taken massive quantities of vitamins, had not done
drugs, and had gone to the gym daily for many years before he became ill, he
died anyway.

Mr. T's partner had died in San Francisco. After the death Mr. T dispersed their
belongings and moved to Chicago – a city where he had lived previously and in
which several family members resided – to live with his sister and to take "time to
heal." After several months he took a job that was well beneath his capabilities to
"get back into practice." After several months he took the more challenging position that he held when he entered treatment.

Mr. T reported that both his family and his partner's had been very supportive
and that he felt his need to mourn had been respected and validated by them. However, in the community he felt like a pariah. Several old acquaintances had become
anxious and then had withdrawn when he related that his partner had died of
AIDS. When Mr. T attempted to go out and meet new people, he quickly became

anxious and gave up his plans, fearing that he would eventually have to tell people about his partner and his own seropositive status. This was in sharp contrast to his previous experience of himself as outgoing and highly social.

In general, Mr. T felt that no one understood or cared to understand, though he was not quite sure what he wanted people to understand. He felt that moving to Chicago had been a mistake; he longed for San Francisco, where he felt being a surviving partner and being seropositive was more readily accepted as the norm rather than the exception. Perhaps there, he thought, people would not treat him differently. Though he assumed he was dying (he knew his lab counts via a research study), he was not being followed by a physician. He resisted my attempts to get him engaged in a medical assessment, stating that when the time came for him to have a physician, he would find one. Though he had developed a number of friends in the seropositive support organization, he was beginning to alienate them. In fact, it was at their urging that he came for psychotherapy.

As treatment progressed, Mr. T related more of his personal experience to me. He continued to carry on elaborate conversations with his deceased partner, and a strong element of idealization of the partner was evident. He felt very embarrassed to relate the extent of these conversations, fearing that he would be labeled as crazy. Severe self-esteem problems were evident: he felt diminished and unable to function as well as he had previously in job or social settings. For example, he panicked at the idea of purchasing new clothes, feeling that everything looked terrible on him; he was profoundly anxious at the idea of looking in the mirror with salespeople nearby. (This is especially interesting in that his partner had died of Kaposi's sarcoma and was horribly disfigured.) It became increasingly clear that Mr. T felt desperately out of control and that his anxiety over feeling out of control was as disabling as his clinical symptoms.

After several weekly meetings Mr. T requested and began twice-weekly sessions. He quickly formed an idealizing transference. Initially, some erotized elements were evident but not to the extent that they threatened to disrupt the treatment alliance. The erotized elements quickly diminished over the next few weeks and were replaced by a more solid idealization of the therapist.

Very quickly, I pointed out that a great deal of what Mr. T was experiencing was due to his being a seropositive surviving partner and that at this point in time after his partner's death he should be getting excited again and probably would be if he were not carrying the same virus that killed his partner. Although I validated and attempted to normalize the continued dialogue or conversations with his partner, I was also interested in what he talked about with his partner. I encouraged him to relate the story of their relationship and of his partner's illness and death. Initially, in a very real way I felt that there were three people in the consulting room: Mr. T, his partner, and myself. Mr. T proved to be a vivid dreamer, and his dreams often beautifully and succinctly summed up the current themes in his treatment. Over the first two months of our work, he related the following three dreams:

> Jim [his partner] and I were on an island in a river. Jim was sick and lying on a cot. The river was raging, it was storming, and there was chaos all around

us. I was worried about keeping him dry and was busy making sure he did not get wet. Though there was chaos all around us, I felt calm inside.

I was going somewhere on a train. All of sudden I was outside of the train. I felt fine until I thought that I should hold on to something, since the train was moving so fast. I panicked when I realized there was only a little rail to hold on to that I could barely get my fingers around.

I was getting on a plane to go to Florida. I sat down in the cramped and shabby tourist section. The stewardess approached and said there had been a mistake, that I was to sit in first-class. She pointed to an escalator that was going up. I rode up and was in a first-class section that had plush seats and huge windows. I became anxious and thought, "I do not belong here; I am going back to tourist where I belong."

The first dream was understood to summarize the common experience of men caring for their ill partners: though their world may be falling apart around them as the partner becomes increasingly ill, the well partner is still sustained by the relationship. He has an important job to do: caring for his ill partner. The sense of duty and the sustaining power of the relationship help the partner to feel grounded and to avoid feeling as vulnerable or buffeted by chaos as he feels in the wake of a disruption in the relationship (or as he will feel on the death of his partner). The second dream was understood as symbolizing the panic that Mr. T came to experience as he realized the world was still moving on, perhaps even toward his own illness, and how little grounded he felt, let alone secure that there would be a relationship that could sustain him the way he sustained his partner. The third dream was understood as relating to Mr. T's own damaged and diminished self-esteem, which ultimately was preventing him from engaging in relationships that could help him feel grounded and secure and, consequently, was enhancing his feeling of not belonging. (The dreams could also be understood as reflecting the deepening transference; the explanations are not mutually exclusive.)

Over the next five months of treatment Mr. T's depression lifted considerably and his anxiety diminished. The dialogue with his partner diminished over the first several months of treatment, and he became more interested in other people. He became increasingly comfortable with himself and was less abrasive in his support group. He pursued other interests; took another, more challenging, job; hosted a holiday party (this was especially significant in that he and his partner were avid entertainers, and each event was very much an effort in teamwork); and eventually began a dating relationship.

The continuing idealization of the deceased partner is often a central component in the complicated mourning process of seropositive partners. This must be handled appropriately and empathically; otherwise, one risks traumatizing, if not enraging, the patient. The idealization cannot be interpreted away; rather, it must be allowed to gradually deflate. One could argue that the patient is gaining a sense of comfort through the idealization at a time when the self may not be able to take comfort in other relationships. As the surviving partner forms a relationship with the clinician – one that will deepen the more the clinician is able to be empathically in tune with his experience of mourning – the transference will deepen and solidify. As this happens, one will also observe that the idealization of the deceased partner gradually wanes.

As in this case, erotized elements may emerge in the transference. If this is not distressing to the patient and does not threaten to disrupt the treatment, no interpretation is in order; the erotized elements will also wane as the transference deepens. If the patient is showing signs of distress, then a discussion that points out that the erotization is a sign of his feeling understood, comfortable, and excited about the possibility that perhaps he is capable of forming new attachments may be called for.

Another aspect of work with these men involves the therapist pointing out to them the distorting influence of seropositivity. While this may potentially be an intellectual intrusion into the dialogue between the patient and the therapist, it offers an important structure with which to help the patient organize his experience. The patient is already feeling depressed, anxious, isolated, and, perhaps most painful of all, weird and different, apart from the rest of the world. The patient often explains his ongoing experience to himself in these terms. Offering the patient the explanation that part of what he is experiencing is due not to his personal pathology but to the distorting effects of something beyond his control helps him organize the experience as something considerably more benign, cuts into the negative experience of self that often comes to dominate the self organization, and offers him the opportunity to relate his fears, connected to the loss of his partner, about his own health and life.

Pointing out the distorting effects of seropositivity also provides the opportunity for the patient to experience with the clinician any angry affect surrounding his experience. Several men expressed considerable anger (once given permission to do so) as they related their feeling of being cheated, of being in a situation that is "unfair." I tend to respond that, yes, they have been cheated, AIDS has taken a great deal away from them, and they have every right to be angry over their situation. This can be especially helpful in that often these seropositive men adopt a "walking on eggshells" approach, fearing that the experience of any angry affect (save perhaps a projected anger toward institutions or unhelpful individuals) may disrupt their equilibrium and bring their world crashing down; essentially, they fear that they will become ill.

Mr. T's selfobject environment was very supportive and responded to his status as a mourner, recognizing his need to gradually regroup and helping him make a new start. However, these responses were primarily to the more readily understandable and recognizable human experience of loss. Unless we know about the complicating and distorting effects of seropositivity on the mourning process, we cannot adequately respond to these individuals. My experience is that they are at once surprised and highly relieved when this complicating aspect of their attempt to mourn is addressed.

Summary

This chapter is a cursory overview of a very complicated yet crucial aspect of the human experience in general and the AIDS crisis in particular. Though discussed in the context of men whose losses occurred in the context of gay relationships and the current epidemic, the beginning reformulation of mourning theory and the process of mourning is applicable to the general population. Clearly, mourning involves more than the mourner and the deceased: the selfobject matrix plays a crucial role in modulating the mourner's affect, subsequently assisting in the formation of the narrative and its integration into the overall structure of the self. The empathic responses of the selfobject environment also serve to orient the mourner back to the world of the living. The mourner's capacity to tolerate the affective dimension of mourning and the environmental response to the mourner's affect and situation in general are factors that may impede or facilitate the process. Another implication of this perspective is that clinicians are more than facilitators of the mourning process; we are, instead, integral participants.

References

Basch, M. (1988). *Understanding Psychotherapy*. New York: Basic Books.

Freud, S. (1912–1913). Totem and taboo. *Standard Edition*, 13:1–164. London: Hogarth Press, 1957.

Freud, S. (1917). Mourning and melancholia. *Standard Edition*, 14:243–258. London: Hogarth Press, 1957.

Friedman, R. (1988). *Male Homosexuality: A Contemporary Analytic Perspective*. New Haven, CT: Yale University Press.

Glaser, B. (1975). *Theoretical Sensitivity*. Mill Valley, CA: The Free Press.

Glaser, B. & Strauss, A. (1967). *The Discovery of Grounded Theory*. Chicago: Aldine.

Goldberg, A. (1990). *The Prisonhouse of Psychoanalysis*. Hillsdale, NJ: The Analytic Press.

Isay, R. (1989). *Being Homosexual*. New York: Farrar, Straus & Giroux.

Kohut, H. (1977). *The Restoration of the Self*. New York: International Universities Press.

Krystal, H. (1990). An information processing view of object-relations. *Psychoanal. Inq.*, 10: 221–251.

Lewes, K. (1988). *The Psychoanalytic Theory of Male Homosexuality*. New York: Simon & Schuster.

Maylon, A. K. (1982). Psychotherapeutic implications of internalized homophobia in gay men. In: *Homosexuality and Psychotherapy*, ed. J. Gonsiorek. New York: Haworth Press, pp. 59–70.

Palombo, J. (1981). Parent loss and childhood bereavement. *Clin. Soc. Work J.*, 9(1): 3–33.

Palombo, J. (1982). The psychology of the self and the termination of treatment. *Clin. Soc. Work J.*, 10(1): 46–62.

Palombo, J. (1991). Bridging the chasm between developmental theory and clinical theory: Part II. The bridge. In: *Annu. Psychoanal.*, 19:152–194. Hillsdale, NJ: The Analytic Press.

Pollock, G. (1961). Mourning and adaptation. *Int. J. Psycho-Anal.*, 42:341–361.

Saari, C. (1986). *Clinical Social Work Treatment*. New York: Gardner Press.

Shane, M. & Shane, E. (1990). Object loss and selfobject loss: A consideration of self psychology's contribution to understanding mourning and the failure to mourn. In: *Annu. Psychoanal.*, 18:115–131. Hillsdale, NJ: The Analytic Press.

Shelby, R. D. (1989). Internalized homophobia as narcissistic injury. Unpublished paper.

Shelby, R. D. (1992). *If a Partner Has AIDS*. Binghamton, NY: Haworth Press.

Socarides, D. & Stolorow, R. (1984/1985). Affects and selfobjects. In: *Annu. Psychoanal.*, 12, 13:105–120. New York: International Universities Press.

Stern, D. (1985). *The Interpersonal World of the Infant*. New York: Basic Books.

Stolorow, R. Brandchaft, B. & Atwood, G. (1987). *Psychoanalytic Treatment: An Intersubjective Approach*. Hillsdale, NJ: The Analytic Press.

Chapter 6

The role of the other in mourning (1996)

George Hagman

Editor's note: This paper grew out of my observations that mourning is a highly social process. As we have seen in earlier chapters my thesis here is that surviving objects play a crucial role in the accomplishment of a number of the major psychological tasks of mourning, some of which I identify below. To illustrate the thesis, the psychoanalytic treatment of a man suffering the aftermath of parental loss in adolescence is presented. The failure of the social surround to assist with mourning is identified and explored, and the treatment implications of the role of the other in mourning are discussed.

This paper was published in 1996 by George Hagman as "The Role of the Other in Mourning" in The Psychoanalytic Quarterly, *Volume 65.*

This paper will discuss the impact of the social context on bereavement – specifically, the role of other persons in facilitating the mourning process. I will discuss the writings of a number of analysts who from diverse perspectives have stressed the importance to bereaved persons of a loving and helpful social surround. Elaborating on the literature, I will attempt to identify eight functions that the other performs and to clarify how these functions promote mourning. These functions are: 1) understanding the reality of loss; 2) working through shock; 3) "holding the situation"; 4) meeting libidinal needs; 5) being a narcissistic resource; 6) facilitating, modulating, and containing the expression of affects; 7) putting affects into words (symbolization); and 8) assisting with the transformation of the internal relationship with the lost object.

In support of my thesis, I will discuss the treatment of a man whose repressed affects related to bereavement became a major focus of analysis. The inhibition of mourning, resulting in part from the failure of the other to provide the above functions, will be highlighted.

In *Mourning and Melancholia* Freud (1917) offered his major contribution to the study of mourning in a brief section that served as the introduction to his discussion of melancholia. He begins with a question:

> In what, now, does the work which mourning performs consist? . . . Reality-testing has shown that the loved object no longer exists, and it proceeds to

demand that all libido shall be withdrawn from its attachments to that object. This demand arouses understandable opposition – it is a matter of general observation that people never willingly abandon a libidinal position, not even, indeed when a substitute is already beckoning to them. . . . Normally, respect for reality gains the day. Nevertheless its orders cannot be obeyed at once. They are carried out bit by bit, at great expense of time and cathectic energy, and in the meantime the existence of the lost object is psychically prolonged. Each single one of the memories and expectations in which the libido is bound to the object is brought up and hyper-cathected, and the detachment of the libido is accomplished in respect of it. . . . when the work of mourning is completed the ego becomes free and uninhibited again.

(pp. 244–245)

The entry on mourning in the 1990 edition of *Psychoanalytic Terms and Concepts*, edited by Moore and Fine, elaborates on Freud's original formulation:

The work of mourning includes three successive, interrelated phases; the success of each affecting the next: (1) understanding, accepting, and coping with the loss and its circumstances; (2) the mourning proper, which involves withdrawal of attachments to and identifications with the lost object (decathexis); and (3) resumption of emotional life in harmony with one's level of maturity, which frequently involves establishing new relationships (recathexis).

(p. 122)

Since bereavement is typically an extremely social experience (Berger et al., 1989; Kalish, 1980), what role if any do others play in the mourning process? Nonanalytic research has shown repeatedly that the availability of supportive others is an important factor in the resolution of bereavement (Bowlby, 1980; Jacobs, 1993; Parkes, 1972; Parkes and Weiss, 1983). Bowlby (1980) notes how "families, friends, and others play a leading part either in assisting the mourning process or in hindering it" (p. 191). The most important function in the facilitation of mourning, Bowlby determined, was the acceptance, even the encouragement, of expressive mourning. Parkes (1972) echoed Bowlby by emphasizing the importance of social support to bereaved persons and the danger of isolation.

Psychoanalytic researchers have also noted the importance of others in mourning. Most prominently it has been claimed that the successful adaptation to loss in childhood depends on the continued availability of parental (or substitute) supports (Furman, 1974; Laufer, 1966; Nagera, 1970; Wolfenstein, 1966). Erna Furman (1974) provides the best discussion of this viewpoint: "Our experience shows that the surviving love objects play a crucial part in the life of the bereaved person and contribute much to the manner in which he deals with his loss" (p. 109; see also Furman, 1986). The surviving love objects offer security and need fulfillment in the midst of loss; and they provide love, which involves empathy and the acceptance of feelings. "Help with mourning is the essence of the surviving love object's role. . . . Mourning alone is an almost impossible task even for a mature adult" (Furman, 1974, p. 114). One crucial area of help is in the expression and regulation of grief; Furman writes: "Sometimes . . . the difficulty in affective expression stems simply from not having anyone who shares feelings or towards whom they can be expressed" (p. 261). In her review of the clinical literature of childhood bereavement, Furman noted the almost complete neglect of the role of others in mourning (pp. 285–286).

Approaching childhood bereavement through the study of its sequelae in adult psychopathology (see Fleming, 1963), Joan Fleming (1972) stated: "The detrimental effects of parental loss depend very much on the age at which the loss occurs, on the character of the preloss relationship, *on the availability of a good substitute, and on the type of relationship maintained with the surviving parent*" (p. 35, italics added).

Recently Shane and Shane (1990) have approached the problem of childhood bereavement from a self psychological perspective. The Shanes point out that in bereavement there is not only the loss of an object, but also the loss of the narcissistic functions of the lost "selfobject."

> Given an adequate supportive environment . . . the child will spontaneously mourn the death of an important loved one. The pain of loss can be borne and the necessary capacity to think, talk and reflect about it can be sustained if the child is helped to mourn rather than stifled by the unempathic criticism and unrealistic standards for mourning behaviors.
>
> (p. 115)

Here the Shanes echo Furman's point that the surviving love object's capacity to appreciate the inner world of the child and to respond appropriately supports the child's self, which, because of the death, has suffered narcissistic injury. Without the presence of this self-supportive environment mourning may be foreclosed.

The assumption regarding childhood loss is that because of the child's immature ego and continued dependence on the surround for survival and for object-libidinal sustaining experiences, the needs of bereaved children are different from those of adults. There is implicit in the childhood literature the assumption that the mourning of adults is less dependent on interpersonal factors. Few analysts, however, would claim that bereaved adults do not benefit from the presence of concerned others. For example, Melanie Klein (1940), in her paper "Mourning and Its Relation to Manic-Depressive States," delineates from an object relations perspective the role of the good object in the internal psychical process of mature mourning. Klein stresses that the resolution of the regression to the paranoid-schizoid position, which characterizes mourning, depends to some extent on the internalization of experiences of support and love from external objects. This internalization of the good object mitigates primitive aggression and facilitates movement toward and through the depressive position, and hence, to the success-ful resolution of the mourning process. Klein writes:

> ... if the mourner has people whom he loves and who share his grief, and if he can accept their sympathy, the restoration of the harmony in his inner world is promoted, and his fears and distress are more quickly reduced.

> (p. 145)

Contemporary infant research and psychoanalytic clinical theory have empha-sized the many functions of the caregiver and social surround in development and maturation (Emde, 1989; Emde and Buchsbaum, 1989; Kohut, 1977; Krystal, 1978, 1988; Lichtenberg, 1989; Stern, 1985; Stolorow, Brandchaft, and Atwood, 1987; Winnicott, 1965). Drive, ego, object relations, and self-development all depend not only on inherent tendency and capacity, but also on reliable and respon-sive caregiving. Recently, these findings have been extended to adult psychology (Dowling, 1990; Dowling and Rothstein, 1989). In addition, it has been accepted that regression due to psychopathology or trauma may evoke archaic states neces-sitating an increased need for helpful environmental response. This is certainly the case during mourning when there is a need for environmental involvement if the complex and difficult tasks of recovery are to be accomplished without lasting impairment. It is important to note that when I say *environmental involvement* I do not necessarily mean psychotherapy, but rather the normal responsiveness of involved and concerned others.

In summary, if we put aside the distinction between adult and childhood bereavement, the psychoanalytic literature is consistent in identifying several key roles for the other in mourning: 1) to assure the continuance of basic living needs; 2) to provide love, empathy, and understanding; and 3) to accept and/or share affect. I would like to expand on these functions and to be more specific regard-ing their psychodynamic implications. To this end I will break down the three functions listed above into eight subgroups and will discuss their relevance to the psychoanalytic treatment of a bereaved adult.

I have identified the eight functions of the other in mourning from a review of the literature on mourning, child development, object relations, and self psy-chology, from personal observations of mourning, and from the psychoanalytic treatment of bereaved adults. These functions frequently overlap, and in certain cases the same behaviors may meet several areas of need (e.g. providing libidinal satisfaction may also meet narcissistic needs).

Understanding the reality of loss. Freud (1917) pointed out how the bereaved initially try to deny loss until, eventually, reality testing prevails. Furman (1974) and Baker et al. (1992) view the development of an understanding about death in general, as well as about the nature of a particular death, as the first task of mourning. Invariably, other people play a crucial part in providing information during bereavement. How one becomes aware of a death is usually with or from others. Whether one is told in a clear, a confusing, or even a deceptive way will affect one's ability to understand. Often persons are deprived of essential details for extended periods after a loss occurs. Empathy (or the lack thereof) can greatly influence how we "take in" the news. The availability of a knowledgeable and caring doctor, policeman, or family member and the ability to ask questions and express doubts repeatedly and fully can assist in the understanding and eventual acceptance of death. In the absence of information and discussion it is easy for denial to take hold. A good contemporary example is the long-term struggle of the families of soldiers missing in action in Vietnam. The absence of concrete knowledge of death often leads to doubt and denial. The initial shock of death and the defenses, which are marshaled to protect against trauma, will be greatly influenced, for good or ill, by the degree of attunement of the messenger, or fellow mourners.

An emphasis on the role of others in the development of the subjective meaning of bereavement is not meant to minimize the importance of intrapsychic factors (Hagman, 1995b). The death of another resonates deep within the unconscious, which powerfully influences the meaning of the loss. For example a violent or otherwise painful death can graphically evoke forbidden aspects of ambivalence leading to anxiety and defense. On the other hand, a quiet, painless death may allow these negatively charged fantasies to remain repressed and outside the domain of the work of mourning. Since it is commonly through communication with others that we learn about an impending or actual death, these others play a key role in our initial experience and understanding of the loss.

Working through shock. Freud, Bowlby, and Parkes have all stressed the existence of an initial "shock phase" when the reality of death is recognized. Once again the issue of ambivalence may contribute to the "shock" experienced in response to bereavement. The realization of a forbidden aggressive wish may lead to an emergency attempt to ward off fantasy and affect and perhaps to deny the reality of the death. The mobilization of more advanced and effective psychological defenses (intellectualization, repression, and identification) may take time. Recognition of ambivalence may be essential during later stages of the mourning process; however, during this early phase the maintenance of psychic equilibrium may require vigorous defensive effort. The presence and involvement of caring others is crucial to the emergence from this period of psychic numbness (Baker et al., 1992). Physical closeness, empathy, and perhaps the sharing of affects such as sadness, fear, and rage allow for the safe emergence of the self from shock. Expressions of love and tenderness and simple acts of caring can serve to convince the bereaved that reality can be endured. On the other hand, the willingness to suspend intimate gestures or comfort may be important in some cases. The acceptance of expressions of negative affects such as anger or hatred may be painful but nonetheless inevitable and essential to the process. In another work I described during this phase "the reflexive fortification of the self in response to a perceived threat of attack on its integrity" (Hagman, 1995a, p. 196). Once again the experience of an attuned response from the social surround provides the necessary "background of safety" for mourning to occur (Sandler, 1960).

"Holding the situation." It has been repeatedly noted that the demands of the changed environment frequently derail the mourning process (Bowlby, 1980; Parkes, 1972). Funeral and burial arrangements, childcare, obtaining and preparing food, and securing financial resources are just some of the multiple tasks with which the bereaved have to be concerned. Winnicott (1965) stressed the key role of basic environmental provision in regressive states. During bereavement it is important that there are others within one's social network that are able and willing to assure that basic needs are met. In many cultures there is a designated member of the community or family who manages the rituals of interment and mourning. During a specified period of mourning, the survivors are provided with food and other supports. Both Parkes and Bowlby have noted how persons isolated from supportive relationships fare badly, principally because of their need to defend against the regression of mourning in the face of basic demands of living. Only when one is assured that one's survival is not in danger can one afford the "luxury" to mourn (Bowlby, 1980). Recently, Slochower (1993) described the holding function of the Jewish custom of "sitting shiva." She argued that these social rituals "enable the mourner to mourn within the context of care. . . . The community . . . provides the mourner with this therapeutic hold. It is reflected in both concrete care and the emotional space within which the mourner is encouraged to experience and express a variety of feeling states" (p. 360). Echoing Slochower, Galatzer-Levy and Cohler (1993) have highlighted the role of ritual and social surround as essential others in bereavement (pp. 329–336).

Meeting libidinal needs. In spite of their seeming withdrawal and lack of interest in the world, bereaved persons continue to need the availability of libidinal objects. Affection, physical closeness, and sexual intimacy can all play a part in the expression of grief and the experience of mourning. On the other hand, there are times when the bereaved would be overwhelmed or otherwise threatened by strong libidinal contact. To this end, the other must remain attuned to the changing needs of the bereaved so as not to impair the unfolding of mourning. Most important, as Freud stressed, it is the lure of reality and the resurgent pressure of libidinal wishes which fuel the recovery process. The continued availability of libidinal objects is therefore a key element in the facilitation of mourning.

Being a narcissistic resource. Jacobson (1965), discussing the psychoanalyses of adult patients who lost parents in childhood, emphasized the narcissistic injury resulting from the loss of a love object. Echoing Jacobson, Shane and Shane (1990) stress that upon the loss of a loved one, the bereaved is not only deprived of the libidinal and aggressive functions of the object but the narcissistic functions which have played a crucial role in the regulation and sustenance of the self (see also Hagman, 1995b). The Shanes note how the narcissistic loss may be less identifiable than the loss of object functions; nonetheless, the attuned presence of a responsive other is a continued need of the bereaved. Clearly, several of the functions noted above can be understood also in terms of narcissistically sustaining experiences. However, I think that it is crucial to differentiate areas of narcissistic vulnerability and need from object relational ones.

Facilitating, modulating, and containing the expression of affect. The close association of grief with mourning has made them virtually synonymous. But mourning may include a range of affects, which, while normal and healthy, seem contradictory to the consciously held relationship with the lost object. These mourning affects may include rage, hatred, fear, joy, hunger, sexual excitement, etc. What is common to all of the mourning affects is their intensity as well as their association with bereavement. Fundamental to the work on this dimension of the mourning process is the ability to express, contain, and modulate these affects. Stolorow and co-authors (1987) have noted: "A process of mourning and grief following loss can occur only if depressive affects can be identified, comprehended, and tolerated" (p. 75). Many analysts and researchers have emphasized the ubiquity and importance of affect expression in mourning, most especially grief (Deutsch, 1937; Lindemann, 1944).

The affective experience of mourning can be characterized as a temporary regression to an archaic state of abandonment, helplessness, and yearning. Parkes (1972) understands grief itself as a desperate attempt to recover the lost object through distressful affect. Stolorow et al. (1987) have noted how mature persons "may revert to more archaic, somatic modes of affect expression in the unconscious hope of thereby evoking the needed response from others" (p. 73). Several authors have given examples of how the absence of other persons with whom to share one's mourning affects leads to pathological outcome (Furman, 1968; Kliman et al., 1969; Moller, 1967; Solnit, 1970). Many others have stressed the importance of meaningful love objects that empathize with and accept the mourner's feelings, but they have not elaborated this point in theoretical terms (Klein, 1940; Lindemann, 1944; Ottenstein et al., 1962; Paul, 1969; Peniston, 1962; Steiner, 1970).

The intensification of ambivalence toward the lost object may lead to conflict. Anger, frustration, and even hatred are felt by the bereaved to be unspeakable. In many cases fellow mourners (and the general cultural ethos) discourage these negative affects. Prohibitive sanctions compound and intensify defense, which may lead to pathological outcome or at least to the partial derailment of mourning. The presence of others who accept and facilitate the expression of the full range of affects aids in the containment, modulation, and resolution of ambivalence. Through emotional responsiveness and empathy, the other person creates an ambiance, which allows for open expressiveness. (Note that this ambiance should not be confused with Western culture's defensive overemphasis on comfort and affect suppression that is meant to block the expression of painful or threatening mourning affects.)

Krystal, Kohut, Emde, and Stolorow have discussed at length the function of the other in the articulation, integration, and developmental transformation of drive and affectivity. Stolorow has noted how emotional attunement assists in the modulation, gradation, and containment of strong affect. This leads to the synthesis of contradictory affective experience and the eventual effective use of affects as self-signals (Stolorow et al., 1987). Krystal (1978) emphasizes that without self-signal capacity, affects tend to herald traumatic states and are thus defended against; emotionality then comes to be experienced as solitary and unacceptable. As Deutsch (1937) and Lindemann (1944) note, the fear of the regressive experience of bereavement may lead to repression and denial and thus to a postponement of mourning. On the other hand, Stolorow notes how mutual sharing and acceptance leads to the integration of affect states into *cognitive-affective schemata*, which are key components of psychic structure (see also Horowitz, 1990).

Putting affect into words (symbolization). The ability to put the mourning affects into words is crucial to engagement in the cognitive-affective work, which characterizes the later stages of mourning. Language does not set this machinery in motion so much as it serves as a primary tool in the ego's effort to bring order to discrepant and/or inchoate impulses, perceptions, and experiences. With language, the experience of the bereaved self is structured and transformed through dialogue. I have noted that one of the primary roles of others in this area is the encouragement of and receptivity to the verbalization of feeling, experience, and memory. The verbal expression of affect (rather than simple physical discharge) allows for affect regulation and more effective engagement in the psychological work of internalization, decathexis, and recathexis.

This creative verbalization during mourning stands in contrast to the frequent use of language as a "balm," a defense against the normal experience of painful reality, fantasy, and affect. Failure to achieve the symbolic representation of affect can lead to its repression or an inability to move beyond the longing and tearfulness that characterize the early stages of mourning. Eventually, the ability to hold the memory of the deceased in mind without significant regression or anxiety is key to the working through of attachment, the transformation of the representation of the lost object internally, and the resumption of a creative involvement in the external world. For example, the presence of depressive symptoms in the bereaved frequently indicates ambivalence. Inevitably, the resolution of ambivalence will depend on the conscious restructuring of negative fantasies and the verbal articulation of ambivalent affects. However, bereaved persons will be reluctant to talk about their pain unless they feel others are understanding, responsive, and accepting.

Assisting with the transformation of the internal relationship with the lost object. All of the foregoing functions serve to create a secure and responsive ambiance in which to mourn. Freud understood the decathexis of the internal representation of the lost object as the essence of the mourning process proper. Others have emphasized the combination of internalization, decathexis, and recathexis (Abraham, 1925; Fenichel, 1945). In addition, the transformation of the internal representation of the lost object invariably involves others.

Clinically, this is seen in the psychoanalytic treatment of bereaved children and adults. Some have noted how the analysis of the transference with these patients not only helps to precipitate mourning, but also plays a part in the resolution of the attachment to the internal image of the lost parent (Fleming and Altschul, 1963; Furman, 1986). Earlier, Klein (1940) discussed how the analyst, as the object of projection and internalization, plays a vital and determining role in the dynamics of the mourning process. On a conscious level, others play a role in the bereaved's reminiscing and during resurgences of mourning. Unconsciously, the bereaved will project aspects of the lost object and re-enact areas of unresolved conflict or longed-for gratification. In most cases the eventual recognition that the new object is not the old one will lead to disillusionment, decathexis, and growth (Fleming, 1972). In other cases of pathological bereavement there may be a continuing compulsion to search for and recover the lost relationship; resolution may then be prolonged, and analysis may be required. In terms of the restoration of the self in mourning, once again the availability of an optimally responsive milieu acts as a *facilitating medium* for the integration of affect and the repair of injured narcissism. In other words, the object is accepted as lost, but the supporting matrix and sustaining psychological nutriments of the self survive (Hagman, 1995a, 1995b).

I would like now to discuss the treatment of a man who suffered bereavement prior to analysis. I will illustrate how the failure of others to provide the functions discussed above contributed to the foreclosure of mourning, and how the analysis of these failures and the provision of specific supportive functions led to the resumption and resolution of the mourning process.

Sam was a 37-year-old mathematics professor who entered psychoanalytic psychotherapy several months after his father's death from cancer. He was seen three times weekly on the couch for five years. Sam's wife had encouraged him to seek treatment because of his growing depression and social withdrawal. He himself was only vaguely aware of a problem.

Sam was a tall, attractive man, somewhat morose, with an introverted, pensive manner. The initial weeks of treatment centered on Sam's work and on his highly intellectual inner life. He read endlessly and was preoccupied with trying to understand the world logically. At the same time he was fascinated by a contradictory idea: that there were limits to logic. Chaos theory was one of his interests, the notion of reality being both ordered and infinitely complex and unknowable. Sam wove endless, vivid arguments in sessions. The only thing he admitted that he might never be able to explain or accept was death.

Sam's mother had died after a seven-year battle with cancer when he was nineteen years old. During the last several years of her life the family (his father and two sisters) became increasingly withdrawn, and eventually the mother's impending death was not talked about in the home. A week after the mother's burial Sam left for college in a distant state.

At the university Sam adopted a disciplined, ascetic lifestyle. He devoted himself obsessively to the study of mathematics. He had infrequent contact with his family, and he did not tell anyone at school about his recent loss. He did not grieve and does not have any memory of his inner state at the time. He developed a tendency to passivity and depressive affect. Many years later, it was Sam's reaction to his father's death, combined with the deepening intimacy of his marriage, which led to a breakdown in Sam's defenses.

Strangely, as Sam recounted his life story in the early sessions, he gave no emotional weight to the tragedy he had suffered. He believed that his had been a comfortable, happy childhood and adolescence. He admitted the facts of his mother's illness and death, but he appeared to give these traumatic experiences little significance. They were just some unfortunate experiences. Sam had remained in a state of numbness and shock which had developed during the years of his mother's decline and which was never worked through after her death. However, over the first six months of treatment, as I interpreted his defenses against recognizing the importance of his history of loss, he became more and more depressed. He could not describe the feelings at first; usually his wife, Mary, noted his mood to him. His intellectual monologues began to lose their drive. My countertransference changed from intellectual curiosity to a sense of deep sadness and longing. I became more convinced that behind Sam's obsessive compulsiveness was an aborted mourning for his parents. It was painful to watch his confused, unknowing experience of sadness. I began to interpret Sam's struggle along these lines.

"My sense is that you may be beginning to feel some sadness about your father's death."

"I don't know . . . maybe . . . it doesn't really make sense."

Sam began to discuss how he tried not to think about his father. In a way, he noted how he had also not thought about his mother's death. No one had thought about it. There had been no one to talk to. "I can't even remember what I felt about it, her cancer or . . . her dying."

Sam noted that after her death he was alone. There was much he felt he had to take care of. He described how, during the years of his mother's illness, he had been forced to care for himself, and afterward at college he continued to be self-reliant. He felt he had no choice. What else could he do? He did not remember feeling sad. There was nothing and no one to remind him. It was all just suddenly over. He was in school. There was little time to think about home. There was no one to grieve with even if he had wanted to, he would tell me.

"At college, I did what I needed to do. There was one odd thing. I was preoccupied with the mail. As if I was hoping to get something . . . something . . . I don't know what."

"A letter from your father . . . or perhaps your mother."

"That's impossible – she was dead, and he never wrote."

He noted how he had withdrawn into himself at school. "I was like a monk. I read and studied. I guess I lost myself in schoolwork. My relationships during that time, they seem shadowy to me now. Like I didn't make contact with people."

Over the next few weeks Sam began to discuss the events of his father's death at length and in vivid detail. He was surprised at how clearly he could recall the events. He said that he had never gone over them with anyone, not even Mary. He recalled that things had improved between him and his father.

"All those years at home and alone at school, I had little contact with him. I didn't even think of him being proud, or being there for me. In a way my success in school felt empty I guess . . . but recently I began to feel that he was interested in me. I guess I had missed that, but didn't know till I began to get it . . . but, my father is dead. I won't ever see him again. I can't believe it. . . ."

For the first time he admitted some feelings of sadness. "I know intellectually I should be sad. I know it . . . but, it's like it turns off right as I feel it."

The next few sessions focused on Sam's teenage years and the family's struggle to cope with the mother's terminal illness. Sam was able to see how there was no place to grieve. No one could talk about it. How could he grieve all by himself? He shared with me his growing recognition that his family had suffered a tragedy from which he had not recovered. He recalled feeling alone, emotionally numb, as his mother was sick and then died. Afterward, he *was* alone.

"You're not all by yourself now."

"I know. I have Mary and I feel like I know more because of therapy, but . . ."

Gradually Sam expressed feelings of sadness and grief in sessions. One day he described how tears at home overcame him the night before. "I couldn't stop crying. I just sat there and cried."

In fact, that night he had had a dream: "In the dream my parents were in a car. I was just standing there watching. The car started off. They were driving away, out west or something. I woke up crying. I was desperate to get here. I felt that if I didn't get to the session I might die."

I added, "The grief and fear were so strong."

"Yeah. I needed to be somewhere safe. I just curled up in bed until it was time to come here. I think Mary was a little freaked out, but she sat with me and just let me cry. It felt like although she was a little scared, she helped me do it. It was okay. Like here – it's okay to be upset. We can talk about it."

Sam began to put his grief into words. During the next few sessions he spoke about his sadness and his longing for his parents. He cried at times and reminisced about sailing with his father and about the last few years when they had felt closer to each other. It was much harder to talk about his mother. That would take time, he admitted. "I need to feel stronger about myself I guess. For years, I was alone. It was like I didn't exist. I need to remember what it was like, what *I* was like."

The dream about his parents expressed not just loss through death, but Sam's exclusion from the oedipal triangle. I understood his intense sadness as in part a defense against aggression mobilized by the return to consciousness of adolescent oedipal fantasies. With this, the work of mourning became intermingled with other areas of conflict. I began to work interpretively in this area as sessions became focused on problems at his work, especially his relationship to the dean of his department. Sam's thesis had come under critical scrutiny by the dean, who found some of Sam's most cherished ideas to be questionable. It became clear that the dean had become the object of the projection of Sam's father transference. Sam's continual experience of rejection and lack of involvement from the dean echoed the problems Sam encountered in his relationship with his father during his teenage years. The expectation of the dean's criticism and rejection arose from the adolescent experience of double loss (the mother's death and the father's withdrawal), which had impaired Sam's mourning and skewed his development.

"He doesn't care about what I'm doing. He won't do things that he should do. I try to get him to respond. He has no time. Why bother?"

Fantasies specific to the lost object typically emerge from repression with the activation of mourning during analysis (Fleming and Altschul, 1963). The working through of the resulting conflicts characterizes the work of object decathexis and the internal transformation of the relationship with the deceased. The re-creation of the lost relationship in one's social reality (which includes the treatment relationship) has been noted by many analysts. At this point, the role of the other is to assist with differentiation, decathexis, and resumption of emotional growth. Through my interpretations I was able to link Sam's experience with the dean with his unresolved issues with his father who Sam believed had abandoned him during the mother's illness and after her death. In addition, it appeared that Sam's frustration and longing disguised powerful competitive and aggressive urges toward the paternal dean. I interpreted how the iconoclastic nature of his thesis reflected his desire to challenge the authority and power of the dean, as he must have longed to as a teenager with his own father who had refused to engage with him or to recognize his age-appropriate assertiveness. When Sam canceled several sessions upon my return from summer vacation, I sensed that the paternal transference had entered the treatment.

"Why bother?" Sam asked. "It didn't seem to matter." He turned away and faced the wall. "It almost feels better facing the wall."

"Away from me."

"I guess so."

"The wall is just as unresponsive, but at least it's there."

"You mean your vacation?"

"I believe your father's unavailability and unresponsiveness left you feeling destitute and desperate for someone to become involved with you, to be a parent to you. At the same time you longed to challenge your father, to prove yourself, but he turned away. You felt defeated by his indifference, and then you must have felt guilty about your anger and competitiveness toward your grieving father. In the end no one was there. You must have felt that he wasn't there when you needed him."

"I sometimes have these dreams. I've never mentioned them. It's just blank, dark, nothing. I wake up terrified, speechless. I haven't realized what they're about. Like everyone and everything is gone. It's the worst fear – like they are all dead . . ."

"On some level you must have lived with that fear for years . . . that your feelings were dangerous."

"Yeah . . . but I didn't even know it. Until now. It's like now, here, I can put it into words. Of course, it's not true anymore. I'm not alone anymore."

"But last week I was gone also."

"And I was alone . . . maybe I had killed you off also."

"So it is safest to turn to the wall. The wall can't be killed off."

For Sam the resurgence of oedipal wishes, normal to adolescence, had occurred in the context of parental and familial tragedy. Normal urges toward competitiveness and self-assertion with the father suffered repression and became self-directed as depression and inhibition. The repression of drive, the derailment of key adolescent developmental processes, and the increasing attachment (rather than individuation) to his parents caused an arrest in the mourning process as well. His failure to integrate powerful ambivalent feelings led to longstanding problems with ambition and adult sexuality. The increasing isolation of Sam's family cut him off from alternative sources of libidinal and narcissistic resources and opportunities. The interpretation of Sam's drive to engage with oedipal objects, the articulation of affects related to his assertiveness and aggression, as well as grief, and the provision of an analytic environment responsive to his inner life facilitated the mourning process as well as the activation and resolution of his infantile neurosis.

Over the next several years Sam's feelings related to the loss of his parents re-emerged from time to time. More important, however, as the treatment began to focus on transference fantasies related to the dean and myself, we began the extended analysis and working through of Oedipal issues (conflicts related to assertiveness and competitiveness) and narcissistic issues (the need for responsiveness, admiration, and idealization). From this viewpoint the completion of mourning will probably be coincident with the completion of the analysis of Sam's neurosis.

Discussion

The causes of Sam's arrested mourning lay both in areas of developmental deficit and neurotic conflict, *and* in the absence of a supportive and facilitative social context. Because Sam was adolescent, his failure to mourn may have also had to do with his developmentally determined incapacity to mourn (Wolfenstein, 1966). In addition, Sam's experiences in life prior to his mother's illness affected his response to the loss and the eventual course of his bereavement (Altschul, 1988; Bowlby, 1980; Furman, 1974). However, I will focus on the role of others in mourning as it pertains to Sam's psychodynamics and treatment. This is not meant to deny the significance of other contributing factors.

Sam and his family spent five years coping with the mother's terminal illness. The family roles were shifted to compensate for the decline in the mother's functions, and the family assumed a number of defenses to ward off anxiety related to the progression of disease, familial deterioration, and the anticipation of death. Two of their primary defenses were the denial of the significance of the family tragedy and the isolation of affect from family communications. This resulted in the development of a family *ethos* forbidding the open expression of the frightening reality confronting them. Sam's family coped, but at the expense of not anticipating or preparing for the emotional consequences of the loss of the mother. Sam had internalized this family ethos. Hence, though he intellectually recognized the loss of his mother and was not unduly stressed by the initial shock of her death, his elaboration of the subjective meaning of his losses and his engagement in basic mourning tasks (which would have required both an internal willingness and ability, as well as the presence and active involvement of others) did not occur. Eventually, years after the death, Sam came to treatment when the defenses against mourning, which he had developed and sustained in his years of isolation, began breaking down. Recognition of his tragic past initiated the mourning process.

I have emphasized the importance of self-security in mourning. To this end, the preeminent function of Sam's analysis was the provision of a "holding environment," sustained and managed by the analyst (an interested and empathically responsive other), which enabled Sam to mourn within a "context of care" (Slochower, 1993). Sam had left his family within days of his mother's death. He found himself confronted with a new and strange environment far from his familiar and relatively secure home. Those who might have shared his grief were not available. The demands of his new life precluded the experience of regression so necessary for mourning. The defenses of repression and isolation (already well established) became compounded in the absence of a responsive and supportive social milieu. Over time the improved availability of and intimacy with his father, his increasingly stable relationship with his wife, and a gradual lessening of defense set the stage for resumption of the derailed mourning process. The secure "hold" of the analysis created a sustained and responsive therapeutic environment which continually countered Sam's expectation of being left alone.

The treatment encouraged the emergence of Sam's needs in the object libidinal and narcissistic sectors. Sam's social, and increasingly psychological, isolation after his mother's death, due to circumstance and defense, led to an impoverishment of libidinal investment. This also impaired his capacity to engage in effective mourning, which is fueled by the tension between a reluctance to relinquish the lost object and an urge for new relationships and gratifying experiences. In treatment, Sam experienced the presence of an interested and caring other as a form of intimacy and nurturance that encouraged and sustained the emergence of unconscious wishes. This was manifest in the gradual development of the oedipal transference (conflicts related to aggression, assertiveness, ambition, and competitiveness in both the professional and sexual spheres). Sam's emergence from depressive withdrawal was both precipitated and marked by the resumption of these oedipal strivings.

In the area of the self, Sam had suffered narcissistic injury through the absence of responsive relationships and milieu. This led to a dependence on increasingly internal, usually intellectual, sources of self-sustenance as well as a vulnerability to narcissistic injury. The expectation of a recurrence of earlier experiences of trauma fueled initial resistances; however, repeated transference interpretations connecting the present with Sam's traumatic past, and the sustained experience of the analyst's empathy, led to the development of the working alliance. The availability of a responsive milieu thus facilitated Sam's utilization of new, narcissistically enhancing experiences – a central task of the mourning process.

Sam's internalization of the family ethos against mourning, combined with the absence of responsive others and the demands of a new life far from home, resulted in defenses against regression, and most significantly, the repression of affect, specifically grief. Sam could not recall crying or the experience of sadness. The articulation and communication of affect became stifled. No one was there to respond; thus the experience of helplessness, longing, and pain that characterizes mourning had to be denied. Sam had to feel that his survival was secure before he could allow himself to grieve (Bowlby, 1980). This took time. Specifically, it was the improvement in his relation with his father, his marriage, and the responsiveness and "holding" of the treatment, which provided the "context of care" which facilitated, modulated, and contained his affect. The episode of tearful panic precipitated by the dream was met with calm support from Sam's wife. He also knew that I would be responsive and interested in his grieving. He finally had the opportunity to put his mourning affects into words. After years of silence he spoke at length about the loss of his parents. Affect, memory, and intellect were gradually and safely merged so as to begin the process of acceptance, integration, and resolution. With words came a means of structuring an otherwise meaningless and traumatic set of experiences. The "work" of mourning could commence.

Most important, Sam's engagement in this "work" involved people: Sam's wife, the dean, and the analyst. Mourning has frequently been compared to the analytic process. The inner attachment to representations of earlier relationships and imagoes and the stubborn relinquishment of these psychical ties and the fantasy dramas which make them so troublesome (while at the same time accessible to our interventions) are at the core of every treatment. Contemporary analysts have repeatedly asserted how the analyst as object of fantasy and "real" other plays a key part in the analysand's eventual liberation from the tyranny of the past. In this sense the bereaved in normal instances makes use of others to perpetuate the past, to receive nurturance and satisfaction from the present, and to push forward securely and effectively into the future.

In Sam's case he had insulated himself in a sterile and lonely present with only fragile ties to a painful past. The future, which typically involves the extension of libido and narcissism into a potential psychical reality, did not exist for Sam, and he found it hard at first to conceptualize it. The future, of course, is unthinkable without hope. Sam's hope was nurtured by the availability of a "context of care" characterized by his increasing openness and the responsiveness of others. To this end, the charged dialogue of the therapeutic relationship became the smithy in which the hard, slow forging of Sam's future was accomplished.

Conclusion

My stress on the importance of others in the mourning process is not meant to deny the role of other factors in pathological outcomes of bereavement. The literature noted throughout this paper is thorough in the exploration of the many factors which have an impact on mourning. What I have tried to identify are the specific functions of these others in the facilitation or obstruction of mourning. Contemporary psychoanalysis, the most articulate psychology in its depiction of the vicissitudes of the dynamic relationship between the self and the object world, seems to me to possess the explanatory capability to describe the often silent and complex interrelationship between our struggle to come to terms with loss and the role others play in this highly intimate process.

References

Abraham, K. (1925). A short study of the development of the libido, viewed in the light of mental disorders. In *Selected Papers of Karl Abraham*. New York: Basic Books, 1953, pp. 418–501.

Altschul, S., Editor (1988). *Childhood Bereavement and Its Aftermath*. Madison, CT: Int. Univ. Press.

Baker, J. E., et al. (1992). Psychological tasks for bereaved children. *J. Orthopsychiat.*, 62: 105–116.

Berger, A., et al., Editors (1989). *Perspectives on Death and Dying: Cross-Cultural and Multidisciplinary Views*. Philadelphia: Charles Press.

Bowlby, J. (1980). *Attachment and Loss, Vol. 3: Loss. Sadness and Depression*. New York: Basic Books.

Deutsch, H. (1937). Absence of grief. *Psychoanal. Q.*, 6: 12–22.

Dowling, S. (1990). *Child and Adolescent Analysis: Its Significance for Clinical Work with Adults*. (Workshop Series of the American Psychoanalytic Association, Monogr. 6.) Madison, CT: Int. Univ. Press.

Dowling, S. & Rothstein, A., Editors (1989). *The Significance of Infant Observational Research for Clinical Work with Children, Adolescents, and Adults*. (Workshop Series of the American Psychoanalytic Association, Monogr. 5.) Madison, CT: Int. Univ. Press.

Emde, R. N. (1989). Toward a psychoanalytic theory of affect: I. The organizational model and its propositions. In *The Course of Life: Infancy*, eds. S. I. Greenspan & G. H. Pollock. Madison, CT: Int. Univ. Press, pp. 165–192.

Emde, R. N. & Buchsbaum, H. (1989). Toward a psychoanalytic theory of affect: II. Emotional development and signaling in infancy. In *The Course of Life: Infancy*, eds. S. I. Greenspan & G. H. Pollock. Madison, CT: Int. Univ. Press, pp. 193–228.

Fenichel, O. (1945). *The Psychoanalytic Theory of Neurosis*. New York: Norton.

Fleming, J. (1963). The evolution of a research project in psychoanalysis. In *Counterpoint: Libidinal Object and Subject: A Tribute to René Spitz on His 75th Birthday*, ed. H. S. Gaskill. New York: Int. Univ. Press, pp. 75–105.

Fleming, J. (1972). Early object deprivation and transference phenomena: The working alliance. *Psychoanal. Q.*, 41: 23–49.

Fleming, J. & Altschul, S. (1963). Activation of mourning and growth by psychoanalysis. In *Childhood Bereavement and Its Aftermath*, ed. S. Altschul. Madison, CT: Int. Univ. Press, 1988, pp. 277–307.

Freud, S. (1917). Mourning and melancholia. *Standard Edition, Vol. 14*.

Furman, E. (1974). *A Child's Parent Dies. Studies in Childhood Bereavement*. New Haven/London: Yale Univ. Press.

Furman, E. (1986). On trauma: When is the death of a parent traumatic? *Psychoanal. Study Child*, 41: 191–208.

Furman, R. (1968). Additional remarks on mourning and the young child. *Bull. Philadelphia Assn. Psychoanal.*, 18: 51–64.

Galatzer-Levy, R. M. & Cohler, B. J. (1993). *The Essential Other: A Developmental Psychology of the Self*. New York: Basic Books.

Hagman, G. (1995a). Death of a selfobject: Toward a self psychology of the mourning process. In *The Impact of New Ideas: Progress in Self Psychology, Vol. 11*, ed. A. Goldberg. Hillsdale, NJ: Analytic Press, pp. 189–205.

Hagman, G. (1995b). Mourning: A review and reconsideration. *Int. J. Psychoanal.*, 76: 909–925.

Horowitz, M. J. (1990). A model of mourning: Change in schemas of self and other. *J. Am. Psychoanal. Assoc.*, 38: 297–324.

Jacobs, S. (1993). *Pathologic Grief: Maladaptation to Loss*. Washington, DC: Am. Psych. Press.

Jacobson, E. (1965). The return of the lost parent. In *Drives, Affects, Behavior, Vol. 2: Essays in Memory of Marie Bonaparte*, ed. M. Schur. New York: Int. Univ. Press, pp. 193–211.

Kalish, R. (1980). *Death and Dying: Views from Different Cultures*. New York: Baywood.

Klein, M. (1940). Mourning and its relation to manic-depressive states. *Int. J. Psychoanal.*, 21: 125–153.

Kliman, G., et al. (1969). Facilitation of Mourning During Childhood. *Presented at the meeting of the American Orthopsychiatric Association.*

Kohut, H. (1977). *The Restoration of the Self*. New York: Int. Univ. Press.

Krystal, H. (1978). Trauma and affects. *Psychoanal. Study Child*, 33: 81–116.

Krystal, H. (1988). *Integration and Self-Healing: Affect, Trauma, Alexithymia*. Hillsdale, NJ: Analytic Press.

Laufer, M. (1966). Object loss and mourning during adolescence. *Psychoanal. Study Child*, 21: 269–293.

Lichtenberg, J. (1989). *Psychoanalysis and Motivation*. Hillsdale, NJ: Analytic Press.

Lindemann, E. (1944). Symptomatology and management of acute grief. *Am. J. Psychiat.*, 101: 141–149.

Moller, H. (1967). Death: Handling the subject and affected students in the schools. In *Explaining Death to Children*, ed. E. A. Grollman. Boston: Beacon, pp. 145–167.

Nagera, H. (1970). Children's reactions to the death of important objects: A developmental approach. *Psychoanal. Study Child*, 25: 360–400.

Ottenstein, D., et al. (1962). Some observations on major loss in families. *Am. J. Orthopsychiat.*, 32: 299–300.

Parkes, C. M. (1972). *Bereavement: Studies of Grief in Adult Life*. New York: Int. Univ. Press.

Parkes, C. M. & Weiss, R. S. (1983). *Recovery from Bereavement*. New York: Basic Books.

Paul, N. (1969). Psychiatry: Its role in the resolution of grief. In *Death and Bereavement*, ed. A. H. Kutscher. Springfield, IL: Thomas, pp. 174–195.

Peniston, D. H. (1962). The importance of death education in family life. *Family Life Coordinator*, 11: 15–18.

Sandler, J. (1960). The background of safety. *Int. J. Psychoanal*, 41: 352–356.

Shane, M. & Shane, E. (1990). Object loss and selfobject loss: A consideration of self psychology's contribution to understanding mourning and the failure to mourn. *Annual Psychoanal.*, 18: 115–131.

Slochower, J. (1993). Mourning and the holding function of shiva. *Contemp. Psychoanal.*, 29: 352–367.

Solnit, A. J. (1970). A study of object loss in infancy. *Psychoanal. Study Child*, 25: 257–272.

Steiner, J. (1970). Group function within the mourning process. *Archives Foundation Thanatology*, 2: 80–82.

Stern, D. (1985). *The Interpersonal World of the Infant. A View from Psychoanalysis and Developmental Psychology*. New York: Basic Books.

Stolorow, R. D., Brandchaft, B. & Atwood, G. E. (1987). *Psychoanalytic Treatment: An Intersubjective Approach*. Hillsdale, NJ: Analytic Press.

Winnicott, D. W. (1965). *The Maturational Processes and the Facilitating Environment: Studies in the Theory of Emotional Development*. New York: Int. Univ. Press.

Wolfenstein, M. (1966). How is mourning possible? *Psychoanal. Study Child*, 21: 93–123.

Chapter 7

Mourning and the holding function of shiva (1993)

Joyce Slochower

Editor's note: The standard model of mourning described mourning as a largely intrapsychic process in which an individual person engaged. Although many would now acknowledge that surviving relationships play an important part in facilitating the process, the specific function of other people is in need of further study. In this pioneering paper, Joyce Slochower discusses the function of the Jewish custom of "sitting shiva" and how the community plays a part in holding (in the Winnicottian sense) the mourning process, thus facilitating the individual's successful work of mourning.

This paper was published in 1993 by Joyce Slochower as "Mourning and the Holding Function of Shiva" in Contemporary Psychoanalysis, Volume 29.

This paper addresses the potential presence of therapeutic factors in a nonanalytic setting. It developed partly in response to a personal experience, and out of my ongoing interest in the therapeutic function of non-interpretive aspects of psychoanalytic process. This factor, which has been variously described, refers to that dimension of psychoanalysis which involves the analyst's symbolic and actual function as a receiver of the patient's experience. In that capacity, the analyst has been said to provide or to represent an environmental mediator (Spitz, 1956), a background of safety (Sandler, 1960), an extra-uterine matrix (Mahler, 1968) or basic unit (Little, 1981), a protective shield (Khan, 1963), a holding environment (Winnicott, 1965a, 1965d), an emotional container (Bion, 1962, 1963) and a transformational object (Bollas, 1987). While some believe that if analysis is to produce change, this non-interpretive factor is always central, others focus on the non-interpretive holding factor in the treatment of only certain patient groups. These include patients needing a regression or suffering from a basic fault (Winnicott, 1965e; Balint, 1968), from narcissistic issues (Modell, 1975, 1976) or from severe borderline pathology (Slochower, 1992). What unifies these varied models is the critical importance given to the analyst's capacity to receive, hold, and survive the patient's intense emotional experiences. When the analyst provides this function (which I shall call the holding function), the subjective aspects of analytic process are largely contained within the analyst. Previously, I have described this non-interpretive holding function as it emerges for patients needing a holding of dependence, of self-involvement, or of rage (Slochower, 1991).

In each case, the analyst does not interpret the patient's experiences, but instead provides a setting that makes their full expression possible. For some patients, the mutual survival of analyst and patient will permit the integration of aspects of the self for the first time.

The analyst's provision of a space within which the patient may contact heretofore unknown aspects of internal life has always seemed to me to be a more complex analytic task than that of offering interpretations. Interpretive work involves communicating our understanding to the patient, and this is an aspect of psychoanalysis for which we have been trained, and through which we derive considerable self-esteem. Non-interpretive work, in contrast, requires that we contain our understanding (or lack thereof), sometimes for long periods. It assumes our ability and willingness to remain potentially present emotionally in the face of the wide range of affective states that our patients may communicate. When non-interpretive work requires that we provide a holding function for the patient, we tolerate the additional strain that may be relieved when we are free to participate more fully as (subjective) observers of analytic interchange.

It was thus with considerable surprise that I discovered this dimension of psychoanalytic experience in a non-analytic setting, provided by people without therapeutic training. The precipitating event was my father's death, and the therapeutic experience took place in the context of shiva (Jewish mourning) observance. This death and mourning stood in stark contrast to a previous loss that took place without shiva, which was far more difficult to assimilate as a result. The present paper addresses the psychological functions involved in shiva. It will be suggested that, in part, the laws of mourning represent both a culturally derived pre-psychoanalytic therapeutic response to the bereaved individual, and an intuitive understanding of the emotional impact on the community of fulfilling shiva requirements. That understanding extends beyond the mourner's obvious temporary need for nurturance and support, and reflects the paradoxical aspects of intimacy inherent in the analytic interchange (Winnicott, 1971; Modell, 1990). Following a brief review of the mourning process and the traditions of shiva, the varied emotional functions of shiva will be discussed.

Loss and mourning

The death of close loved ones is always a profound and wrenching experience. Such loss, whether expected or not, whether dreaded or wished for, contains a traumatic element. This is especially so when the loss is of a central and irreplaceable relationship – of parent, sibling, spouse or child. The mourning process itself is a complex one. Freud (1917) believed that mourning, a "normal" variant of depression, involved feelings of painful dejection, a loss of interest in the outside world, lost capacity to love, and an inability to engage in everyday activities. He understood mourning as allowing the libido to slowly and painfully detach from the loved object.

Abraham (1924), in contrast to Freud, suggested that normal mourning and (neurotic) depression are similar in that both result in lowered self-esteem and can involve ambivalent feelings toward the lost object. Abraham further noted that the mourner deals with the pain of loss by introjecting, rather than detaching from the loved object. The importance of the mourner's yearning for the lost object was also underlined by Bibring (1953) and Jacobson (1957).[1]

Klein (1975) underlined the inevitable sense of guilt and fear of retaliation following such loss. She related this to the work of the infant in the depressive position.

> The poignancy of the actual loss of a loved person is greatly increased by the mourner's unconscious phantasies of having lost his internal "good" objects as well. He then feels that his internal "bad" objects predominate and his inner world is in danger of disruption . . . Fears of being robbed and punished by both dreaded parents – that is to say, feelings of persecution – have also been revived in deep layers of the mind. I should say that in mourning the subject goes through a modified and transitory manic-depressive state and overcomes it.
>
> (1975, p. 353)

For Klein, then, the mourner must contend with his grief, guilt, hatred and self-hate, and also feelings of triumph over the dead person. Klein felt that this work reflects the reinstatement and reintegration of the original depressive position. Winnicott (1965c) similarly believed that mourning, like depression, required a resolution of guilt and a sense of responsibility for the death. Winnicott understood the source of these feelings to be the destructive wishes that inevitably accompany loving.

Bowlby (1960, 1980) described several emotional responses to the death of loved ones. These are: a focus of thoughts and behavior on the lost object; feelings of hostility that may be directed in a variety of ways; appeals for help; feelings of despair, withdrawal, regression and disorganization; and finally, reorganization of behavior toward a new object. He noted that in normal mourning anger is, in fact, inevitable, and may be directed toward the lost object. Bowlby questioned the centrality of the identification process in the resolution of mourning and emphasized the varied emotional processes involved.

Loss of a loved person gives rise not only to an intense desire for reunion but to anger at his departure and, later, usually to some degree of detachment; it gives rise not only to a cry for help, but sometimes also to a rejection of those who respond (1980, p. 31). Thus, psychoanalytic theorists emphasize the intense but varied internal dynamics involved in mourning (see Siggins, 1966, for a review of this literature). There is some disagreement concerning the degree to which mourning is analogous to or different from neurotic depression. Certainly, the mourner differs from the neurotic in that the lost object is absent both symbolically and in reality. Further, mourning, unlike neurotic depression, is at least ideally a somewhat circumscribed process, and is spontaneously curative. It is evident that the intensity of an individual's mourning will depend on the nature of the mourner's relationship to the deceased, on the relative emotional health of the mourner, and also on the circumstances of the death. The affective tone of the mourning process will vary depending on whether the mourner's reactions primarily involve feelings of abandonment, relief, guilt, rage, etc. Nevertheless, when the loss is a significant one, the individual's need to integrate it remains a constant feature. During the period of mourning, the mourner suffers from a powerfully diminished capacity to be involved in the world of real relationships or activities. Instead, the mourner is taken up with the task of avoiding, experiencing and expressing grief about the loss, of sorting out memories and conflictual feelings about the death and about the dead person, and of living through a temporary depression. This depression in part concerns a sense of having been abandoned by the deceased loved one. Ultimately, the work of mourning will allow the mourner to give up the lost relationship as a real, alive one, while forming and preserving an internal relationship to the lost object in all its complexity.

Death and Jewish tradition and law

All cultures recognize the mourner's need to express respect for the dead person and grief at the loss (see Mandelbaum, 1959, for a discussion of the social function of funeral rites in some other societies). Some aspects of the Jewish laws pertaining to death and shiva have their origins in the Biblical period (cf. Gen. 50:15; Lev. 10:20; Amos 8:10); many were developed during the Rabbinic period. These laws are most complex; they address not only the mourner's and community's behavior during the week of shiva, but also during the days before burial and for eleven months after death as well. Only a broad outline of the customs relating to the shiva week itself will be described here. (See Lamm, 1988, for a full and detailed discussion of the laws of mourning and references to relevant texts). While it is primarily religious Jewish communities that observe the laws of mourning in detail, aspects of shiva observance have been widely incorporated among non-observant Jews as well.

Jewish tradition describes five stages of mourning, each with its own laws and customs. It should be noted that one sits shiva only for parents, siblings, children, and spouse. These relationships are deemed the most central and least replaceable in life, and thus deserving of a formal mourning. The first stage of mourning begins with death and lasts until burial. Most of the laws concerning this period involve honoring the deceased. From the moment of death, the body is watched, and shortly before burial it is bathed, dressed, and placed in a casket, usually by members of the mourner's own community. Burial itself is designed in such a way that its impact is stark; an unadorned wooden casket (or, in Israel, a shroud without a casket) is used; at the cemetery the coffin or shroud is covered with earth by the mourner(s) and members of the mourner's family and community. The emphasis on honoring the deceased may provide a much needed activity for the mourner who is too shocked by the death to begin the actual work of mourning. During this phase (*aninut*) all social amenities as well as most positive religious requirements (i.e. laws pertaining to religious acts of ritual observance, such as reciting prayers) are suspended for the mourner. Every attempt is made to shorten this period by arranging that burial take place as soon as possible, and mourning itself begin. This is considered both respectful of the deceased and in the best interests of the mourner.

The mourner's loss is first concertized in the custom of *Keriah*. Either at the moment of death or at the funeral, a tear is made in the mourner's outer garment. This garment will be worn throughout the week of shiva, which formally begins when the mourner returns home from the burial. The mourner washes his hands prior to entering the home (this symbolizes a cleansing following contact with death). All mirrors (traditionally associated with vanity) are covered. A symbolic meal of condolence is then eaten. It is traditionally provided by the community, not by the mourner, and includes foods associated with life, such as bread and hard-boiled eggs. A memorial (*yahrzeit*) candle is lit; it will burn for the seven-day shiva period.

Traditionally, shiva lasts for seven days (although in certain circumstances, *Shabbat* and holidays interrupt or actually cancel the shiva period). Throughout shiva, the mourner ordinarily remains at home (but travels if the shiva house is elsewhere and the mourner cannot reside there for the week). During the entire shiva week, the mourner and the community take up the task of speaking about the deceased and about the mourner's loss.

The laws of shiva alter virtually every aspect of ordinary social behavior for both mourner and visitor. The mourner's grief is concretized in a variety of ways; he/she does not wear leather shoes (traditionally associated with comfort and vanity). Similarly, the mourner neither bathes (though exceptions are made for those who find this restriction very difficult) nor changes clothing, particularly the rent garment. The mourner refrains from using cosmetics, cutting hair, shaving and engaging in sexual relations. The study of Torah is also forbidden, as such study is believed to bring joy. The mourner is free to walk, stand, lie, or sit but only on a low stool or chair.[2] Contrary to popular belief, the chair need not be hard or uncomfortable. Instead, this low seat symbolizes the mourner's lowered emotional state. The mourner does not rise to greet the visitor; in fact, the front door is left ajar in order to free the mourner from this obligation. The mourner is excused from all household tasks (cleaning, laundering, etc.) and does not prepare or serve food for others or for him/herself. Thus, the mourner is freed from all social obligations and distractions, and is expected to be involved solely with the mourning itself.

Visitors to the mourner operate under similarly unusual rules. A visit (shiva call) to a mourner is considered its own good deed and obligation (*mitzvah*). In traditional settings such calls are paid by most of the mourner's community, whether or not they were personally involved with the deceased or with the mourner. Callers generally come unannounced at any time during the day or evening; thus, for much of the day, the mourner is involved in verbal contact. The purpose of the shiva call is explicit: to offer the mourner the consolation of contact during a time of loneliness or despair, and to provide an opportunity to speak about the loss and to share memories of the deceased. Callers are not permitted to greet the mourner; instead, they wait until the mourner notices and greets them. The mourner, who may choose to speak of the dead person, of other things, or to remain silent, must initiate conversation. The caller does not initiate or direct the conversation in such a way as to distract the mourner from the work of mourning unless the mourner indicates such a need. Thus, at times, the caller may simply sit silently with the mourner; at other moments, the caller may be engaged in conversation of more or less emotional depth. The caller, who is not expected to stay long, does not say good-bye, and, instead, utters a traditional phrase, "May God comfort you among the mourners of Zion and Jerusalem." The mourner remains seated, and does not respond to the caller's statement with a farewell greeting.

At the end of the seven-day shiva period, the mourner is expected to "get up," i.e. to resume daily activities in most respects. However, during the subsequent thirty days (*shloshim*), certain activities (such as attending parties) designed to bring joy are curtailed. Many male mourners refrain from shaving throughout *shloshim*. This represents a most powerful and visible expression of the mourner's state of bereavement. In fact, for a full eleven months following a death, the mourner continues to concretely acknowledge this loss by saying *Kaddish* in synagogue daily, and, in the case of a parent's death (a loss lacking the possibility of even partial replacement), also limiting social activities and festivities.

The emotional function of shiva

The laws of shiva are most complex, and in large measure derive from ancient religious tradition and beliefs about death. Clearly, shiva serves a variety of religious functions for the community and for the mourner. Since shiva is a social and not an analytic interchange, the intrapsychic function of the shiva experience, and how the individual mourner assimilates it, will be variable, and often somewhat obscure from the caller's point of view. Certainly, my own response to shiva was highly subjective, colored by my relationship with my father as well as by my idiosyncratic response to these traditions. I have, however, heard both from my patients and my friends that shiva was extremely helpful in ways not unrelated to my own experience. I thus hope that this personal description may have some generality.

From the moment of my father's death, I derived considerable comfort from the knowledge that his body was cared for and watched by my own community rather than by strangers. At the cemetery, I found something both raw and compelling as my own family and friends covered the unprettified casket. The possibility of denying death was absent and its shock was intense. In that context, I returned home and remained there for a week. I was both protected from and deprived of the external distractions that might be viewed as relieving the pain of loss; I neither worked, nor shopped, cooked for myself or my family, etc. Yet I was far from alone; a stream of shiva callers appeared who set aside their own concerns and allowed me to talk about my father when I needed to, and about other things when I did not. They came and left unrequested, and thus freed me from the burden of having to ask for company that I did not always know I needed; at the same time, they made it possible for me to retreat in privacy when I wished to do so. Many shiva callers brought food; few ate mine. Some were close friends or relatives; many were more casual acquaintances, yet most made it possible for me to talk, to stay with the feelings of loss as long as I needed to. Their farewell greeting offered the comfort of community ("May God comfort you among the mourners . . ."), reminding me that I was not alone in this experience. I emerged from this very intense week of remembering exhausted but relieved. My recovery did not end there, but was steady, and at the year's end I found myself largely at peace with this loss.

How did shiva help? These laws altered virtually every aspect of ordinary social behavior for both myself and the shiva caller in ways that made the denial of death nearly impossible. I was required to express my grief (whether felt or unfelt at any moment) in multiple concrete ways: my shoes, clothing, lowered chair, etc., underlined my state of mourning and interfered with the possibility of "putting on a face" (false self) to the world. Yet the callers' visits, even people's farewell greeting, required no acknowledgment from me. This prohibition against ordinary greetings and farewells was awkward for many of us, yet it served as a compelling reminder of the visit's non-social nature. The custom requiring that the caller wait for me to speak first similarly provided a structure that facilitated a direct response to me and to death by making it harder for any of us to escape into social convention.

Thus, shiva customs force the community (and sometimes also the mourner) to face the mourner's loss in a far more direct way than might be comfortable. Shiva, then, would seem in part to be designed to facilitate grieving; virtually all activities that might take the mourner away from the loss are withdrawn. During this period, the caller is required, in a sense, to temporarily set aside personal concerns, troubles and joys, and any discomfort about the shiva call itself, in order to provide a space within which the mourner can experience loss.

The holding function of shiva

It appears that a central concern of shiva tradition is to enable the mourner to mourn within the context of care. This care is to be given freely, and does not require an expression of need on the mourner's part. A particularly compelling aspect of shiva involves the creation of an emotionally protective setting for the mourner that is reminiscent of the analytic holding environment. The community of shiva callers collectively provides the mourner with this therapeutic hold. It is reflected in both concrete care, and in the emotional space within which the mourner is encouraged to experience and to express a variety of feeling states. The mourner is, in a sense, permitted to use people within the community without regard for their own needs (i.e. ruthlessly) in ways that parallel the holding provided both the infant and the patient in need of a regression (Winnicott, 1965b, 1965e, 1971).

Subjective aspects of the shiva call

Shiva, then, creates a potential holding environment. The holding function of shiva addresses a particularly important aspect of the mourning process. The provision of this hold may, however, obscure the fact that the caller also functions as an observer, or as an "enmeshed observing-participant" (cf. Fromm, 1964; Hirsch, 1987) in the shiva situation. The shiva caller is a subjective participant to the extent that the mourner or the mourner's loss makes an emotional impact on the caller. Shiva calls often evoke in the caller memories of related losses (or of anticipated losses), or feelings associated with other dimensions of the mourner-caller relationship. The caller's personal reactions may result in a fuller understanding of the mourner's experience, or may become interference, much as the analyst's subjectivity impacts the patient. If the caller chooses to share his/her own memories or reactions with the mourner, the mourner may experience a direct sense of connection to others at a time characterized by acute loneliness. Alternatively, such revelations can be disturbing and distracting, reflecting an impingement from the mourner's point of view. The caller's ability to make use of his subjectivity in communicating with the mourner has the potential to tremendously enhance the therapeutic effect of the visit. Nevertheless, it is clear that the structure of shiva is not designed to encourage the caller to express personal reactions. It is instead the holding function of shiva that predominates. While holding does not deny the caller's subjectivity, it does require that the caller largely contain it in order to provide the mourner with an emotionally protective setting.

The caller's response to the mourner

Since the shiva call is intrinsically an interpersonal event, the caller will inevitably be affected by variations in the mourner's capacity to directly experience and express grief. The shiva call is probably simultaneously easiest and most difficult when the mourner's grief is palpable. Here, the caller's sense of emotional responsibility to the mourner is considerable. At the same time, the mourner's appreciative response is likely to be both gratifying and reassuring in that the shiva caller inevitably doubts the usefulness of the visit. The caller who facilitates the mourner's repeated expression of intense and painful feelings about the loss may provide the deeply grieving mourner with a non-regressive opportunity (Modell, 1988) to work through earlier painful feelings about that relationship. This requires, however, that the visitor tolerate the difficult feelings generated by the subject of loss. These feelings can be quite intense. To the extent that the visitor has failed to assimilate his own feelings about death, such a shiva call may be acutely stressful. Even, however, the caller who has dealt with death directly must now set aside these personal experiences to be there for the mourner in ways that may parallel aspects of the non-interpretive analytic position. The caller may feel moved and caring of the mourner but burdened by the weight of this task. This situation nevertheless offers the caller a sense of purpose in that the mourner clearly needs the caller to be present.

At some moments, the mourner's intense self-preoccupation emerges with a force that tends to leave the caller feeling emotionally obliterated. To the degree that a mourner is defended against grief, that grief may emerge in a diverted form or may be apparently absent. At times, grief appears as a flat focus on the self accompanied by an apparent disinterest in and imperviousness to the shiva caller. When the mourner is someone with little tolerance for emotional experience, a powerful need not to feel grief may be communicated. The mourner may behave as if nothing is wrong, as if the shiva call were, in fact, a social visit. This stance is unlikely to elicit feelings of empathy in the caller. Instead, the caller, perhaps like the analyst reacting to a narcissistic patient (Modell, 1976), may feel bored, shut out, even judgmental of the mourner's apparent lack of grief. Yet shiva tradition requires that the caller remain with the mourner, and not demand that the mourner changes, i.e. express real feelings. Here, the caller is required to remain emotionally available with a mourner who appears at best oblivious to the purpose of his presence, while containing whatever feelings this position evokes.

To the extent that the mourner's own feelings about the death are complex and involve guilt about past actions or inactions, feelings of hatred toward the dead person, etc. (cf. Klein, 1975), the mourner is likely to experience expressions of concern ambivalently. The caller's caring presence can intensify the mourner's guilt about felt failures vis-à-vis the deceased. At other moments, the caller's sympathy may enrage the mourner by its inadequacy in the face of loss. The mourner may react to the caller with irritation, or respond with anger or guilt to these expressions of sympathy. In such a context, the caller would need to tolerate both whatever personal feelings are generated by the death itself and the feeling of being unappreciated, unhelpful, or even hurtful to the mourner. It would require that the caller not withdraw out of annoyance or out of anxiety about the usefulness of the shiva call. By remaining emotionally present but not intrusive, the caller communicates confidence to the mourner about both the caller's and the mourner's ability to survive the onslaught of difficult feelings generated by the grieving process.

The paradox of shiva

The therapeutic relationship, which is unlike anything else in ordinary social experience, has been described as a paradoxical one in that it involves simultaneously contradictory dimensions. The therapist is a "real" and "unreal" object to the patient; the therapeutic interplay involves an ongoing mix of different levels of experience and reality. Modell (1990) and Pizer (1992) underline, with Winnicott (1971), the role of real and "as if" elements in the analytic setting. The analytic boundary both permits and protects this paradox, which occurs in the transitional space that analysis creates. In similar ways, the rules of shiva create an extraordinary social situation. In this setting, which represents a kind of transitional space, the relationship between mourner and caller is also characterized by paradox. For a limited and circumscribed time and in a fixed place, the shiva caller functions in a highly specific, rather artificial way with a person temporarily in need. The shiva caller's purpose is to provide a therapeutic presence for the mourner. Yet the caller can never fully "know" what the mourner's experience is like, and may not even be emotionally involved with the mourner. In fact, the shiva caller performs a function for the mourner that is unlikely to extend far beyond the context of shiva. The mourner and caller do not, however, ordinarily challenge the meaningfulness of shiva even if it is clear to both that shiva's end will also bring an end to the caller's attentions. It is within this space that a therapeutic process may take place. What is intrinsic to this paradox is the willingness of mourner and caller (patient and analyst) not to challenge the artificiality of the shiva (or analytic) setting, and, instead to tolerate its ambiguities.

Protection of the caller in shiva

The laws of shiva, as seen in this context, are designed for the protection of the mourner, and make powerful demands on the caller. To require that a person who may have little psychological sophistication tolerate the range of feelings evoked by a mourner is a considerable demand. The laws of shiva do, however, take into account the vulnerability of the community. Interestingly, the shiva caller is protected in ways similar to the protection provided the analyst by analytic parameters. Shiva calls are short, ordinarily paid not more than once by any individual. Instead, the mourner's larger community takes on this obligation. The community, falling lightly on its individual members, thus shares the holding function of shiva. Although the caller allows the mourner to set the tone and content of the conversation, the caller is provided the same protection of time that is inherent in the structured analytic hour. Similarly, it is the caller, not the mourner, who typically sets the time of his call and of its termination, retaining, perhaps, the potential to express hatred in this way (Winnicott, 1949).

On the seventh day of shiva, the mourner must "get up," whether emotionally "ready" or not. The caller is thereby automatically freed from obligation at the end of the shiva week. Further, shiva is interrupted by *Shabbat*, and is actually cancelled by major holidays. These laws may in part reflect the community's need to remain involved in life, in joyous or religious events that supersede even the needs of the individual mourner. Thus, shiva laws place the mourner's needs within the larger context of community needs. The caller is protected in ways similar to the analyst who takes weekend breaks and summer vacations despite the patient's need for analysis. Of course, the mourner (like the distressed patient) may be quite unable to suspend grief just because *Shabbat* or a holiday[3] interferes. Thus, shiva fails here, and the mourner is left to cope with being dropped. To the extent that this failure in adaptation to the mourner's needs was preceded by a period of good enough adaptation, however, it may be strengthening rather than traumatic. A break in the shiva experience can begin to draw the mourner back into life, much as the mother's gradual failures facilitate development in the infant and as a disruption in holding may promote an integrative process in the patient (Winnicott, 1971).

These laws make quite evident that while Jewish tradition views the mourner's needs as great, they are not paramount in that they do not consistently override the needs of the shiva caller. In fact, it may be that the limits placed on the mourner's needs are actually what permit the community to tolerate the very great demand that is made of it during the period of shiva observance.

Certainly, it is not uncommon that the practice of shiva fails to hold the mourner, because neither the mourner nor the community can tolerate the massive onslaught of anxiety generated by such an experience. Shiva also cannot function effectively in the absence of some degree of cohesive community. This cohesive community is absent for too many. What is nevertheless most compelling is the power of these shiva laws to meet an individual's intense regression in its varied aspects, while still protecting the needs of the larger community. Shiva is in many ways a brilliant adaptation to universal human need, reflecting the capacity of society to temporarily provide a holding for its members while ensuring that the larger community remains an ongoing concern.

Dedication

In memory of my father, Harry Slochower, with thanks to S. P. Kaplan and to M. M'at.

Notes

1 Since my focus is on the mourner's emotional needs, and not on mourning per se, I will not attempt a comprehensive review of theories of mourning.
2 Actually, these prohibitions originally involved wearing shoes of any kind, and sitting anywhere other than the floor. The ancient mourner was thus placed in close emotional and literal proximity to the deceased (Tractate Semachot, 6:1).
3 When shiva coincides with a major holiday that results in its interruption or cancellation, the therapeutic function of shiva may fail in ways that leave the mourner traumatically unprotected. Here, it seems that the community's ritual observance overrides the mourner's needs in ways that may interfere with the resolution of grief. Several patients have confirmed this. Adaptation to the mourner's needs was preceded by a period of good enough adaptation; however, it may be strengthening rather than traumatic. A break in the shiva experience can begin to draw the mourner back into life, much as the mother's gradual failures facilitate development in the infant and as a disruption in holding may promote an integrative process in the patient (Winnicott, 1971).

References

Abraham, K. (1924). A short study of the development of the libido: Viewed in the light of mental disorders. In: *Selected Papers on Psychoanalysis*. London: Hogarth.
Balint, M. (1968). *The Basic Fault*. London: Tavistock.
Bibring, E. (1953). The mechanism of depression. In: P. Greenacre (ed.). *Affective Disorders*. New York: International Universities Press.
Bion, W. R. (1962). *Learning From Experience*. London: Heinemann.
Bion, W. R. (1963). *Elements of Psycho-Analysis*. London: Heinemann.
Bollas, C. (1987). *The Shadow of the Object*. New York: Columbia University Press.
Bowlby, J. (1960). Grief and mourning in infancy and early childhood. *Psychoanal. Study Child*, 15: 9–52.
Bowlby, J. (1980). *Loss: Sadness and Depression*. New York: Basic Books.

Freud, S. (1917). Mourning and melancholia. *Standard Edition, Vol. 14*. London: Hogarth.

Fromm, E. (1964). *The Heart of Man*. New York: Harper and Row.

Hirsch, I. (1987). Varying modes of analytic participation. *Journal of the American Academy of Psychoanalysis*, 15: 205–222.

Jacobson, E. (1957). Denial and repression. *J. Am. Psychoanal. Assoc.*, 5: 61–92.

Khan, M. (1963). The concept of cumulative trauma. In: *The Privacy of the Self*. New York: International Universities Press, 1974.

Klein, M. (1975). *Love, Guilt and Reparation*. New York: Delta.

Lamm, M. (1988). *The Jewish Way in Death and Mourning*. New York: Jonathan David.

Little, M. (1981). *Transference Neurosis and Transference Psychosis: Toward a Basic Unity*. New York: Jason Aronson.

Mahler, M. (1968). On human symbiosis and the vicissitudes of individuation. *J. Am. Psychoanal. Assoc.*, 15: 740–763.

Mandelbaum, D. G. (1959). Social uses of funeral rites. In: H. Feifel (ed.). *The Meaning of Death*. New York: McGraw-Hill.

Modell, A. H. (1975). A narcissistic defense against affects and the illusion of self sufficiency. *Int. J. Psychoanal.*, 56: 275–282.

Modell, A. H. (1976). The holding environment and the therapeutic action of psychoanalysis. *J. Am. Psychoanal. Assoc.*, 24: 285–307.

Modell, A. H. (1988). On the protection and safety of the therapeutic setting. In: A. Rothstein (ed.). *The Therapeutic Action of Psychoanalytic Psychotherapy*. Madison, CT: International Universities Press.

Modell, A. H. (1990). *Other Times, Other Realities: Toward a Theory of Psychoanalytic Treatment*. Cambridge: Harvard University Press.

Pizer, S. A. (1992). The negotiation of paradox in the analytic process. *Psychoanal. Dial.*, 2: 215–240.

Sandler, J. (1960). The background of safety. *Int. J. Psychoanal.*, 41: 352–356.

Siggins, L. D. (1966). Mourning: A critical survey of the literature. *Int. J. Psychoanal.*, 47: 14–25.

Slochower, J. (1991). Variations in the analytic holding environment. *Int. J. Psychoanal.*, 72: 709–718.

Slochower, J. (1992). A hateful borderline patient and the holding environment. *Contemp. Psychoanal.*, 28: 72–88.

Spitz, R. (1956). Countertransference. *J. Am. Psychoanal. Assoc.*, 4: 256–265.

Winnicott, D. W. (1949). Hate in the countertransference. *Int. J. Psychoanal*, 30: 69–74.

Winnicott, D. W. (1965a). Dependence in infant-care, in child-care, and in the psychoanalytic setting. In: *The Maturational Processes and the Facilitating Environment*. New York: International Universities Press.

Winnicott, D. W. (1965b). The development of the capacity for concern. In: *The Maturational Processes and the Facilitating Environment*. New York: International Universities Press.

Winnicott, D. W. (1965c). The mentally ill in your caseload. In: *The Maturational Processes and the Facilitating Environment*. New York: International Universities Press.

Winnicott, D. W. (1965d). Psychiatric disorder in terms of infantile maturational processes. In: *The Maturational Processes and the Facilitating Environment*. New York: International Universities Press.

Winnicott, D. W. (1965e). The theory of the parent-infant relationship. In: *The Maturational Processes and the Facilitating Environment*. New York: International Universities Press.

Winnicott, D. W. (1971). The use of an object and relating through identifications. In: *Playing and Reality*. New York: Basic Books.

Chapter 8

Self experience in mourning (1995)

George Hagman

Editor's note: The standard model of mourning focused on the work involved in relinquishing the lost object. Changes in self-experience resulted from identifications with the object as a means to resist giving up the attachment. In the following chapter, I explore the narcissistic impact of bereavement and the consequences of the loss of the functions that the object served in self-experience. This is not meant to minimize the importance of object loss; rather I want to explore a dimension of bereavement and mourning which has been neglected.

This paper was published in 1995 by George Hagman as "Death of a Selfobject: Towards a Self Psychology of the Mourning Process" in The Impact of New Ideas: Progress in Self Psychology, *Volume 11, edited by Arnold Goldberg, the Analytic Press, an imprint of Taylor & Francis, New York and London.*

The psychoanalytic theory of mourning has changed little from Freud's original formulation (Freud, 1917) despite the extensive theoretical and clinical literature on the subject. Primary emphases on decathexis and identification related to object loss has remained consistent regardless of school of thought and clinical method. The purpose of this chapter is to review the psychoanalytic model of mourning from a new perspective: the psychology of the self. My thesis is that mourning is essentially the transmuting internalization of the structure and function of the lost selfobject. I intend to offer a revision of the models of mourning as formulated by Bowlby (1980) and Parkes (1987), with an emphasis on the transformation of the lost selfobject's narcissistic function as the primary goal of the work of mourning. After a brief literature review, I expand on my thesis and propose a reinterpretation of the stages of mourning along self psychological lines. This is followed by a discussion of the role of the selfobject ambience in the facilitation of the mourning process. In closing, a treatment implication of a self-focused approach to mourning is reviewed.

Literature review

Because the psychoanalytic theory of mourning deals primarily with the internal, psychical fate of the lost object, the impact of loss through death on the self can only be inferred from classical theory. Freud's original notion regarding decathexis and identification implies ego change (and therefore, one would assume, self-experience), but only secondarily, as the ego alters itself in an attempt to retain the object tie. Freud's understanding of melancholia certainly assumed an altered experience of self, as hostility becomes inwardly directed; however, once again, this is in reaction to object loss. In addition, because the mourning theory predated the structural model and the terms *ego* and *self* were essentially interchangeable in Freud's thinking at that time, his mourning theory can be viewed as an early conceptualization of the bereaved self which was never fully elaborated by him.

Freud recognized the limits of his focus on object loss. As he contemplated the affective intensity of grief, Freud (1917) wrote, "Why this compromise by which the command of reality is carried out piecemeal, should be so extraordinarily painful is not easy to explain in terms of economics. It is remarkable that this painful unpleasure is taken as a matter of course by us" (p. 245). Later, in an appendix to his work on anxiety (1977), Freud attempted to explain the pain of loss in terms of frustrated libido; although there was logic in the explanation, it failed to capture the unique agony of grief. In the end, as he himself apparently saw, Freud's model of mourning did not adequately explain the full impact of bereavement on the affective experience of the bereaved – the almost bottomless well of despair and pain that can only result from an experience of severe injury. His model may be useful in understanding the cognitive aspects of change during mourning, but it does not have the explanatory power regarding the affective impact of bereavement.

Edith Jacobson (1965), discussing the psychoanalyses of adult patients who lost parents in childhood, emphasized the narcissistic injury resulting from the loss of a love object. She wrote:

> Evidently children experience the loss of a parent . . . as a severe narcissistic injury, a castration. . . . The fact that in such children . . . the lost object becomes glorified, tends to raise that object's narcissistic value and meaning to the point of turning it into the most precious part of their own self which has been lost and must be recovered.
>
> (p. 209)

Colin Parkes (1987) touched on this idea in his discussion of identity issues in adult mourning, saying, "If I have relied on another person to predict and act in ways as an extension to myself then the loss of that person can be expected to have the same effect upon my view of the world and of myself as if I had lost a part of myself" (p. 114). He was struck by the frequently violent imagery that the bereaved use in describing their painful inner experiences. Some speak of a sense of their "inside being torn out," leaving "a horrible wound," a "gap," or "unhappy void." Others experience an exquisite fragility of the self; as one widow put it, "I feel terribly fragile. If somebody gave me a good tap I'd shatter into a thousand pieces" (pp. 114–116). Parkes stated specifically that there is "empirical justification . . . that the pain of grief, like physical pain, is the experience of damage to the self" (p. 116). Leon Grinberg (1964) spoke directly to this issue in his article on guilt and mourning. He said that object loss could be experienced as an attack on the self: "in any object loss there occurs simultaneously a loss of parts of the self, which leads to its corresponding process of mourning" (p. 368). The "cohesion" of the self is experienced as endangered, its integrity threatened. The person experiences "psychical pain" as "certain parts of the self" are experienced as menacingly lost. Psychoanalysis, Grinberg said, "gives the patient the possibility of recovering excluded parts of the self as well as the possibility of giving up those aspects which must inevitably be lost in the process of development." Through analysis, "the ego (*self*) will exhibit reparative tendencies towards itself, which will permit it to become stronger and better balanced" (pp. 370–371). In spite of Grinberg's emphasis on Kleinian theory, he speaks powerfully in support of a psychology of the self in mourning.

To this end, Morton and Estelle Shane (1991) recently offered an important contribution to the study of mourning in which they enhanced the psychoanalytic model with concepts derived from self psychology. In their article, they stressed that to focus solely on the experience of object loss in mourning means that "the loss of narcissistic support from that person" (p. 117) will be missed. The Shanes pointed out how the narcissistic needs of the bereaved must be met by an empathic, responsive caregiver and milieu for the selfobject loss to be resolved. They suggested that chronic self-disorders might develop when the bereaved fails to access selfobject functions in compensation for the loss. In this way, they believe, the trauma of death and selfobject failure can be mitigated so that the mourning process can proceed and be resolved successfully.

However, they did not go so far as to suggest a revised model of mourning based on their findings, and therefore, they missed the opportunity to utilize the full explanatory range and power of self psychology. Expanding on the Shanes' thesis, I offer a comprehensive reworking of the "standard" clinical model of mourning from the point of view of the psychology of the self. To this end, I attempt to show how the loss of the specific, unique, and distinct nature of the selfobject is one of the core issues in bereavement and how the rupture of the seemingly irreplaceable selfobject bond ineluctably leads to much of the affective turmoil and dramatic, psychic change processes of mourning.

Finally, it is important to note the work of Ulman and Brothers (1988) on posttraumatic stress disorder (PTSD). It is their belief that in PTSD there is a "shattering and faulty restoration of central organizing fantasies of self in relationship to others" (p. 20). Vulnerability to trauma is "determined by the degree to which the self (in relation to selfobject) remains organized around archaic and illusory notions of personal grandeur or idealized merger with the omnipotent" (p. 15). Because the self-as-fantasy constitutes the fundamental psychic reality or subjective frame of reference (the fundamental "meaning structures" of the self), the "shattering" of the central organizing fantasies can be devastating to the self, resulting in the severe dissociative symptoms of PTSD. Although bereavement does not necessarily result in this type of "shattering" of the self, the bereaved does not experience a disillusionment and disorganization of subjective experience. Therefore, I agree with Ulman and Brothers that what are clinically important are the vicissitudes of unconscious and conscious fantasy organization and the impact of selfobject loss on the structure and regulation of the affective life of the self.

Self-experience in mourning

Each person's self-experience crystallizes over time through interaction with others, whose activities and responses come to be experienced as parts of the self (selfobjects). The selfobject is the internal, affectively charged experience of the other. The quality and dynamics of function of the selfobject in the repair, sustenance, and regulation of the self over time is the area of study of self psychology. As the self matures, there is a gradual decrease in the person's dependence on object interactions for the maintenance of self-structure; nevertheless, throughout life, all persons continue to require positive selfobject experiences within an inter-subjective context. In the case of the death of a loved one, this selfobject bond is ruptured, thus precipitating the mourning process.

I believe that Kohut's (1972) concept of "transmuting internalization" can be helpful in our reconceptualization of the mourning process. In his early model of mental self-structure, Kohut proposed that, in response to situations of "optimal frustration," the self takes into its own structure, through a process of breaking down and transforming, the narcissistic functions of the selfobject. Kohut likened this process of reworking the selfobject tie and internalizing its functions (so as to free them from dependence on the object) to the work of mourning. Stolorow, Brandchaft, and Atwood (1987), in a recent reformulation of Kohut's concept, asserted that the formation of self-structure occurs not in a state of frustration, but as a direct result of the process of restoration of the ruptured selfobject bond in the context of an experience of "optimal empathy" and "affective responsiveness" (see also Terman, 1988, and Bacal, 1985). In other words, Stolorow et al. stressed that the self evolves within an intersubjective context characterized by attunement and responsiveness. This has important implications for the understanding of the role of survivors in the provision of a facilitative and supportive selfobject milieu, the availability of which is a prerequisite for successful mourning.

Kohut (1972) conceptualized transmuting internalization as a developmental process in which the archaic functions of the selfobject, either in early childhood or in the context of analytic treatment, are transformed into autonomous psychic structure. However, in the case of normal mourning, the selfobject is not of an archaic nature and the bereaved possesses a sufficiently internalized and mature self-structure. Nonetheless, as Kohut stressed, even the mature self relies on others for selfobject experiences that, though not necessary for the "survival" of the self, are utilized by the person to maintain normal and fully functional levels of self-cohesion, vitality, and initiative. Therefore, the death of a loved one is experienced as a "self-crisis" that confronts the individual with a specific task, necessitating psychic work, of which only a person with adequately internalized self-structure is capable. In fact, when assessing the impact of a particular bereavement on the self of an individual, it is important to explore the extent to which the bereaved experiences the loss as a threat to his or her personal survival. Given this, we must keep in mind that the selfobject concept refers to a psychological experience that, in healthy individuals, remains available despite the physical death of the other. The normal mourning process that I discuss involves the gradual transformation of the nature of the psychological experience of the essential other (selfobject) into a form that no longer requires the other's presence. However, in cases of pathologic bereavement, the psychological experience of the essential other is dependent on his or her presence, and with that loss, the bereaved's self may be experienced as so damaged that the risk of depression, and perhaps death, is high, as is the possibility (in some cases) of psychotic decompensation. Admittedly, in spite of the continuing cohesion of the self, normal bereavement is also experienced in terms of intense psychic pain and affective turmoil. In fact, it is in the area of the selfobject's function in regulating affective experience in even the maturely developed self that the process of transmuting internalization in mourning is so crucial.

Many authors have stressed the function of affects in self-experience. Contemporary analytic theorists place affectivity, the regulation of affect, and the structuralization of affects in the center of their theories. Recent contributors from self psychology have also emphasized the primary role of the selfobject in the affective dimension of self-experience. To this end, Stolorow et al. (1987) have made an important contribution to our understanding of affect and the selfobject. They wrote that

> selfobject functions pertain fundamentally to the integration of affect into the organization of self-experience, and that the need for selfobject ties pertains most centrally to the need for attuned responsiveness to affect states in all stages of the life cycle.
>
> (p. 67)

It is through selfobject experiences that our affective life is differentiated and our experience of self articulated. Selfobjects function to synthesize affectively discrepant experiences, which is essential to an integrated sense of self. It is through the selfobject that we acquire tolerance of affect states and the use of affects as internal signals by which we manage our inner and outer lives. Selfobjects assist the person in the development and maintenance of cognitive-affective schemata, which provide stability, cohesion, and vitality to the self-experience.

Stolorow et al. stressed that the healthy functioning of the self and the continuing cohesive experience of self arises from the presence, reciprocal activities, and affective attunement of the object. Earlier, Bowlby (1980) described how the object plays a crucial role as an activating stimulus and terminating stimulus, thus playing an important part in self-regulation. The selfobject experience is also such a circular system requiring the attuned presence, actual or *potential*, of both self and object. Mourning ensues when this bond is ruptured and the intersubjective, mutually regulatory system breaks down.

As stated previously, I see mourning as the transmuting internalization of the structure and function of the selfobject (the "organizing fantasies" of the self) in response to the death of a loved one. The network of cognitive-affective schemata (self-organizing fantasies) sustained by and within the selfobject tie is traumatized, broken down, reworked, and gradually transformed in such a way as to maintain the integrity of self-experience and restore self-cohesion and vitality. Although mourning can be said to occur following any selfobject loss, it is typically the loss of those selfobjects that have been relied on to repair, sustain, and regulate aspects of the nuclear self that results in a full state of mourning. However, it is important to note that in these cases, the self has not necessarily been dependent on the selfobject in an archaic sense; therefore, the loss, though painful, does not traumatize or damage the core self-structure. Successful resolution of mourning will largely be determined by the structural integrity, cohesion, and resilience of the nuclear self as well as the availability of adequately attuned, compensatory selfobjects. Pathologic mourning will typically result when the nuclear self is primarily organized around archaic selfobjects, in which case the core of the self has remained poorly structuralized and vulnerable to disruption.

Unfortunately, the nature of the focus of this chapter does not allow a complementary discussion of mourning for the lost object as an object in its own right, apart from its selfobject functions. The highlighting of the transmuting internalization of selfobject functions does not mean to imply that the experience of "object loss" is not important – far from it. However, over the years the psychoanalytic literature has dealt extensively with the problem of object loss, and my goal here is to explore an area that has been neglected. Future discussion includes issues related to what Shane and Shane (1990) called *otherness*: "The range of experiences in adult life where one serves the needs of another, where that other's emotional requirements are perceived to have priority over one's own. . . . The capacity to serve as a self-regulating other (selfobject) becomes an essential attribute of good-enough otherness" (p. 490). When one extends the concept of *otherness* to *loss*, one sees an additional side of mourning – that is, not only the loss of selfobject functions, but also the loss of what life would have provided for the other. This viewpoint has particular applicability to our understanding of a mature parent's loss of a child or spouse. Without a doubt, the loss of a relationship in which one had been empathically immersed has its own special pain, its unique tasks and processes.

The stages of mourning?

Most contemporary psychoanalytic models of mourning are highly influenced by the stage models of Bowlby and Parkes, which are considered to be the "standard" models of bereavement. However, the Parkes/Bowlby models are derived primarily from ethologically based research and are therefore confined to an objective, experience-distant viewpoint. The approach that I take here accepts the phenomenological accuracy of much of Parkes and Bowlby's research findings; however, I utilize insights from self psychology to propose an alternate interpretation of their data, so as to capture, in a experience near, subjectively focused model of bereavement previously unobserved aspects of the psychological process of mourning as a transmuting internalization of the selfobject function of the deceased person.

Hence to avoid the reified, somewhat reductionistic approach of the Parkes/ Bowlby model, I list five critical experiences which characterize the mourning process. Although I discuss each experience separately, in reality the bereaved may experience them in a fluid fashion and, at times, there may be little distinction between them. It is probably best to see this model as largely of heuristic value – more honored in the breach than in practice. Prior to the discussion of each dimension of mourning, I include a quote from first-hand experiences with mourning that I believe will be helpful in the analysis to follow.

Rupture of the selfobject bond (shock and self crisis)

Upon the unexpected news of his beloved daughter Jean's death, Mark Twain (Moffat, 1982) reflected:

> It is one of the mysteries of our nature that a man, all unprepared, can receive a thunder stroke like that and live. There is but one reasonable explanation of it. The intellect is stunned by the shock and but gropingly gathers the meaning of the words. The power to realize their full import is mercifully wanting. The mind has a dim sense of vast loss – that is all. It will take mind and memory months and possibly years to gather the details and thus learn and know the whole extent of the loss.
>
> (p. 6)

"Reality-testing has shown that the loved object no longer exists" (Freud, 1917). The news of death is accompanied by a state of shock, disbelief, and numbness (Parkes, 1987). The recognition of the "fact" of the death may be sudden or protracted, and this will determine the length of this stage. Internal equilibrium is "frozen," and the experience of the self is dominated by apprehension, perhaps acute nonspecific anxiety, and dread. Disorganization and fragmentation of self does not yet occur during this phase. In fact, there may be a heightened sense of organization and focus within the self-experience in response to the immediacy of the trauma. Many practical issues and problems may have to be dealt with. The experience of the bond to the deceased may in fact be intensified. There is also, frequently, a defensively motivated split between the awareness of the event of the death and a belief in the survival of the deceased. As Freud (1917) noted, "opposition (*to giving up the object*) can be so intense that a turning away from reality takes place" (p. 244). Sometimes, the denial of the reality of the loss may be vigorous and stubborn. The "self-state" of this phase can best be characterized as a reflexive fortification of the self in response to an attack on its integrity. Eventually, in normal cases, the bereaved will seek to evoke the customary responsiveness of the lost selfobject, thus entering Stage 2.

Attempts to restore the tie with the old selfobject (searching)

Toby Talbot (Moffat, 1982) reflected on her sorrow at her mother's death:

> Grief comes in unexpected surges. As when nursing, and anything can trig-
> ger the onrush of milk. An infant in a carriage or a child crying, but also a
> traffic light changing, water running, a dog barking . . . Little alarms these
> are, transmitted to that network of nerves, muscle, hormone, tissue, and cells
> that constitute the physical self. Mysterious cues set off a reminder of grief. It
> comes crashing like a wave, sweeping me in its crest, twisting me inside out.
> Then recedes, leaving me broken. Oh, Mama, I don't want to eat, to walk,
> to get out of bed . . . Nothing matters . . . I wake from sleep in the middle of
> every night and say to myself, "My mother is dead."
>
> (p. 106)

The recognition of the reality and finality of death precipitates emergency
attempts to retain, or recover, the selfobject bond (Parkes, 1987). Archaic affective states occur as the person struggles to restore contact with the dead. Crying,
screaming, and sobbing are primitive appeals from the archaic self to the lost
selfobject. "The person may revert to more archaic . . . modes of affect expression
in the . . . hope of thereby evoking the needed responses from others" (Stolorow
et al., 1987, p. 73). Yearnings for merger with the idealized object and fantasies of the presence of an admiring, loving object frequently accompany these
affective storms. In spite of their painfulness, these affective states (in terms of
self-experience) are attempts to restore the selfobject bond, at least momentarily.
Gradually the experience of the selfobject's unavailability and lack of response
leads to lessening attempts to regain the bond, and acceptance of the reality of
loss begins to set in. The self-state may be characterized as one of intense, psychical pain (grief) in response to the recognition of self-injury. Emergency attempts
to restore the self through action (crying for the deceased, pining) and fantasiz-
ing (dwelling on memories of the dead) are resorted to. The selfobject bond with
the deceased is broken. The self-experience is unstable and ultimately begins to
fragment.

Disruption of self-experience (psychic disorganization)

The following passage by Talbot (in Moffat, 1982) conveys the despair that may
be experienced during the middle phase of mourning:

> Life is a death sentence. Better not to give yourself to anything. The more
> you give, the more is taken from you. . . . I find myself drowning, engulfed
> by the disorder of the current, wanting to seize her hand to bring me to shore.
> Missing her so. Futilely trying to recapture the profile of elusive contours and
> shapes. To crystalize that deceased being. To evoke that palpable presence,

the voice, inflections, and rhythms, the silences, expressions, gestures, stance, gait, the birthmarks, the quirks. But the subject . . . becomes indistinct.

(p. 107)

In the wake of the rupture of the selfobject bond, the self may be experienced as depleted and empty, and temporary disintegration and fragmentation of the self may occur. The object is dead, and its function in sustaining the self is lost. The person may experience depression, diffuse anxiety, sleeplessness, hypochondriasis, confusion, and loss of positive investment in life. The availability of a responsive, affectively attuned milieu of supportive compensatory selfobjects is crucial for this stage to be endured, the powerful affect states to be resolved, and the mourning process to be accomplished. The self-state of this phase results from the disintegration of fantasy structure and the disruption of self-experience. The integrity of the structures, which had previously contained and regulated the bereaved's affects, is disturbed. Periods of calm acceptance are shattered by storms of grief, panic, and rage. Despite the extremity of the self, it is important to note that, in most cases, the cohesiveness of the nuclear self is not affected. It is only in cases of pathologic bereavement that the core of the self may be damaged. In normal bereavement self-disintegration is only partial and temporary, as eventually, the person spontaneously engages in the process of self-restoration.

Restoration of the self (psychic reorganization)

Later in her bereavement Talbot (Moffat, 1982) noted feelings of recovery and a renewed sense of self:

> Slowly I find myself being weaned from her material presence. Yet filled with her as never before. It is I now who represents us both. I am our mutual past. I am my mother and my self. She gave me love, to love myself, and to love the world. I must remember how to love. . . . Piece by piece, I reenter the world. A new phase. A new body, a new voice. . . . It is like a slow recovery from sickness, this recovery of one's self. . . . My life now is only mine.

(p. 111)

Freud (1917) described the psychical process of this stage from the point of view of drive psychology. He said that the giving up of the object is "carried out bit by bit, at great expense of time and cathectic energy, and in the meantime the existence of the lost object is psychically prolonged. Each single one of the memories and expectations in which the libido is bound to the object is brought up and hyper-cathected, and detachment of libido is accomplished" (p. 245). Later, Freud and other analysts would add identification with the lost object to this process (Abraham, 1925). Freud stated in *The Ego and the Id*: "It may be that . . . identification is the sole condition under which the Id can give up its objects" (p. 29). Abraham (1925) was even more explicit when he noted how the bereaved affects "a temporary introjection of the loved person. Its main purpose is . . . to preserve the person's relation to the lost object" (p. 435).

In self psychological terms, what Freud observed was the process of transmuting internalization of the selfobject into permanent self-structure which can continue to provide needed functions such as self-affirmation, mirroring, merger, twinship, and so forth, consistent with the function of the selfobject prior to the death. This is accomplished through a painful process of internal revitalization of residual selfobject functions that are gradually structuralized as an enduring, conscious image of the dead or transformed fully into the fabric of self-experience. As previously noted, Freud himself observed this process in the bereaved's compulsive recall of innumerable memories of the dead, but he stressed only the processes of identification, decathexis, and object removal. What has been missed up to this point is how memories of the deceased also evoke lost self-experience. The bereaved's memories are not simply of the deceased; they also reestablish momentarily (however partially) the narcissistic function of the lost object. To this end, these "memories" are not just static dead images from the past. They also have a dynamic, selfobject function in the maintenance and restoration of the bereaved's current self-state. Little by little, as these "lost" selfobject functions are revoked independent of the object's presence, many are "microinternalized" (Kohut, 1977), becoming part of the bereaved's self-structure. The ultimate objective of this stage is *not* the relinquishment of the selfobject bond (although one of the goals of mourning is for the self to no longer depend on the presence of the deceased), but the restoration of the cohesion and vitality of the self through transformation and adaptation of the selfobject and its functions within the self-structure. Ultimately, the selfobject may eventually be integrated into the self, maintained intact as a fantasy (perhaps experienced as spiritually present) to be evoked as necessary to assist in the maintenance or repair of the self, or obtained from other relationships. It is a crucial point that this internal, psychical work cannot be fully successful unless there is adequate development of self-structure prior to the loss so that there is "maturationally preformed receptivity for specific introjects" (Kohut, 1972, p. 49) and the mourning process occurs within the context of a responsive selfobject relationship and selfobject milieu/surround. As I describe in an upcoming section, the availability of "optimally responsive" selfobjects not only plays an essential role in the facilitation of mourning, but also makes a vital contribution to the creation of new self-structure and, thus, the restoration of the self (Bacal, 1985; Stolorow et al., 1987; Terman, 1988).

Creativity (new identity)

In the following passage from a short story, Thomas Mann (Moffat, 1982) wrote of the serenity and renewed pleasure in life that can follow successful bereavement:

> Is not life in and for itself a good, regardless of whether we may call its content "happiness"? Johannes Friedemann felt that it was so, and he loved life. He . . . taught himself with infinite, incredible care to take pleasure in what it

had still to offer. A walk in the springtime in the parks surrounding the town; the fragrance of a flower; the song of a bird – might not one feel grateful for such things as these? . . . how tenderly he loved the mild flow of his life, charged with no great emotions, it is true, but full of a quiet and tranquil happiness which was his own creation.

(p. 266)

Having restructured the self after loss, and thus having regained the needed selfobject functions lost due to the ruptured selfobject bond, the person is motivated to reengage actively in the selfobject milieu and form new relationships. There is a joyful reinvestment of the restored self in new experiences and initiatives. There is an experience of greater affective stability, renewed vitality, and self-cohesion. However, the final outcome of the mourning process is not solely determined by the quality of social activity; more essential is the renewed integrity of self-experience. In most cases, the self-state has returned to its pre-loss condition; in others there may be an experience of self-diminishment, and still in others, an experience of self-enhancement and liberation (Pollock, 1989).

The ambience of mourning

Successful mourning occurs in the context of a responsive, supportive, and facilitative selfobject milieu (Shane and Shane, 1991). Without this empathic ambience and self-sustaining environment, the bereaved (having endured a traumatic self-injury) may not spontaneously engage in the process just described. There may, in fact, be an inhibition or distortion of mourning, as the person resorts to defensive measures to shore up the self in the absence of essential selfobjects. Optimally, in our society, this selfobject milieu is composed of the community, its mourning customs and rituals, and the bereaved's family. In a recent article, Joyce Slochower (1993) discussed the function of the custom of sitting shiva in Jewish culture as a facilitative milieu that provides holding and empathic responsiveness to the bereaved. This viewpoint could certainly be extended to the psychological function of mourning rituals in many cultures. However, more characteristic of modern Western society is the primary role of a relatively small network of relationships characterized by individual caregiving.

Stolorow et al. (1987) stressed this caregiver's role in creating a relationship of "affective responsiveness" to facilitate adaptation to loss and self-development. Adapting Stolorow's concepts to the condition of bereavement, it can be said that the caregiver must tolerate, absorb, and contain the bereaved's affect states, which presuppose that they do not threaten the organization of the caregiver's sense of self. They should function to "hold the situation" (Winnicott, 1960, p. 229) so that it can be integrated. The caregiver's selfobject function gradually facilitates the restoration of the capacity for self-modulation of affect and the ability to assure a comforting attitude toward oneself. Consequently, such affect will not entail irretrievable loss in the self. The expectation that restitution will follow disruption is implicitly communicated, providing support for the bereaved's sense of self-continuity and confident hope for the future (Stolorow et al., 1987).

Murray Bowen (1985) gave a moving account of his work with a young widower and his three latency-age children. The young man had come to Bowen overwrought with grief and confused regarding problems arising from his wife's sudden death. An important concern was how to manage his own grief without traumatizing his children. With Bowen's support, empathy, and expert advice, the father came to be able to grieve with his children in an open yet strong and reassuring manner. He was able both to protect the children from various stressors and to facilitate their direct involvement in the mourning rituals and experience of their mother's death. Eventually, the father arranged for a viewing at the funeral parlor for himself and the children. He set up a time for them to be alone with the mother, so they could mourn her together. Bowen wrote:

> The father did a detailed account of the children's visit. . . . The children went up to the casket and felt the mother. The five-year-old son said: "If I kiss her, she could not kiss back." All three spent some time inspecting everything, even looking under the casket. The eight-year-old son got under the casket and prayed that his mother could hold him in her arms again in heaven. . . . He took a small pebble . . . and placed it in his mother's hand. The other children also got pebbles and put them in their mother's hand. Then they announced, "We can go daddy." The father was much relieved at the outcome of the visit. He said, "A thousand tons were lifted from this family today."
>
> (p. 334)

In Bowen's account, the father was able to access valuable selfobject functions from Bowen, who was available as a responsive, calm, empathic presence, providing structure and self-regulatory assistance to the father. He then internalized Bowen's involvement and integrated his own grief and the needs of his children so as to facilitate a healthy mourning process for his family. In the end, he created a facilitating situation, which he then "held" for his children. Because of him, they could grieve their mother's death in the ambience of their father's strength, love, and protection. Through the father's eyes, Bowen vividly captured the positive impact of an empathic selfobject surround. The children investigated the body of their mother with curiosity and tenderness. Because of the father's involvement, they were able to "be themselves" during their final moments with their mother, as they said goodbye to her in their fashion. In terms of the children's long-term adaptation to the loss of their mother, Bowen claimed, from a brief follow-up a few years later, that he did not observe any evidence of pathological sequelae from the death. Admittedly, Bowen's later assessment was informal and perhaps superficial. However, many studies of childhood parent loss have confirmed the general truth of his observation that the chances for successful adaptation to loss are greatly improved when the child is provided with continuous, responsive, and supportive parenting from adult survivors (Krupnick, 1984).

Finally, it is important to note that, although I have emphasized the transmuting internalization of the functions of the lost selfobject, it is also true that the bereaved person, during and after the period of mourning, may utilize a number of other selfobjects that continue to be available after the death. Also, one of the outcomes just noted in the discussion of Stage 5 is a renewed ability either to seek out and use new selfobjects as replacements for the lost functions of the object or, perhaps, to meet different selfobject needs. In both instances, the responsive selfobject surround makes possible a normative and not unfortunate outcome of loss, (i.e. the replacement of the selfobject with other, perhaps somewhat different, selfobjects or group of selfobjects that serve functions similar to the lost selfobject).

Treatment issues

From the perspective of self psychology, the goal of mourning is the restoration of the self after the rupture of a primary selfobject bond. What psychoanalysts have failed to see is the bereaved patient's struggle to transform the bond with the lost selfobject in order to secure its regulating functions within the self. Given this, the most important function of treatment is to support and protect this process by means of the analyst's empathic attunement and "holding" of the situation. The reduction of anything potentially traumatic within the analytic environment is essential. Special strategies, such as confronting the patient with the reality of death or stimulating abreaction, are invariably damaging to the empathic hold and must be avoided. Bereaved persons are exquisitely sensitive to failures in empathy and will resist and defend themselves against anyone who might, even inadvertently, interfere with the mourning process.

In the treatment of the bereaved, the focus of analysis should be on the person's struggle to repair, sustain, and regulate the self subsequent to the rupture of a crucial selfobject bond. The goal of mourning is not decathexis, but the retention of the lost selfobject functions through transformation of self-structure. The unfolding of the bereaved's selfobject needs for mirroring, merger with an idealized other, companionship, and self-efficacy in the transference provides an experience of empathic attunement and responsiveness, thus facilitating the mourning process. In a properly managed treatment, the patient not only engages in a process of transforming the selfobject functions, but also internalizes the supportive ambience of the optimally responsive analytic relationship.

E. K. Rynearson (1987) described the treatment of a woman who suffered from a refractory, pathologic bereavement subsequent to the death of her teenage son. He pointed out how every effort to encourage the final resolution of mourning failed. In spite of years of therapy and a generally good treatment relationship, the woman remained despondent and deeply attached to the memory of her dead son. The patient would even say how she found the treatment "helpful enough," but "it will never bring my son back," she would add despairingly. Despite all efforts, the patient remained determined to continue her lonely vigil. "I began to wonder out loud," Rynearson wrote, "how her dying son might help in reviving our therapy." He asked the patient to compose a letter from her son. He noted, "It did not feel contrived or unnatural to seek some caring and strength from an internalized 'presence' that had needed so much from us." The patient composed a series of moving and beautiful letters as if from her son, an admiring and supportive tribute to her as a mother. Rynearson concluded,

> We now look to David (the son) as a part of herself that is increasingly able to help us by becoming more alive and nurturant. David remains an obsession, but he also advises and guides as a mother would a child. I cannot say precisely what is changing in this dissociated, highly traumatized and tangled attachment, but my patient and I, and now David, are all working together.
>
> (p. 497)

Rynearson's clinical approach is not a self psychological one; however, I believe that his change in treatment strategy, as just described, was consistent with the findings of self psychology, and although he may not necessarily concur, his renewed approach to his work with the patient can be usefully interpreted along self psychological lines. To this end, it may be concluded that his insight into the selfobject nature of his patient's continuing relationship with her dead son arose from his empathic emersion in his patient's state of bereavement. He became aware of the "function" of the selfobject, as he explored with the patient the positive, self-sustaining, self-repairing, and self-regulating nature of the woman's "moribund" attachment to her son. Rynearson's initial treatment goal of encouraging the patient to give up her investment in the dead threatened his patient's self-security and provoked a chronic "resistance" to the working alliance. Once he ceased to promote decathexis and began to explore the functions of the selfobject in the areas of affirmation, mirroring, and merger needs, he noted a change in the ambience of the treatment and a revitalization of the treatment relationship. Not having a self psychological viewpoint, he was not able to conceptualize his intervention and formulate his insight as an interpretation that might have been of use to his patient. Nonetheless, his intuition regarding the positive function of the bond with the son allowed him to move beyond a chronic and painful treatment impasse in the general direction of recovery.

The mourning process can be said to be successfully concluded when the self is once again experienced as cohesive and vital, with a renewed capability and motivation for the effective use of selfobjects in the repair, sustenance, and regulation of the self. This does not mean that the lost selfobject has been abandoned – far from it. Many who have recovered from bereavement maintain powerful attachments to the dead as selfobjects, which continue to serve vital functions. In other cases, the selfobject may be fully integrated into the self, as the attachment to the dead fades from awareness. Self psychology provides us with a powerful clinical tool with which we can attune ourselves to the bereaved's struggle to maintain the integrity of self-experience in spite of the appearance of regression and suffering. It has been, perhaps, our own fear of self-injury and loss that has driven us to encourage and hasten an end to mourning, often blinding us to its self-restorative function.

References

Abraham, K. (1925). A short history of the development of the libido. In: *Selected Papers of Karl Abraham*. New York: Brunner Mazel, pp. 418–479.

Bacal, H. (1985). Optimal responsiveness and the therapeutic process. In: *Progress in Self Psychol., Vol. 1*, ed. A. Goldberg. New York: Guilford, pp. 202–226.

Bowen, M. (1985). *Family Therapy in Clinical Practice*. Northvale, NJ: Aronson.

Bowlby, J. (1980). *Attachment and Loss, Vol. 3*. New York: Basic Books.

Freud, S. (1917). Mourning and melancholia. *Standard Edition, Vol. 14*. London: Hogarth Press, 1957, pp. 243–258.

Freud, S. (1977). Inhibitions, symptoms and anxiety. In: *Standard Edition of the Complete Psychological Works of Sigmund Freud*, eds. J. Strachey & A. Strachey. New York: Norton.

Grinberg, L. (1964). Two kinds of guilt: Their relation with normal and pathological aspects of mourning. *Int. J. Psycho-Anal.*, 45: 366–371.

Jacobson, E. (1965). The return of the lost parent. In: *Drives, Affects, Behavior, Vol. 2*, ed. M. Shur. New York: International Universities Press, pp. 193–211.

Kohut, H. (1972). *The Analysis of the Self*. New York: International Universities Press.

Kohut, H. (1977). *The Restoration of the Self*. New York: International Universities Press.

Krupnick, J. (1984). Bereavement during childhood and adolescence. In: *Bereavement: Reactions, Consequences and Care*, eds. M. Osterweis & M. Green. Washington, DC: National Academy Press, pp. 99–141.

Moffat, J. (1982). *In the Midst of Winter: Selections from the Literature of Mourning*. New York: Random House.

Parkes, C. (1987). *Bereavement: Studies of Grief in Adult Life*. Madison, CT: International Universities Press.

Pollock, G. (1989). *The Mourning-Liberation Process*. Madison, CT: International Universities Press.

Rynearson, E. K. (1987). Psychotherapy of pathologic grief and bereavement: Revisions and limitations. In: *The Psychiatric Clinics of North America, Grief and Bereavement. Vol. 10, No. 3*, ed. S. Zisook. Philadelphia: W. B. Saunders.

Shane, M. & Shane, E. (1990). The struggle for otherhood: Implications for development in adulthood of the capacity to be a good-enough object for another. In: *New Dimensions in Adult Development*, eds. R. Nemiroff & C. Colarusso. New York: Basic Books, pp. 487–499.

Shane, M. & Shane, E. (1991). Object loss and selfobject loss: A contribution to understanding mourning and the failure to mourn. *Annu. Psychoanal.*, 13: 115–131.

Slochower, J. (1993). Mourning and the holding function of shiva. *Contemp. Psychoanal.*, 29: 352–367.

Stolorow, R., Brandchaft, B. & Atwood, G. E. (1987). *Psychoanalytic Treatment: An Intersubjective Approach*. Hillsdale, NJ: The Analytic Press.

Terman, D. (1988). Optimal frustration: Structuralization and the therapeutic process. In: *Learning from Kohut: Progr. Self Psychol., Vol. 4*, ed. A. Goldberg. Hillsdale, NJ: The Analytic Press, pp. 113–125.

Ulman, R. & Brothers, J. (1988). *The Shattered Self: A Psychoanalytic Study of Trauma*. Hillsdale, NJ: The Analytic Press.

Winnicott, D. W. (1960). *The Maturational Processes and the Facilitating Environment*. New York: International Universities Press.

Chapter 9

Detachment and continuity

The two tasks of mourning (1997)[1]

Robert Gaines

*Editor's note: Traditionally psychoanalysis has emphasized the central impor-
tance of decathexis, or detachment from the lost object. This has resulted in a
neglect of the need to accept the absence of the deceased, but at the same time preserve a sense of relationship and continuity. In this paper Robert Gaines explores
the processes behind both disengaging from the lost person and at the same time
maintaining a sense of connection in the face of loss. The importance of continuity
in the relationship with the lost person is emphasized by several of the authors in
this volume and is one of the defining claims of the New Mourning Theory.*

*This paper was published in 1997 by Robert Gaines as "Detachment and Conti-
nuity: The Two Tasks of Mourning" in* Contemporary Psychoanalysis, *Volume 33.*

In psychoanalytic theory, the essential work of mourning has been defined as
the acceptance of the irrevocability of the loss, and the progressive decathexis of
the lost object, which frees the mourner to make new relationships and find new
satisfactions. This is the detachment task of mourning. From this perspective,
pathological or incomplete mourning results from an inability to relinquish the
object, with consequent denial of the finality of the loss and unconscious fantasies
of undoing and reunion.

Emphasis on the need to detach from the lost object has obscured another aspect
of the work of mourning, which is to repair the disruption to the inner self-other
relationship caused by the actual loss. The individual needs to reconnect the severed bond, now on an exclusively internal basis, and to maintain the availability
of a sustaining inner relationship. This is the task I call "creating continuity." The
mourner is thus faced with the difficult project of simultaneously making room for
new investments while consolidating the old.

Both of these tasks of mourning have their roots in Freud's thinking. The task
of detachment is the one most often associated with Freud's (1917) work and the
one emphasized in subsequent psychoanalytic approaches.[2] As I detail later, this
is because the detachment process in mourning derives from and succinctly illustrates the basic assumptions of drive psychology. The task of creating continuity
has remained incompletely conceptualized, most likely because it draws on, and
extends aspects of, the relational point of view embedded in Freud's thinking.

In what follows, I trace the emergence of both of these aspects of the work of mourning in Freud's thinking and consider some of the reasons for the emphasis on detachment, as well as the limitations of viewing mourning only as a process of detachment. I then discuss some of the reasons why individuals need to maintain continuity with lost objects, why this need should be regarded as a task of mourning, and the ways in which detachment and maintaining continuity work together in mourning. I illustrate the task of creating continuity with a sketch of Anna Freud's mourning for her father, and conclude with some thoughts about successful mourning generated by this perspective.

Before proceeding, some terms used in the discussion should be defined and clarified. What I call creating or maintaining continuity[3] refers to those "internalizing actions," taking place after object loss occurs, that repair, modify, expand, or intensify preexisting internalizations of the lost object, so as to enable the individual to continue to experience a sense of inner connection and meaningful relation to that object, and to maintain this connection over time. It also includes such varied activities as visiting a grave, conversing with friends, donating money to an institution, or making a career change that support these internalizations. In this discussion I am following Schafer (1968) in using internalization as the most inclusive concept, referring to "all those processes by which the subject transforms real or imagined regulatory interactions with his environment, and real or imagined characteristics of his environment, into inner regulations and characteristics" (p. 9). Implied in this definition is the assumption that there are a variety of modes or processes of internalization. Each mode has its own structural and experiential characteristics. Introjection, incorporation, and identification are the most frequently discussed modes of internalization. Another mode of internalizing, not usually referred to by name, involves taking in a specific aspect or pattern of a relationship, wherein self and other are represented in interaction with each other (what Schafer calls "regulatory interaction").

Introjection and detachment and continuity in Freud's thinking

The placing of detachment from the lost object as the central task of mourning emerged in Freud's (1917) original formulation of the mourning process. As Freud depicted him, the mourner at first finds himself filled with painful thoughts of the lost person. Events, actions, and objects of all kinds evoke with pain and longing the memory of the departed. Every moment of the day brings new memories and longings, each of which must be responded to with the reminder, "this no longer exists," "this can never be again." For some time, the mourner craves the return of the lost one and tries to hold on to him or her. But gradually the longing subsides, the reality of the loss is accepted, the lost individual is decathected as a libidinal object. When the needs fulfilled by the lost person are freed and can be met by another, the mourning is complete. The mourner's problem, in this conceptualization, is essentially an economic one. His libido is bound up in a departed object.

He experiences no satisfaction and may feel quite empty. Only when his finite quantity of libidinal energy is detached from the lost object and can be invested in a new object does he recover. This brief, elegant, yet detailed statement has become one of the most familiar and influential in Freud's writings. It has been the source and foundation for all later psychoanalytic theorizing about mourning.

Nonetheless, Freud's thinking about the concepts he used in his analysis of mourning and the process of mourning itself continued to evolve. He moved beyond the exclusive focus on detachment and toward recognition of the task of continuity. This came about through his growing appreciation of the role of identification. In *Mourning and Melancholia* (1917), Freud contrasted normal mourning, where detachment takes place, with depression (melancholia), where identification with the ambivalently regarded object occurs. Later Freud realized that identification is not a pathological process, but occurs normally as a mechanism to help the child adapt to changes and losses in the relation to his parents, and is actually one of the major ways in which development occurs (Freud, 1921, 1923). Later still, Freud (1933) indicated his awareness that identification can also be part of mourning, stating, "If one has lost an object or has been obliged to give it up, one often compensates oneself by identifying oneself with it and by setting it up once more in one's ego, so that here object choice regresses, as it were, to identification" (p. 63). In contrast to the earlier formulation (1917), here Freud explicitly suggests that some new internalization of the object occurring after the loss is a frequent part of mourning.[4] Freud did not carry this line of thought further. He did not question whether identification (or some form of internalization other than identification, as is often the case) might be not only a frequent accompaniment to mourning, but also actually an invariant and necessary part of it. Rather, in all of his references to the topic, including his last major statement on mourning (1926), Freud made it clear that the function of identification, when it occurs, is to facilitate the work of detachment. Because of his commitment to the idea that the work of mourning is a process of decathexis of the object, which is such a pure and parsimonious application of his early drive theory, he did not note the seeming contradiction in the abandonment of the object being facilitated by strengthening of the inner relationship to that object.[5]

Despite this evolution of Freud's thinking, the detachment model of mourning became the centerpiece of psychoanalytic thinking about mourning. The task of detachment was used to explore mourning in childhood and adolescence (E. Furman, 1974; R. Furman, 1964, 1973; Nagera, 1970; Wolfenstein, 1966, 1969), pathological mourning (Deutsch, 1937; Volkan, 1981), and mourning as a process of adaptation[6] (Pollock, 1961, 1989). The usefulness of viewing mourning as a process of detachment stems from at least two factors. First, it is a simple but powerful fact of life that coming to terms with a loss must involve some relinquishing of hopes, dreams, and other future expectations, some acceptance of possibilities that will never be. The idea of detaching reflects this aspect of mourning. It also offers a compelling description of the individual's inner process of relinquishment: the struggle to hold on to life as it was, the step-by-step letting go of wishes and plans, and the gradual acceptance of the new reality. Second, the idea of detachment offers an explanation for the phenomenology of pathological mourning. What stands out in cases of pathological mourning is a syndrome characterized by a relatively brief or shallow period of overt grief, a conscious acceptance of the reality of the loss, and numerous behaviors, dreams, affect states, and transference reactions indicative of unconscious fantasies of undoing the death or of reunion with the lost object. Alternatively, there may be a period of intense grief and absorption with the loss, which never really ends and forever after remains an obstacle to resuming normal life. In either case, the individual in the midst of pathological mourning is unable to detach from the lost object; in fact, he is overly involved with it. This, however, is not the only possible explanation of the symptom picture. Hypercathexis of the lost object can also be a compensatory attempt to prevent a real or fantasied inability to maintain a sense of connection to the internal representation of the lost object.

Limitations of detachment and the need for continuity

While the concept of mourning as a process of detachment has proven useful, limitations appear if we attempt to account for all aspects of mourning in terms of a detachment process. In the detachment model, the mourner's problem is essentially one of distribution of libidinal energy. His libido is invested in or stuck to an object that is no longer there. But why is it so difficult to release it? Why does it usually take a long and arduous struggle to transform the relationship to the lost object? From the point of view of libido theory, it is not self-evident that this would be so. Libidinal energy is, by definition, highly displaceable. As Freud (1915) stated, in the libidinal equation of drive, aim, and object, the object is the most variable element. A healthy young woman at a party can be very attracted to one young man, but if he rebuffs her, she can easily become attracted to another. Why can't the mourner do this? The adhesiveness of the mourner to her object is not a property of the libidinal drive, but of the object tie itself.

To make the point in a different way, it can be observed that a mourner, in a lonely moment, seeks out the sexual embrace of another, responds fully in a physical sense, yet finds his inner sense of isolation and loss only briefly, if at all, assuaged. If it were otherwise, we would consider the relationship to the lost object to have been shallow, and would question the man's capacity for any meaningful relationship at all. And what of the situation of a parent–child relationship, where the elements of libidinal satisfaction are, at most, highly derivative? Epidemiological research has shown that child bereavement is even more difficult to resolve than spousal bereavement (Rubin, 1993). Today we recognize that the relation to another has many more functions, or that it needs to be considered from more points of view, than libidinal satisfaction alone. These functions evolve over the course of both child and adult development. A partial list includes allaying separation anxiety; building blocks for internalizing a stable representational world and sense of self; opportunities for actualization of identity; narcissistic affirmation and vicarious narcissistic gratification; sense of purpose in life; and transcendence of narrow self-interest. Libidinal objects can be exchanged one for another, but significant relationships, with their multiplicity of functions and their formative role in an individual's inner world, cannot be replaced. They must be maintained, and new relationships added to the old.

The limitation of viewing mourning as exclusively a process of detachment is illustrated by another important question: What is the fate of the departed object and the relationship to that object? The concept of detachment seems to imply that the libidinal investment is withdrawn from the lost object and reinvested in a new one. The old, empty relationship is now irrelevant and presumably fades away. This, of course, could not be and is not the case. The detachment-process model of mourning derives from clinical theory proposed prior to the development of the structural theory and our awareness of the role of object relations in creating and maintaining ego and superego structures. It fails, therefore, to make explicit what happens to the relationship to the lost object. For example, a bereaved child whose sense of safety in the world, whose definition of self, and whose model of his future all derive from his internalization of his relationship to his departed parent cannot detach himself from that relationship. Clearly what is required is not some simple relinquishing of the relationship, but some transformation of it, so that the inner relationship can continue to be animated without ongoing nourishment from an actual relationship. As Loewald (1962) described it, "Mourning involves not only the gradual, piecemeal relinquishment of the lost object, but also the internalization, the appropriation of aspects of this object, or rather, of aspects of the relationship between the ego and the lost object which are 'set up in the ego' and become a relationship within the ego system" (p. 500). This is what I refer to as the creation of continuity.

The need to create this kind of continuity is most obvious for children, who so clearly need their parents to fuel their rapid growth, but it is also present for adults. We are accustomed to viewing the child as needing parental objects to build and maintain inner structure, but we do not usually think of adults in this way. Adults, however, continue to use the relationship to their parents to maintain a stable inner structure as well as to modify that structure to meet evolving adaptational needs. Further, adults also use current object relationships, to spouses and children, to consolidate and maintain the various self-other representations that are the foundations of their inner world, and they rely on those relationships to add the aspects of inner structure that must accrue during the phases of adult development.

Relationships to one's parents continue to be needed and continue to evolve during adulthood, before and after their deaths. As one becomes a parent, enters middle age, faces one's own death, one continually revisits, revises, and reuses the relationships to one's parents. Increasing identification with one's parents after one becomes a parent is often observed. The need to use one's parents this way exists whether they are dead or alive. While parents are alive, this reorganization of one's perception of them and relationship to them can be assisted by new experience and by the parents' own participation in a review of the past. If the parent is dead, this reorganization of the relationship and reapplication of it to the present and future will take place largely internally (unless siblings or family friends are available to contribute to it). Some aspects of the relationship to one's parents only become relevant after they are gone. Specifically, the memory of how a parent dealt with aging and impending death can be a very important legacy for an individual. Identification with the model provided and the sense of connection and continuity with one's parents are particularly meaningful and are needed as one copes with the fears of isolation and abandonment often associated with the idea of death.

The constitutive role, vis-à-vis inner structure, of current adult relationships is less often described. It is well recognized that transferences from parental relationships can cause problems in marital relationships. It is equally true that there is a positive way in which spouses transfer parental roles onto each other, providing, at various times, basic nurturance, auxiliary ego support, and superego reinforcement previously provided by parents. The mental representation of one's spouse "takes over" for, or "blends in" with, the parental images, giving them animation that time, distance, or death has eroded. At the same time, the new qualities of the spouse add to, modify, and enrich the original internalizations of the parents.

In addition, over time, the life created together with a spouse and children comes to occupy a special place. The individual's developmental need for a sense of having lived a full, meaningful life is largely met by these experiences (Erikson, 1950). The need for this sense of a full life does not diminish, but, in fact, increases over time. The loss by death of a spouse or child threatens the stability of the inner structure built on the relationship to that individual. One cannot easily "start over." One's past connections cannot be "let go" without leaving a gaping hole in one's inner world. Some way to preserve the presence and meaning of the lost relationship, even as one attempts to find new satisfactions, is necessary.

Interestingly, although Freud's theoretical formulations did not fully integrate this aspect of mourning, his personal wisdom did. In a letter to Binswanger after the death of his son, Freud (1929) said,

> Although we know that after such a loss the acute state of mourning will subside, we also know we shall remain inconsolable and will never find a substitute. No matter what may fill the gap, even if it were filled completely, it nevertheless remains something else. And actually this is how it should be. It is the only way of perpetuating that love which we do not want to relinquish.
>
> (p. 386)

The task of creating continuity

While the process of creating continuity has been alluded to by Freud (1933), Loewald (1962, 1978), and others, the conception of creating continuity as a task in mourning has not been fully appreciated. Instead, as in Freud's letter to Binswanger, the capacity to maintain the inner sense of connection is often taken for granted. This is not so surprising, because the task of creating continuity often is carried out successfully, and sometimes silently (unconsciously). If not focused on, it can go unnoticed. Nevertheless, it is an active process, one that takes psychological work, and a successful outcome is not automatic. At every stage of life, the factors that make for difficulties in creating continuity vary, as do the resources available for the task. Three factors are discussed below to illustrate this concept, without attempting a comprehensive list.

Figuring most prominently in childhood and adolescence, but relevant in varying degrees throughout life, is the developing capacity for object constancy. The concept of libidinal object constancy, as it has come to be understood and used, tends to describe the development of this capacity as occurring earlier and more decisively than is warranted. This obscures the role of the development of object constancy as a factor in the ability to create continuity.

The arrival of libidinal object constancy, between ages two and four, is frequently treated as if it were the end point in the developmental line of object constancy rather than the beginning of the buildup of truly stable inner relations to objects which can survive frustration, absence, and death. As A. Freud (1965) emphasized, the so-called attainment of libidinal object constancy is actually more a turning point at which the child passes from predominantly need-satisfying relations to objects toward more or less constant relations in which the object can be cathected, whether or not a need is present, and whether or not the individual is being gratified by the object. She stresses that the relation is now relatively constant, but by no means totally so. During early childhood, a long absence or permanent separation can disintegrate or significantly impoverish the inner relationship to the absent object. The capacity to maintain the continuity of relationship to a dead object is quite limited.

Over the course of childhood and adolescence, the individual develops the capacity to tolerate longer and longer separations from a parental object and still maintain an active inner connection. During the second separation-individuation phase in adolescence, the individual decathects the parental objects and seeks new objects (Blos, 1967). Also part of this process is an increasing internalization of the relationship to the parents, which significantly reduces the need for the actual relationship. By the end of adolescence the individual is ready to leave the parental home and live independently without parental substitutes, while still maintaining an inner connection to the parental figures.

Wolfenstein (1966, 1969) has suggested that only after the decathexis of the parents during adolescence, which she terms "trial mourning," is the individual capable of mourning an actual loss (that is, letting go of the object as opposed to requiring a substitute replacement). It might be added that only after the degree of object constancy that follows the internalization process of adolescence has been achieved does the individual begin to be able to maintain the continuity necessary to cope adaptively with loss.

However, the end of adolescence does not achieve the full development of the capacity for object constancy. During the gradual growth of object constancy in childhood and adolescence the parents are always there. After a young person leaves home, the actual contact usually does not cease; it only becomes less frequent. Even for the person who has fully completed the separation-individuation process of adolescence, further developmental adjustments to increasing separation from, and decreasing reliance on, the parents lie ahead. In progressing along this developmental line, the individual becomes increasingly better prepared to cope with permanent loss by death, which always presents a further challenge to the capacity for object constancy. This sense of object constancy as a mode of relating, which can and must continue to evolve throughout the life cycle, parallels a similar point of view developed by Solnit (1982).

Another factor affecting the individual's ability to maintain continuity is conflict. It has been frequently noted that the aggressive component of an intensely ambivalent relationship complicates mourning. The loss is experienced unconsciously as the result of death wishes toward the individual. This creates unbearable guilt or fear of retaliation, and so the reality of the loss is denied. This dynamic also disrupts continuity. Denial of the reality of the loss places the lost object in a psychological limbo, which prevents maintaining a meaningful connection.

Conflict over aggression has seemed most central to mourning because the detachment process involves, in a sense, a "psychological killing," or putting in the grave, of the lost object (Volkan, 1981). From the point of view of creating continuity, however, which is a psychological reanimation of the lost object relationship, a variety of conflicts are relevant. In fact, any conflictual element in relation to the lost object that has been dealt with by maintaining distance, distrust, and resentment will interfere with mobilizing the positive elements of the relationship that can be used to maintain continuity.

A very different set of factors involved in the creation of continuity has to do with the individual's family and social network. The creation and maintenance of continuity is not easily carried out alone. For many people it is difficult to maintain the internal image without the opportunity to express it aloud and share it with others. Partly, this has to do with the role of language in preserving memory. Both the expression of feelings and images in words and the repetition and sharing of those narratives with others are known to enhance memory. Also, the very act of communicating one's experience of a lost relationship has the effect of "bringing it alive" that is different from inner contemplation. Further, other people's appreciation of the lost object validates and enriches the solitary mourner's inner image. Other's observations about the mourner's relationship to the lost object can add to an understanding of what the relationship consisted of, what it meant for the individual, and how it is relevant to his life now and in the future. The availability of other people with whom to share the connection to the lost object helps mourners to bring the relationship into the present context, making it part of their shared ongoing lives. In a very important way, inner construction of objects draws on shared social construction of those objects (Silverman, Nickman & Worden, 1992).

Individuals who have suffered a loss often feel as though they must choose between maintaining a connection to the lost object and moving forward. Although this is an inevitable inner struggle, the actual interpersonal context sometimes exacerbates the problem. For example an adult who has lost a spouse may find a potential new mate who is unable to tolerate any connection to the former spouse; or a child who has lost a parent may face a remarriage wherein one or both parents cannot bear any continued loyalty to the departed spouse. These sorts of situations complicate the individual's mourning process and increase the difficulty of maintaining continuity.

The relationship of detachment and continuity

Before considering the relationship between the tasks of detachment and continuity, the differences between maintaining continuity and the refusal to detach from the object, as seen in pathological mourning, must be clarified. Clinically, the distinction must be made carefully, and requires not just external observation, but access to fantasies and feelings, as well as a sense of the individual's movement over time. Conceptually, the difference can be clearly stated. Creation of continuity refers to all those processes, conscious or unconscious, that affirm the emotional connection to an object explicitly recognized as gone. On the other hand, fantasies of reunion, of undoing the death, or of an ongoing relationship in some magical, timeless place are part of denial operations, not part of creating continuity. Besides the distortion of reality they entail, such fantasies implement a kind of fixation in time. This may manifest itself in the fear that moving forward in life or making decisions will provoke loss, in waiting for things to happen instead of pursuing them, in setting up situations to pursue contemporary "lost objects" who are displaced versions of the original one, in yearning for an idealized time in one's past, and so on. These patterns oppose the carrying forward into the present and future, which characterizes the maintaining of continuity. In creating continuity, a link is made between the past and present; the ongoing connection is used to support new investments or to expand or enrich the self. Thinking through a problem the way one's parent used to, adapting a departed spouse's approach to resolving interpersonal conflict, and devoting time to a charity that fights a disease one's child died of are examples of processes that create continuity. Creation of continuity has a bittersweet quality. It is always simultaneously a balm for and a reminder of the pain of the loss. Creation of continuity and detachment are both processes that oppose denial and wishful clinging to the object. In fact, they work together in a dynamic relationship.

The feelings associated with the loss and the prospect of life without the lost object are extraordinarily painful and threatening. At first there is little in the way of solace, of a "silver lining," or a lesson to be learned that we often look for to ease a painful situation. The creation of continuity comes into play as just such an inducement to accept reality, a softening of the pain of letting go. The individual makes a trade-off in psychic reality, letting go of the actual relationship but holding on to, perhaps intensifying or making new use of, the inner relationship. The implicit thoughts follow such lines as "although my mother is gone, I can still fulfill her dream that I become . . ." or "even though my husband is gone, I will always cherish the memories of our years together." This is, I believe, what Freud (1933) was referring to when he spoke of using identification to compensate oneself after a loss.

The dynamic relationship between creating continuity and detaching has another important aspect. Loss forces the individual into a painfully passive position. In losing a loved one we are impinged on by an event the outcome of which we cannot influence or alter. The processes of "letting go" and "saying good-bye," which are part of detaching, may be necessary for making room for new possibilities, but they do little to relieve this painfully passive position. They are part of reality that we are forced to accept. Creation of continuity, on the other hand, is experienced as the individual reasserting himself as the active agent, making commitments and planning for the future. It is part of a process of ego remobilization. While creation of continuity may contain an illusion of power to defy fate and time, it is just the kind of illusion, created in play or "transitional space," that Winnicott (1971) identified as being at the root of creativity and the sense of personal initiative. The individual cannot recover from a loss until he can reestablish some sense of active determination and control in the very area where the loss has deprived him of all control.

Anna Freud: An illustration of continuity in mourning

The life of Anna Freud provides an excellent example of the role of creating continuity in mourning. The special circumstances of her life, including the thorough interweaving of her personal and professional lives, the availability of published biographical material, and the fruits of her capacity for self-observation and self-analysis (which, at times, focused directly on conflicts surrounding the struggle to maintain continuity), provide an unusual window into the inner workings of this process. Her life and her coming to terms with her father's death illustrate the need for continuity, the challenge an individual faces in creating continuity, and the ways that the creation of continuity assists the mourning process.[7]

To evoke the need for continuity that Anna Freud felt after the loss of her father, it is necessary to sketch in certain aspects of her character development and her relationship with her father. She was the youngest of six siblings. She did not have a close relationship with her mother, who favored her sister Sophie, two years older. This gap was partially filled by a very close relationship with her governess, and by the special fondness her father had for his spunky, mischievous daughter, who he nicknamed "Black Devil." From her earliest years, Anna Freud was plagued by bitter sibling rivalry with Sophie, as well as by very painful feelings of being left out or left behind by the group of older siblings. This matrix of relationships and feelings fueled a very intense oedipal period. Anna was strongly drawn to her father, with very little balancing by way of attraction to her mother. Being close to her father and winning his love were ways to assuage the accumulated hurts and disappointments. Anna resolved this potentially intractable oedipal situation with a compromise solution that might have been a recipe for disaster for someone else, but for her, with her particular gifts and temperament, became the foundation for an unusually creative and productive life. In this compromise, Anna did not follow the typical oedipal pattern of relinquishing wishes for the father and identifying with mother. Instead, she held onto her wishes for a special relationship with her father, but apparently repressed all the sexual components of these wishes. Later in life, this compromise formation was buttressed by renouncing her self-interest in her tie to her father and substituting a selfless devotion to his physical welfare and to his life goal, the advancement of psychoanalysis (this is the defense of altruistic surrender, which she introduced into the psychoanalytic literature; A. Freud, 1936).

Also supporting this unusual compromise was a strong identification with her father. She could replace the more oedipal tinged wish to have her father with the more acceptable one of wanting to be like him. Equipped with her special talents, this goal was actually attainable, and its achievement softened the inevitable disappointments associated with the wish to have her father to herself. This compromise formation, while certainly subject to many strains, was a workable one for her. On the negative side, she retained a strong masculine identification and never developed certain aspects of her femininity, including being a mother. The data on her sexuality is limited. From what is available, it appears her sexuality was significantly inhibited. The plus side of her development, however, clearly outweighs the negative. She established and maintained an intimate relationship with her life companion, Dorothy Burlingham; she was a generous and engaged friend to many people; she took on a leadership role within her extended family; and she took care of her father, easing his suffering and prolonging his productive time, right up to his last day. Her accomplishments in her work (her father's work, too) were, of course, of truly legendary proportions. Throughout her life, her tie to and identification with her father and his cause were always at the center of her existence.

At the time of her father's death in 1939, Anna Freud was forty-four. She had already begun her relationship with Dorothy Burlingham. Psychoanalysis and her father, however, were the main focus of her life. She had been for some years a training analyst, a leading psychoanalytic educator, a leader of the international psychoanalytic movement, and a major theoretical contributor to psychoanalytic thinking. She was in daily contact with her father, both as intellectual and work companion and as the chief organizer and major provider of the nursing care his illness required. In short, her life revolved around her actual interaction with her father and her involvement in her father's work, which had become, in a thoroughly integrated way, her own work.

As might be expected, Anna Freud's mourning for her father took time and effort. Despite her close relationship to him and the thorough integration of that relationship into her life, the achievement of a sense of continuity after he was gone did not come easily or automatically.

Her early reactions to her father's death showed some warning signs that difficulty in mourning might lie ahead. Her overt grief reaction was somewhat attenuated, and she returned to seeing patients five days after the death. This was consistent with her character style of constricting the display of intense emotions, and also with her (and her father's) commitment to never giving in to adversity. But it also seems to reflect an underlying fantasy that life could go on as if nothing had happened, as if he were not gone. She was quite angry with her father's British doctors and expressed the feeling that if his German surgeon, Doctor Pichler, had been available, he would not have died. This conscious idea that her father should not be dead seems to have derived from an unconscious one that he was not "really" gone yet. Almost immediately after Freud's death, she began collecting all of his correspondence from friends and colleagues. This large, time-consuming task, while of enormous historical importance, also served to keep her immersed in his presence and implemented the fantasy of somehow defying death and holding on to him.

As time went on, she threw herself, as usual, into her work and into helping others. She maintained a busy analytic practice and was a financial resource for her extended family. She and Dorothy Burlingham opened and operated the Hampstead War Nursery. This was a huge undertaking and a tremendous service to the children of her new country. However, some of the old enthusiasm was missing. A few months after her father's death, she told Dorothy Burlingham that she was feeling detached, that her life felt like a place she was only visiting. Similar feelings continued to plague her beyond this initial mourning period.

In time, these troubling feelings led her to begin working, theoretically and self-analytically, on the problem of mourning. Her first notes for her paper "About Losing and Being Lost" (first written as a complete draft in 1948, delivered as a lecture in 1953, and finally published in 1967) date from this 1942 period of self-reflection. The paper is based largely on her experience and makes direct, though unacknowledged, reference to her own dream material (Young-Bruehl, 1988). This dream material is recorded in her 1942 notes. It centers on a recurring dream theme in which her father returns. He is wandering the landscape, lost and lonely. He reproaches her for neglecting him and implores her to come to him. She is overjoyed to see him, though feels guilty for having been avoiding him. Sometimes there is a tender reunion, which also feels like a failure to maintain a necessary renunciation, but sometimes there is not.

Anna Freud's notes of this time do not indicate her understanding of her dreams and her mourning experience. Evidently she did not make much progress in resolving her issues at this time. We know that the recurring dream reappeared in her life a few years later. The very title, "About Losing and Being Lost," already conceived at this time, however, seems to refer, in her poetic, allusive style, to several ideas. One is the painful experience of her father as a "lost soul." Another is that she has "lost" her father. This second implication of the word "lost" is that through some unconscious action of her own, she has let him slip away. A third is that she herself now feels "lost." These ideas were not developed systematically, and her work on these ideas and her own mourning were pushed into the background by the nearly round-the-clock, seven-days-a-week effort to run the Hampstead Nursery and maintain her practice.

In 1946, after the frightening and exhausting war years, Anna Freud was bed-ridden for a couple of months with pneumonia. She had suffered losses of friends and relatives, and she was also concerned with the large number of psychoanalysts killed by the Nazis. While ill, she was again preoccupied with images of her father as a "lost soul" and with thoughts of her father's suffering at the end of his life. During this time, the dreams of his return recurred, and her self-analysis of her mourning experience was resumed.

The insights she developed during this second period of self-analysis became the basis of "About Losing and Being Lost," although, as I explain later, that paper does not contain all of her thoughts about mourning. Her observations about mourning became organized around the concept of identification. Her analysis of her recurring dream was that she had projected her own feelings of loss and abandonment onto the image of her father and then identified with them through him. The result of this was her preoccupation with his suffering and with the damaged state of psychoanalysis. The representation in the dream of Freud as a "lost soul" reflected her feeling that way, and his wish for her to come to him was her own wish for him to return to her.

In her paper, she emphasized two aspects of this process. First, a person who has suffered a loss sometimes will defend against the experience of his or her own feelings, attributing them to the lost object who is experienced as a forlorn, rejected ghost. Second, the loser's feelings of abandonment in reaction to the current loss reflect earlier feelings of rejection and neglect. In Anna Freud's case, they reflected the rejection she felt from her older siblings and from her father's commitments to her rivals, her mother and Aunt Minna. The realization that her current feelings were a new version of an old problem (one she had become aware of during her misguided attempt at analysis with her father) helped her get a better grip on them.

Anna Freud's paper does not contain a final insight, which proved extremely helpful in resolving a central conflict in her mourning, and which relates directly to the issue of continuity. After her father's death, she felt trapped between two dangerous alternatives. If she moved forward with her life, she would "lose" her father. If she clung to him, or wished to join him, she was renouncing her own life. For example, during the 1946 period she dreamed she married a young doctor, and then discovered her father and mother had disappeared in Paris. She searched for them and her mother was found, but not her father. Her insight was to realize it did not have to be an either–or choice; she could find a way to bring her relationship with her father forward. She could not bring back the past, but she could use it to animate and guide her present and future.

Anna Freud's relationship to her father's ideas added another layer to this conflict, and influenced the way she expressed her own ideas. Her father, and other analysts following him, had emphasized the task of detachment in mourning. However, her own thinking was leading her in the direction of the importance of identification and the task of maintaining continuity. To be loyal to her father, she would have to give him up. To give him up would be to betray her insight, forego her personal solution. The only path was a compromise. Publicly, she stayed close to her father's thinking. Thus, even though her paper is focused on the problem of losing and the role of identification in dealing with loss, she stops short of making explicit the positive role of identification in resolving mourning. In fact, she concludes her paper by saying that the "lost soul" of the mourner's dream can only find its eternal rest after the mourner has "performed the difficult task of dealing with . . . bereavement and of detaching . . . hopes, demands, and expectations from the image of the dead" (A. Freud, 1967, p. 19).

Privately, however, she took her thoughts on identification further and extended them to include the contribution identification makes to resolve mourning. She expressed these thoughts some years later in a letter to Ralph Greenson, following the death of his analyst and friend Max Schur. She said, "I agree that mourning is a terrible task, surely the most difficult of all. And it is only made bearable by the moments, which you describe so well, when one feels fleetingly that the lost person has entered into one and that there is a gain somewhere which denies death" (Young-Bruehl, 1988, p. 314). Earlier she had written to Anna Kris Wolff, after the death of her father Ernst Kris, "As you know, I am an expert in 'good fathers,' and even in losing a good father. The saving thing is that one never really loses them in spirit if they have been good enough. And anyway, one has something to live up to" (Young-Bruehl, 1988, p. 369). In these remarks, Anna Freud is describing explicitly the role of creating continuity in resolving mourning.

To recap, I have described how Anna Freud found herself, during a period of illness in the winter of 1946–47, once again preoccupied by thoughts of her father, his illness, his death, and his status as a "lost soul." She realized that this was an indication of incomplete mourning and attempted to work self-analytically and theoretically on the issue of mourning. She struggled with the tension she felt between the conventional wisdom that mourning involves a process of detachment and her own sense of needing some connection to her father. During this period of self-analysis, and afterward, she came to better grips with her mourning by permitting her identification with her father to sustain her and to evolve in its own way. Following this there was, as there often is when obstacles to mourning tasks have been overcome, a great release of creative energy. She entered a period of intense writing activity. There was also a renewed enthusiasm for the future, and she began the time-consuming process of creating the Hampstead Nursery and Training Center.

In a pattern that is characteristic of creating continuity, we can observe that Anna Freud did not "live in the past." She did not try to re-create life as it was when her father was alive. Rather, she used his outlook, his values, and his hopes for the future to inspire and guide her, and as a foundation for her own continued development and creative contribution. While she was vigilantly protective of her father's public image and intellectual heritage, her own work was forward looking. In the decades after her father's death she embraced Hartmann's (1939) suggestion that psychoanalysis needed to become a more general psychology, and that to do so, it needed to incorporate the study of normal development. This was a major reorientation of psychoanalytic thought. Similarly, her belief that psychoanalysis had to incorporate the data of direct observation along with reconstructions from adult analyses was highly innovative. She was also animated, during the years after her father's death, by his values and standards (Coles, 1992). The Hampstead Clinic's unwavering commitment to helping the underprivileged and severely disabled actualized a belief that psychoanalysis should be used for the betterment of society, and its contributions be extended to as many needy individuals as possible, a belief that she and her father had shared, but that he never had the opportunity to implement in a direct way. Finally, it should be noted, after her father's death she increasingly became a leader in her own right. Fairly late in life she overcame her shyness and dislike of travel to become the preeminent public spokesperson for organized psychoanalysis. At the same time, she battled with the psychoanalytic establishment over issues that were important to her, such as the value of child analytic training and the training of nonmedical analysts.

Continuity and successful mourning

What is the optimal outcome of mourning? Mourning is sometimes referred to as being "finished" or "completed." These terms have more relevance to the task of detaching a lost object and reinvesting in a new object. That sort of task can, perhaps, meaningfully be considered to be finished when the transfer of libidinal investment has occurred. Even in that situation, the possibility of reverting back to the old attachment at a time of frustration or disappointment with the new object is never entirely eliminated. From the point of view of maintaining continuity (that is, adaptation to the inner loss), however, mourning clearly does not end. One continues the psychic work of maintaining the continuity forever. As one goes along, this may be done with less pain, strain, or conscious effort, and with a differing mixture of accompanying affects. At other times, developmental changes may require reactivation of the process. For example, a single woman of twenty-five with a conflictual relationship to her mother may mourn that mother's death adequately by maintaining a loose identification with her mother's career aspirations for her and entering into a new relationship with a female work mentor. If she later marries and has a child, she may feel a need for a deeper connection to her mother, and struggle to find the continuity she needs. Consciously or unconsciously, she will review her relationship to her mother, perhaps now with more tolerance of her mother's faults, and find aspects of her mother's mothering that she can identify with and use.

From this point of view, mourning is not something that can be finished. Rather, it is a process that is carried on continuously, at times nearly quiescently, and then, at times of change or developmental progression, it is reintensified as one again confronts the sadness of one's loss and experiences in a new way the need for a sense of continuity and connection with one's departed objects.

This conceptualization of mourning allows for a more flexible, individualistic evaluation of how well or poorly someone is mourning. All mourners are not expected to fit the linear model of loss, acute grief, detachment, and reinvestment.

It is expected that periods of grief and feelings of emptiness or abandonment will recur episodically and need to be worked through. It is expected that investment in new objects will occur in varying degrees and that continued emotional involvement with the departed will also continue in variable manifestations and degrees of conscious awareness.

Summary

The idea that the major task of mourning is detachment from the lost object has been examined critically. Mourning is more accurately conceived of as involving both processes of "letting go" and of "holding on." Loss of an object threatens inner object ties and identifications, which are the basis of a secure inner world and a sense of security in the world. Mastery of this threat is achieved through the process I have termed the creation of continuity. Creation of continuity is distinguished from the various forms of denial of loss by the fact that in creating continuity there is always explicit, even if unconscious, recognition that the object is gone. Creation of continuity always has a bittersweet quality, but, in tandem with the process of detachment, it helps the mourner move forward in life.

The process of creating continuity is often carried out smoothly and without conscious awareness, but it does require psychological work. At other times a person may suffer feelings or symptoms that reflect a failure to maintain continuity, and this can seriously complicate mourning. Awareness of the task of creating continuity and its possible derailment can be helpful in treating complicated mourning. For instance an overemphasis on conflicts around the need to detach can exacerbate mourning complications that derive from difficulty maintaining continuity. The perspective on mourning that develops from consideration of the task of creating continuity also heightens awareness that mourning is not something accomplished in one period of time and then left behind. While the acute phase of grief comes to an end, the challenge of coping with a loss continues throughout the lifespan.

Notes

1 I would like to express my appreciation to Robin Gaines, M.S.W., Jonathan Cohen, Ph.D., Benjamin Lapkin, Ph.D., Raul Ludmer, M.D., Pasqual Pantone, Ph.D., Donnel Stern, Ph.D., and Ronald Taffel, Ph.D. for their encouraging and thoughtful responses to earlier versions of this article.
2 As Stroebe, Gergen, Gergen, and Stroebe (1992) note, this emphasis has permeated the broader field of psychological approaches to grief, as well as the popular culture. So-called grief therapy centers on a sequence of detachment, emancipation, and finding a new object. Self-help books such as Judith Viorst's *Necessary Losses* (1986) emphasize the same theme. Stroebe et al. make the additional point that models of normal mourning are much more culture-bound than we realize. They contrast our contemporary Western emphasis on detaching, which they refer to as "severed bonds," with the Victorian emphasis on maintaining a connection to the dead, which they refer to as "broken hearts."

3   Throughout I will be using these phrases interchangeably; maintaining continuity is, per-
    haps, more precise, whereas creating continuity is more evocative, capturing more of the
    idea that after loss, something new must be added or must be done to hold on to the sense of
    inner connection and move forward with it into the future. Incorporation is a mode of inter-
    nalizing that is heavily influenced by primary-process thinking (being based on fantasies
    of literally having a person inside oneself), and thus lend themselves more to denial of the
    reality of a loss. Higher order identifications and internalization of regulatory interactions,
    in both of which the recognition of the realistic and separate existence of the object play a
    dominant role, are the modes of internalizing that support maintenance of continuity.
4   Actually, credit for the first clear statement of this observation should go to Abraham
    (1924), who stated, "introjection occurs in mourning in the healthy person and the neu-
    rotic, no less than in the melancholic . . . its main purpose is to preserve the person's
    relations to the dead object" (p. 353).
5   Throughout his discussions of identification, Freud (1921, 1933, 1940) consistently
    makes a distinction between identification and object choice. Identification expresses
    the wish to be like someone, object choice (or object tie) the wish to have someone.
    Identification is an attachment, perhaps a narcissistic attachment, as contrasted with
    object choice, which is a libidinal investment. It is within the context of this distinction
    that identification can be understood as replacing a lost object. From a contemporary
    point of view, this distinction does not hold up. Wanting to be like and wanting to have
    are both instances of personal activity in relation to an object. Both are wishes that
    express and implement a relationship. They are not mutually exclusive, and can coexist
    with various other wishes and fantasies in constituting a relationship.
6   In almost a mirror image of Freud's thinking on mourning, we note in the work of later
    psychoanalytic theorists of mourning that they also recognize that internalization can
    accompany mourning, but they do not integrate this into their conceptualizations of the
    mourning process. For instance, Pollock (1961) describes, very briefly, identifications
    occurring after mourning is completed. Wolfenstein (1969) describes an unusual case of
    relatively successful mourning occurring in a child, which is assisted by the exceptional
    presence of a strong identification with the departed parent. E. Furman (1974) observed
    that identification often occurs in mourning and functions to facilitate the essential pro-
    cess of decathexis. This is the closest approximation to the view being developed here.
    However, it makes internalization an aspect of mourning subsidiary to the main task
    of detachment, and does not recognize that internalization, via identification or other
    means, is a task that is not always accomplished.
7   The biographical material in this section is drawn from *Anna Freud: A Biography*
    (Young-Bruehl, 1988). Separate citations are only made for quotations or references to
    published material.

References

Abraham, K. (1924). A short study of the development of the libido, viewed in the light of
    mental disorder. In: *Selected Papers of Karl Abraham M. D.*, tr. D. Bryan & A. Strachey.
    New York: Basic Books, 1968, pp. 418–501.
Blos, P. (1967). The second individuation process of adolescence. *Psychoanal. Study Child*,
    22: 162–186.
Coles, R. (1992). *Anna Freud: The dream of psychoanalysis*. New York: Addison-Wesley.
Deutsch, H. (1937). Absence of grief. *Psychoanal. Q.*, 6: 12–22.
Erikson, E. (1950). *Childhood and society*. New York: W. W. Norton.
Freud, A. (1936). *The ego and the mechanisms of defense*. Norton: New York.
Freud, A. (1965). *Normality and pathology in childhood*. New York: International Univer-
    sities Press.

Freud, A. (1967). About losing and being lost. *Psychoanal. Study Child*, 22: 9–19.

Freud, S. (1915). Instincts and their vicissitudes. *Standard Edition, Vol. 14*, pp. 109–140.

Freud, S. (1917). Mourning and melancholia. *Standard Edition, Vol. 14*, pp. 237–258.

Freud, S. (1921). Group psychology and the analysis of the ego. *Standard Edition, Vol. 18*, pp. 65–143.

Freud, S. (1923). The ego and the id. *Standard Edition, Vol. 19*, pp. 1–66.

Freud, S. (1926). Inhibitions, symptoms and anxiety. *Standard Edition, Vol. 20*, pp. 75–174.

Freud, S. (1929). Letter to Binswanger. In: *The Letters of Sigmund Freud*, ed. E. L. Freud. New York: Basic Books, 1960.

Freud, S. (1933). New introductory lectures in psychoanalysis. *Standard Edition, Vol. 22*, pp. 1–182.

Freud, S. (1940). An outline of psychoanalysis. *Standard Edition, Vol. 23*, pp. 141–207.

Furman, E. (1974). *A child's parent dies: Studies in childhood bereavement*. New Haven: Yale University Press.

Furman, R. (1964). Death of a six-year-old's mother during his analysis. *Psychoanal. Study Child*, 19: 377–397.

Furman, R. (1973). A child's capacity for mourning. In: *The Child in His Family: Impact of Disease and Death*, eds. E. J. Anthony & C. Koupernik. New York: Wiley, pp. 225–231.

Hartmann, H. (1939). *Ego psychology and the problem of adaptation*. New York: International Universities Press.

Loewald, H. (1962). Internalization, separation, mourning, and the superego. *Psychoanal. Q.*, 31: 483–504.

Loewald, H. (1978). Termination analyzable and unanalyzable. *Psychoanal. Study Child*, 43: 155–166.

Nagera, H. (1970). Children's reactions to the death of important objects: A developmental approach. *Psychoanalytic Study of the Child*, 25: 360–400.

Pollock, G. H. (1961). Mourning and adaptation. *Int. J. Psychoanal.*, 42: 341–361.

Pollock, G. H. (1989). *The mourning-liberation process. 2 vols*. New York: International Universities Press.

Rubin, S. (1993). The death of a child is forever: The life course impact of child loss. In: *Handbook of Bereavement*, eds. M. S. Stroebe, W. Stroebe & R. O. Hansson. Cambridge: Cambridge University Press, pp. 285–299.

Schafer, R. (1968). *Aspects of internalization*. New York: International Universities Press.

Silverman, P. R., Nickman, S. & Worden, J. W. (1992). Detachment revisited: The child's reconstruction of a dead parent. *American Journal of Orthopsychiatry*, 62: 494–503.

Solnit, A. J. (1982). Developmental perspectives on self and object constancy. *Psychoanal. Study Child*, 37: 201–220.

Stroebe, M., Gergen, M. M., Gergen, K. J. & Stroebe, W. (1992). Broken hearts or broken bonds: Love and death in historical perspective. *American Psychologist*, 47: 1205–1212.

Viorst, J. (1986). *Necessary losses: The loves, illusions, dependencies, and impossible expectations that all of us have to give up in order to grow*. London: Simon & Schuster.

Volkan, V. (1981). *Linking objects and linking phenomena*. New York: International Universities Press.

Winnicott, D. W. (1971). *Playing and reality*. New York: Tavistock.

Wolfenstein, M. (1966). How is mourning possible? *Psychoanal. Study Child*, 21: 93–123.

Wolfenstein, M. (1969). Loss, rage, and repetition. *Psychoanal. Study Child*, 24: 432–446.

Young-Bruehl, E. (1988). *Anna Freud: A biography*. New York: Summit Books.

Chapter 10

Some observations of the mourning process (2010)

Otto Kernberg

Editor's note: In this essay Dr. Kernberg reports on and discusses the results of an investigation he conducted with bereaved colleagues. Augmenting his findings from his clinical psychoanalytic practice he proposes some modifications to the traditional analytic understanding of bereavement and mourning. Most importantly, he argues that the impact of bereavement and the unfolding of the mourning process may in fact be ongoing and even lifelong as the internalization processes of the bereaved leads to permanent structural changes in the superego. He shows that these changes are not for the purpose of decathexis and relinquishment; rather they establish a permanent psychological connection to the deceased person. As Dr. Kernberg states in his final paragraph, "We may now conclude that identification is a complex process that includes, at least, the internalization of a relationship with the significant other, the modification of the self-representation as influenced by the object representation, and the maintenance of that internalized object relation."

This paper was published in 2010 by Otto Kernberg as "Some Observations on the Process of Mourning" in the International Journal of Psychoanalysis, *Volume 91.*

Author summary: The main proposal of this paper is that normal mourning is not completed after six months to a year or two as suggested in earlier literature, but may bring about a permanent alteration of psychological structures that affect various aspects of the mourning persons' lives. These structural consequences of mourning consist in the setting up of a persistent internalized object relationship with the lost object that affects ego and superego functions. The persistent internalized object relationship develops in parallel to the identification with the lost object, and the superego modification includes the internalization of the value systems and life project of the lost object. A new dimension of spiritual orientation, the search for transcendental value systems, is one consequence of this superego modification.

Background

The origin of this paper was a personal, painful, extended experience of mourning that gradually raised serious questions in my mind about some generally assumed characteristics of grief and mourning. Is it really a time-limited experience that is completed with a process of identification with a lost object (Freud, 1917)? Is the work of mourning completed with a reworking of the depressive position and the reinstatement of the good internal object, as well as with the process of identification mentioned before? What is involved in the processes of reparation that are so central in the mourning process (Klein, 1940)? Are there aspects of mourning that have not been given sufficient attention in our understanding of the experience? I have tentatively reached the conclusion that perhaps mourning processes do not simply end, but, rather, evolve into more lasting or permanent aspects of psychic structures that have not been explicated fully in the corresponding literature.

In light of these questions, I reviewed my past analytic experiences, particularly the treatment of patients who had undergone significant mourning processes in the course of their analysis. My attention was drawn particularly to a patient who, after many years of a happy marriage, had lost his spouse as a consequence of an automobile accident. His analysis, originally started because of his severe obsessive-compulsive personality features, became marked by a mourning process that overshadowed the last four years of his treatment. Although this analysis took place a number of years ago, I had, at the time, recorded very detailed process notes of sessions, and the abundance of the material of that case permitted me to review that analysis, under the impact, it must be said, of my own mourning experience, the loss of my spouse.

In what follows, I shall briefly describe the relevant developments in the treatment of this patient, including my interpretive approach then, and point to issues that now draw my attention and that I would now see as more important and requiring a broader frame for their understanding than what determined my interventions at that time. I shall then explore certain mourning experiences in a sample of persons who had undergone severe mournings, and where, I believe, new evidence emerged regarding the viewpoints I developed in the course of these explorations.

A mourning process triggered during an analysis

The patient was a 51-year-old man who had started analysis three years earlier because of a rigid, obsessive-compulsive personality structure that had caused serious problems for him in his business relations with colleagues, superiors and subordinates, and had gradually improved throughout his analysis. He was the son of a domineering, successful businessman, whose rage attacks had successfully controlled his wife and children. The patient had a submissive and fearful attitude toward his father that, in the course of the years, had gradually shifted into an open rebelliousness. It was the anxiety he experienced when confronted with what he interpreted as the authoritarian attitudes of his business superiors that had originally brought my patient into treatment. My patient's mother was a woman who, while being submissive to her husband, was rather indulgent with their children – three daughters and one son, the patient – and in chronic conflict with her husband around the degree to which she supposedly failed to discipline them. The mother was also withdrawn and somewhat aloof, and, other than the general submissive attitude toward the father expected from them, the children were left to themselves much of the time. Only when my patient was ill would his mother be concerned about him, as she was, apparently, quite hypochondriacal about any physical symptoms affecting herself or the children. She also had a closer relation to her daughters – the patient was the youngest in the family, and during the treatment it emerged that he felt quite lonely and isolated in what he perceived was mostly a 'women's home'.

The patient had been married for 28 years, and, while he felt that he loved his wife deeply, they had frequent conflicts around his obsessive insistence on rigid schedules and plans, and his over-involvement in his work, as she saw it. She complained that he did not really seem interested in her life, while he felt that she was chronically attempting to make him feel guilty. Yet, all in all, they both felt assured of their mutual love and, throughout the years, their relationship had remarkably deepened and was furthered along during the treatment.

At the time of the treatment to be examined, the patient's obsessive concern with time, precision, and placement of objects and the inhibition in his work had significantly improved. At this point, however, after their son and their daughter had left home to pursue their lives in other cities in connection with their respective professions, his wife died because of the consequences of a severe automobile accident. Now the analysis shifted radically into the analytic work with his mourning process.

He experienced a severe depression of several months that gradually evolved into what might be described as more normal grief that, however, persisted throughout the next three years of treatment. In my view at that time, it was not yet completely resolved by the time we jointly decided that it was reasonable to end his analysis. During the sessions, he still expressed intense guilt feelings for not having paid sufficient attention to his wife's needs. He remembered, again and again, the many circumstances in which she had been expressing her love and he had been taking it for granted, and he spent endless hours in internal dialogues with her and with intense grief over her loss. He repeatedly went through her belongings, letters and photographs, and over a period of months sought out the priest of his church for spiritual consolation. He struggled with persistent, repetitive feelings that his wife must still, somehow, exist in outer reality, and became concerned with the question of life after death. He had not been active in the church, but now experienced a deep sense of longing for faith in the possibility of an eventual reunion of his and his wife's souls.

This patient had presented much more limited periods of mourning after the death of both his parents, which occurred during the early years of his marriage, and his present mourning experience brought to the surface the incomplete mourning of these earlier losses, particularly the death of his mother. I interpreted his present, deep and protracted mourning reaction over many months. This work focused on his inordinate feelings of guilt and his desperate wish for an opportunity to redeem himself, both regarding his wife and in connection with old conflicts with his mother, the sense of chronic loneliness in his early childhood, and the repression of his anger for what he experienced as his mother's preference for his sisters. A reworking of the mourning over the death of his mother became part of the present analytic work. However, the patient persisted in the elaboration of an internal relationship with his wife over the entire four-year period of the analysis that followed her death, without showing, after approximately two years, any sign of a depression or even of a mourning reaction as far as his daily life was concerned. However, in his fantasy life, both during and outside our sessions, he continued an intense dialogue with her. He felt that he owed it to her to dedicate whatever was left of his life to repair and compensate for the limitations of his expression of his love for her while they lived their life together. This moral obligation, as he experienced it, became a source of consolation: he felt it was a way to enrich his life and to maintain contact with his wife.

In the last year before the end of his analysis, he established a new relationship with a woman from the same cultural background as his dead wife. He fell in love with her and this relationship culminated in their marriage a few months before the termination of his analysis. He loved his new wife, but this new relationship consistently reactivated memories of his first marriage, with a pressing urge to modify and correct the limitations that he now felt he had evinced with his first wife, in a wish to change and repair old problematic behavior in the new relationship.

At the time of the termination of his analysis, I wondered whether I had been missing the analysis in sufficient depth of unconscious guilt and aggression regarding his own mother. While the patient seemed to be functioning well in his life with his new wife, and had changed significantly in his relationships at work and in his social life, I felt puzzled about what seemed like the relentless presence of his first wife and her impressive influence on his present life. It was as if the mourning process had evolved into significant characterological changes, as well as the maintenance of an internal relationship with his wife, rather than being completed, after a reasonable time, by a process of identification and 'letting go'.

Now, retrospectively, after a deep personal mourning experience, and the review of other cases with similar experiences to those I had with this patient, and the exploratory interviewing of a selected number of persons who had experienced a loss of a spouse after many years of a happy relationship, I would approach the final stages of this analysis somewhat differently. While retracing the present mourning process to its antecedents in the patient's infantile development – and, eventually, his reaction to the forthcoming end of the analysis, I think now I would be more attentive to the ongoing mourning process related to the loss of his wife, his ongoing internal relationship with her, and the influence of this relationship on the restructuring of his superego. At the same time, I would be more attentive to the transference function of reinstating and maintaining that internalized relationship with her, while bringing it to life in the relation with the analyst. This double function of the mourning process – superego restructuring and maintaining the relationship – I now believe, deserves further exploration.

I am tentatively suggesting some new ways of conceptualizing the psycho-dynamics of normal mourning. Regarding the utilization of diagnostic interviews of persons whom I have not seen in analysis, the question could be raised whether the corresponding findings may really reinforce psychoanalytic hypotheses. This is a limitation of what follows, but, I submit, the similarity of certain reactions in all these cases reinforces the merit of further psychoanalytic exploration of these proposals.

Some phenomenological observations

What follows are the experiences gathered in interviewing persons known to me personally and who were willing to be interviewed, all of whom having had the experience of the loss of a spouse after many years of a happy relationship. Obviously, these are not psychoanalytic observations per se, although these interviews were based on a psychoanalytic perspective. Also, I had already observed clinical features found in patients undergoing mourning processes in other patients, features that replicated surprisingly those of extended mourning without the clinical depression seen in the case I have reported before. And the conscious and pre-conscious manifestations that could be observed in these interviews, I believe, strengthens the hypotheses regarding the unconscious processes that, I am suggesting, may be common features of normal mourning. Also, in exploring the mourning processes of other patients who had lost significant others in the course of their treatment, I had become particularly concerned with the nature of mourning and the grieving process. In the interviews, my focus was on the different components of the mourning process, their duration and their influence on the life of the affected persons. As a personal experience of my own had been the initial stimulus for this exploration, I was particularly concerned with avoiding, as much as possible, the influence of my own experiences on the evaluation of the information that I was receiving.

To begin, practically all the persons I interviewed related the experience of shock following the death of a beloved one, the intense emotional conviction that the person was still there, in some unreal world, which for deeply religious persons was consonant with a rational conviction following their particular religious belief. One woman told me: 'I know that his soul is somewhere. I have spent much time thinking how our love on the earth will come together with the love of God in an eventual redemption of the souls, and what will happen to the negative feelings that are so painful in one's memories . . . will jealousy and envy still exist?' Various persons quoted Joan Didion's autobiographical book, *The Year of Magical Thinking*, and C.S. Lewis's *A Grief Observed*, the latter as the basis for the movie *Shadowland*. In fact, several had not only seen the film, but remembered it in surprising detail after many years. One deeply religious person, a leader of a major educational psychological center, speaking about a beloved deceased person, said with deep conviction: 'I know that we shall meet again.' Others, without religious convictions, stated very clearly that the person they lost in reality continued to exist in their mind, and in the mind of those who knew and loved the deceased. Talking about the lost love object with these others evoked the comforting presence of the loved one, who lived on in their minds. This experience would not decrease its intensity over many years.

But that experience, in turn, seemed only a reproduction of an ongoing process of internal relating to the person who had died, with intense longing, painfully missing the reality of a life lived together, and with the reactivation of the sense of regret over not having used the time together more completely, more intensively. That regret reflected feelings of guilt that, remarkably, were more intense the more fundamentally satisfactory and loving the relationship had been. Persons with a chronic ambivalent relationship and who, one might assume, had good reasons to feel guilty, showed many fewer tendencies in this regard.

One woman, describing the sudden death of her husband of 22 years, with whom she had had a very fulfilling relationship in terms of their sexual life, their mutual expectations and interactions in daily life, and their orientation toward values, social life, and intellectual and ideological aspirations, described the sense of concern after his unexpected death following shortly after a routine medical examination in which he had been given a clean bill of health. Had she been contributing to causing his death from a heart attack because she had been too demanding, originating stress in his life? Over many months this concern pained her and continued in spite of repeated reassurances by professionals, including the physicians who had examined the husband for various reasons and at different times.

While loss related to sudden death tends to trigger intense feelings of guilt and regret in the survivor, death following a lengthy and painful illness may cause intense pain recalling the suffering of the deceased person, a painful recreation and elaboration of the weeks and months of decaying health, and the cycles of hope and despair that usually characterize those terrible times. During the struggle for survival, the immediate tasks – keeping hope alive for the dying person and the person who loves him/her – leave little time or mental space for mourning. The working through of these experiences comes later with long-term grieving.

One man was reviewing in his mind the experiences of a 40-year marriage to a woman he had loved deeply and who died after an extended struggle with metastatic breast cancer. Innumerable moments of their lives together kept emerging in his mind, such as invitations on her part to spend time together in travels that his work had kept him from, and his lack of sufficient support, as he now saw it, of her career and education. A consistent reaction to these painful feelings, that persisted over many years, was his effort to recreate, in his mind, the hopes, expectations, and plans that his deceased wife could not achieve, her desires that remained unfulfilled, and her projects that remained interrupted, with efforts to actively carry out what she would have wanted to achieve or would have wanted him to do.

Another woman, who had been very dependent on her now deceased husband who would take care of all their problems of daily life, felt that it was his wish that she now become more independent and capable of relying on herself. She felt a sense of strength and satisfaction in fulfilling his wishes, a redemption from her feelings of guilt over her excessive passivity with him by changing her behavior in the direction that he would have wished her to go.

The death of a beloved person is, of course, a well-known stimulus for an effort to carry out a social function in memory and in the name of the deceased. One wife established a professional fellowship in the field in which her husband was an expert, and one man made enormous efforts to the effect that the artistic production of his wife be acknowledged and appreciated after her death.

Psychologically, what seemed important to me listening to these persons was their sense of a relationship to the lost person that actively continued by virtue of reparative endeavors which the mourners felt were expressions of love and regret for lost time and opportunities that would be appreciated by the lost partner. One man said that, 30 years after her death, he still consulted with his wife whenever it came to important decisions regarding the relationship to their children.

At the same time, several persons noted that they acquired attitudes that were similar to those of the person who had died. One man felt that something in him had died as well, and that there was a split between one part of himself that felt alive and one that felt as if he had crossed over into a different world to be with his lost wife. Another man commented thoughtfully over the strange combination of having changed, as if he had taken his lost wife into himself, while yet maintaining an ongoing relationship with her in his mind, and wondered, half jokingly, 'Is that schizophrenia?'

What I wish to stress is the combination of the – well-known – identification with a lost object in the sense of a modification of the self-representation, on the one hand, and the persistence of an internal object relation with the lost person. The process of identification really involves the transformation of the self-representation under the influence of the representation of the significant other – as Freud and Jacobson had pointed out – and, at the same time, the persistence of the internalized relation between self and other as a stable psychological structure. I am using advisedly the term 'structure' to refer to the permanence and the functional quality of this mental dyadic relation between self and object representation.

I mentioned earlier the emotional conviction that the person that has been lost is still there in some form in external reality: even in non-religious persons this may take very concrete forms through hallucinatory experiences. For example, one man felt that he was being touched in a caressing way by his deceased wife during the first month after her death, and he had difficulty in explaining to me, years later, whether that was an experience in reality or whether he was dreaming. A woman mentioned, somewhat embarrassed, that she would write letters to her deceased husband with a strong conviction that he would be able to obtain the content and the meaning of these letters because of her action. She put them away, with the fantasy that, eventually, she would be able to show them to him. While these acute experiences and behaviors tend to subside over time, the internal conversation and interaction with the loved and lost person continue, as I mentioned before, over many years.

The pain of mourning gradually decreases, but may be reactivated with full intensity even after years, such as during the interviews that I carried out. In fact, it was impressive how intensively most people reacted to my tactful efforts, over a time-span of two to three hours, to raise questions about the persistence of a mourning process, and how, before my eyes, the intense pain over the loss of the person would re-emerge, with particular characteristics: first, the simple pain over the loss of somebody deeply loved, the regret over the final nature of it; second, the pain over the interruption of the life project of the other person, of what the deceased person, if alive, would want to achieve; third, the pain over the responsibility to carry on alone a world built together, with a sad awareness that, with their own future death, that world would finally disappear. It was as if the exploration of this pain would bring alive the words of Goethe: 'We die twice: first, when we die, and then when those who knew us and loved us die' (Goethe, 1972 [1809], p. 331). And fourth, the pain over the loss of a deep dependency on the loved person that has clearly parental, perhaps mostly maternal features. This signifies, if one explores it further, the reactivation of all mourning processes that the individual has experienced before the traumatic loss of the beloved person, and points to the underlying reactivation of the depressive position.

An efficient, apparently self-assured businessman referred to the fact that, whenever an unexpected crisis developed, a momentary sense of anxiety and despair would overcome him that, in his experience, could be controlled by his calling his wife, who had died four years ago. Under conditions of such critical moments, he would feel as if he were an abandoned child, and an intense longing for her with an upsurge of deep sadness would follow.

As an illustration of the pain over the fact that the lost person would miss out on something that was so dear to her, a usually controlled mental health professional, whose wife had died five years ago, attended the graduation from elementary school of a granddaughter to whom his wife had been very close. Suddenly, in the middle of the ceremony, his feeling of pleasure shifted into sadness and a barely controlled outburst of tears as he thought how happy his wife would have been if she were present at this moment.

The pain over the abrupt ending of the life project of the lost person is also illustrated by the grieving reaction of a widower when he faced the paintings of a certain expressionist painter whose life his wife had been exploring in the context of solving the riddle of certain symbolic objects that repeated themselves in many of his paintings. He felt knowledgeable about what she was after, but incompetent to be able to follow it through, and while he was attracted to the work of this painter it was a joy mixed with pain every time he saw one of his works.

One woman expressed the concern over the loss of a shared world upon her own death: she said, 'One of the things I am most sad about when I think of him is that, when I die, all I knew about his world in the old country, his childhood, his struggle for independence, will be lost.' The internally felt need to transmit to a future generation the knowledge about the life of the person whom one has lost is a powerful incentive for biographical writing.

Thus the pain over the loss of a beloved person is composed of several currents and maintains its influence on the personality over many years. The identification with the lost person, particularly with traits that one admired and missed, is a source of strength and, indeed, fosters the experience of a sense of overcoming the mourning process.

In this regard, Freud's observation that the mourning process is completed with a process of identification is confirmed in everyday experience. At the same time, however, the presence in one's mind of the relation with the lost object goes on, and the sense of guilt over the loss that Freud ascribed mostly to pathological mourning, but that Melanie Klein proposed as a fundamental aspect of all mourning processes in their reactivation of the depressive position, clearly seems confirmed by the consistent observation of guilt feelings, perhaps particularly in persons who had the least reason for feeling guilty.

As mentioned before, persons with severe, chronic conflicts with the person they lost and who, rather than denying, were conscious of their own ambivalence seem to show fewer feelings of guilt, in contrast to cases where a profound repression of the aggression against the lost person would emerge as the syndrome of pathological mourning, an expression of unconscious guilt. In my study of borderline patients, mourning processes most frequently were accompanied by intense rage and resentment at the lost person for having abandoned the surviving partner – a regression to paranoid–schizoid mechanisms, and, in the case of narcissistic pathology, the absence of any mourning process is a typical characteristic development. Narcissistic personalities who, instead of grieving, develop an intense paranoid reaction against those they feel able to blame for the death of the lost partner, spouse, child or parent are thus protected from the painful mourning process that patients with more normal internalized object relations have to confront.

Regarding the reactivation of past mourning processes, one man who lost his spouse remembered with strong feelings the agony of his father following the death of the patient's mother. He wished he could have been aware, at that point, of what he now had become aware of and helped his father while, at the same time, if his father were alive now, they could console each other. One woman, because of the serious conflicts and mutual alienation she had experienced with her mother, remembered a rather ambivalent and, retrospectively, superficial mourning experience at her death. Following, however, the mourning process over the death of her husband years ago, she felt a surge of longing for her mother, spent much time reflecting on her mother's feelings and motivation, and experienced fully a double mourning process for her husband and her mother. This belated working through of a previously repressed mourning process in the light of a later one is not infrequent.

The psychodynamics of mourning

The psychoanalytic literature on mourning processes is mostly concerned with pathological mourning – mourning as part of depression, both neurotic and melancholia (Akhtar, 2000; Coyne, 1985; Fiorini, 2007; Frankiel, 1994; Grinberg,

1992; Kogan, 2007; Pollock, 1975). Beyond the classical contributions of Freud (1917), Melanie Klein (1940) and Edith Jacobson (1971), there is little reference to normal mourning processes. The present study is focused on the phenomenological and structural aspects of normal mourning process on mourning that is not part of a clinical depression.

What follows is undoubtedly influenced by a recent personal experience of mourning, and is at risk of missing, therefore, the necessary objectivity of an adequately distant exploration. As mentioned before, I have tried to gain some objectivity about the questions triggered by my own experience by interviewing a number of persons who had undergone a significant loss of a spouse within the past 10 to 20 years, with the explicit purpose of studying their mourning experiences, and who had given me ample evidence that they did not suffer from a significant personality disorder. Naturally, my experiences with patients in analysis and psychoanalytic psychotherapy provide the general background to this presentation.

My observations regarding the process of 'normal' mourning stem from a psychoanalytic viewpoint of the processes of severe mourning experienced by persons who, both in their general personality functioning and from the descriptive aspects of their mourning processes would not be considered cases of 'pathological mourning'. The latter is reflected in the characteristic clinical aspects of excessively severe or prolonged mourning, clinical depression, irrational guilt feelings, the development of regressive features of personality functioning, or other symptoms linked to that process. The main proposals derived from my observations are the following.

Mourning, in contrast to Freud's (1917) initial assumption, but recognized by him in later years (1960 [1929]), is not a time-limited process. Freud concluded that mourning is completed through a process of unconscious identification with a lost object, and by the compensatory gratitude for being alive, in contrast to the beloved person who has died. Melanie Klein (1940) proposed that an adequate resolution of the reawakened processes of the depressive position and its elaboration completes the work of normal mourning. This is a fundamental contribution to the understanding of normal as well as pathological mourning. While Freud clarified the dynamics of melancholia, Melanie Klein clarified commonalities of normal and pathological mourning, as well as their differences in terms of the normal reactivation of the dynamics of the depressive position or the failure of this process with the dominance of regressive manic or paranoid–schizoid processes. I believe it is the process of unconscious identification with the lost object that needs to be re-examined, and the extent to which the reality of an object loss determines new processes within the depressive position.

To begin, the process of identification refers to the modification of the representation of self under the influence of the representation of a significant other (Jacobson, 1964). But this may not be all in the case of relatively normal persons who have suffered a significant loss, particularly that of a spouse with whom they had an optimal relation over many years. In fact, the traumatic loss of a spouse under such circumstances is relatively under-emphasized in the literature on mourning, where the mourning of parental figures, of one's children, and the losses that children experience upon the death of parents are focused upon much more frequently. And yet clinical observations indicate the enormously traumatic aspects of the mourning of a life partner of many years.

From my interviews, as well as my own experience, I propose that what is also involved in this process of identification is the setting up of a permanent relationship between the representation of self and the representation of the lost object, the combination of an intrapsychic presence of that object and the awareness of its objective permanent absence. From a different perspective, Gaines (1997) proposed that the two tasks of mourning include detachment from the lost object as well as maintaining continuity in the connection with that object. It is the dynamics and structural implications of that permanent aspect of the mourning process that I wish to focus upon. I propose that this objective absence in the presence of an intense subjective experience of the permanent relation between self and the lost other is at the center of the painful experience of loss and the compensatory processes this situation engenders. This intrapsychic duality acquires the characteristics described by Freud and Melanie Klein, namely, an idealization of the lost object and the reactivation of significant previous mourning processes linked to the reactivation of the depressive position. Clinically speaking, past mourning processes are reactivated with their elements of guilt feelings and reparative efforts. As Melanie Klein has stressed, the more ambivalent the relation with the lost object had been, the greater the guilt feelings over the real and fantasized aggression toward the lost object. And, insofar as ambivalence is a universal character of human relations, this process may also be observed consistently. But not only conflicts over aggression are involved here.

Regarding the working through of the depressive position, the reality of guilt over opportunities lost, over failure to appreciate what one had until it was gone, cannot be retraced totally to past internal aggressive impulses now integrated with loving ones toward the lost object. Exaggerated guilt over past experiences also illuminates the limitations that daily reality imposes throughout time. Daily reality militates against the full appreciation of a loving relationship, and only retrospectively emerges the possibility of a perspective that fully illuminates the potential implications of every moment lived together. The paradox of the capacity to only appreciate fully what one had after having lost it, a profoundly human paradox, cannot be resolved by communicating this experience to others. It is an internal learning process fostered by the painful, yet creative aspect of mourning.

There is now no possibility of correcting past shortcomings and failures, no possibility for redressing realistic grievances, no opportunity to make up and try to be a better mate. Objectively, there is now no more forgiveness nor repair. Working through the limitations and failures stemming from the past cannot be carried out now in an objective relation to the lost object.

But reparative processes are possible by other mechanisms that deserve further attention. The desires, aspirations and ambitions of the person who has died, particularly the wishes for his or her own life and future, as well as for the life and future of the person who mourns, and for other persons who were central in the love and concern of the lost person may be experienced by the person in mourning as a mandate, a command, a moral obligation to fulfill the wishes and hopes of the deceased. They become part of the mourner's superego, not as an impersonal aspect of superego demands and prohibitions, but, rather, are preserved as highly personalized relations with the lost object.

Guilt, remorse and reparation: these are intimately related, but not equivalent, nor necessarily linked aspects of the mourning process. Unconscious guilt, massive and overwhelming, as the basis of severe depression, is related to unconscious aggression to the ambivalently loved, lost object, consciously represented by overvalued or even delusional self-depreciation and devaluation, if not even more disguised by a wide array of typical depressive delusions involving the self and the external world (Jacobson, 1971).

But conscious guilt, whether normal or neurotic, is usually associated with remorse, that is, conscious regret for aggressive behavior toward the lost love object, whether through actions, neglect or abandonment. Remorse is the foundational impetus for reparation, the impulse to undo the aggression in an attempt to compensate or atone for the real or imagined damage done to the lost object. But, beyond atonement, there may be a growing impulse to redeem oneself by means of personal change, constructive action, and striving to be a 'better person' in ongoing and new relationships. Remorse and guilt are, as Melanie Klein suggested, the origin of the reparative drive. But remorse is not always followed by the urge for reparation: in cases of narcissistic personality structure, remorse may be subverted to the 'suffering' of the survivor, a self-limited response that does not lead to reparative action. Guilt feelings that do not lead to reparation or its equivalent changes in behavior are a defensive neutralization of the very guilt, sometimes indicative of significant superego pathology.

In the course of normal mourning, however, grief creates a powerful reparative impulse, strengthening the internalized object relation with the lost object as an aspect of preconscious experience, and fosters the development of new value systems, a part of superego, and particularly ego ideal structures. There is a growth of the motivation and capacity to relate daily life with ethical aspirations and meanings. The regret over opportunities lost, over the loss of the finite relationship in reality, and the full illumination of the value of the relationship with the lost object is the driving motivation for this development. As part of this ego and superego development, at any point of the remaining life of the mourning subject, the mourning process may be reinstated: perhaps particularly at those moments of quiet reflection when the past re-emerges as part of the growing sense of continuity of the time experience as part of the maturation throughout the life-cycle.

Another aspect of this experience is the strengthening of the normal development of a subjective, personal past world shared with the lost object that differentiates itself from the experience of present daily reality: a normal, delicately evolving, life enriching yet subtly sad experience of the historical dimension and transient nature of life. It is a normal, subliminal but lasting mourning experience that is punctured by the acute experience of loss of the past when a present event evokes it. It may well be that both types of mourning experience reinforce each other.

The objective manifestations of mourning, such as a persistent, low-toned sadness, a potential for intense episodic sadness activated under the many circumstances that bring into sharp focus the memory of the lost person, the occasional intense pain as memories related to the lost person emerge in present interchanges with others, and a certain degree of internal withdrawal under circumstances that evoke past experiences shared with the lost person may have all subsided after a year or two as manifest symptoms. And yet, over many years, I am proposing that this becomes a permanent trait of the personality that evolves in the context of such a mourning process: the poignant memory of the lost person remains fully and intensively present, together with moments of an acute sense of pain and sadness. This reaction can be triggered at any time, and often catches the mourning person by surprise.

There are well-known circumstances that activate this permanent, internalized relationship: first, the individual's experience of new, beautiful, emotionally intense moments that one knows would have been appreciated intensely by the person who is lost, a sadness that he or she cannot be here to enjoy an experience related to what was so important to him or her. Second, there are moments in which a rapid, instantaneous understanding of the meaning of an event transcends the practical reality of the immediate situation and condenses many memories, understandings and convictions in one single instance, one idea: now the person with whom that awareness could be shared, the only one who would immediately comprehend all the elements involved, is absent. At the bottom of such experiences lies a common world, constructed with the lost person over many years, that now remains only in memory, its presence felt in absence. Third, there is the fulfillment of aspirations that the deceased did not live to see, for example, the growth of a child or grandchild. And, of course, above all, the simple longing for the person who has been lost, the yearning for the recovery of a shared mutual dependency with all its loving and regressive implications of safety and familiarity, the underlying longing for the reunion with beloved parental figures on whom one depended are a powerful context for the emergence of those other triggers of an ever renewed sense of mourning and longing. And, then, there are the dreams in which the dead person is alive, interacting with the dreamer, at times reassuring the dreamer as part of the manifest content of the dream that this is not an illusion . . . followed by the painful awakening to reality.

Happily, the enduring nature of these experiences in the normal course of grieving does not imply a libidinal fixation on the past that permanently limits the capacity for new investments. Libidinal investments are not a zero-sum capacity. To the contrary, the expansion of moral values and ethical commitments related to the mandates that reflect the desires and aspirations of the person who died, whose life project was interrupted, are frequently a powerful stimulus to reparative action of the survivor providing a sense of purpose. They become, as mentioned before, ethical commands and aspired-for ideals. Reparative processes, in short, expand into spiritual demands.

The impulses to repair and stimulate psychological growth, the capacity to learn from experience and to enrich new love relations with the lessons derived from the loss of the past one are present. The capacity to love anew increases with the tolerance and elaboration of mourning as a permanent process. In fact, the capacity to love again may become enriched by this perennial mourning process that combines the gratitude for a new relationship with the gratitude for a new opportunity to fulfill the mandate of the lost object. Normal mourning, I propose, enhances the capacity for loving. This experience of a new opportunity to love must necessarily include the belief that the lost loved ones would want us to find new happiness and go on with our lives, perpetuating the feeling of their presence in their absence. And the loving understanding on the part of the new object of the elaboration of a past loss may enrich the new relationship. Needless to say, all this may go terribly wrong under pathological circumstances, and we know more about those situations from our clinical work.

To mourn a lost loved object and yet to be able to love again . . . without abandoning the love for the lost object nor truncating the mourning process itself is an important and yet neglected aspect of normal mourning. It runs counter to the traditional assumption of a mechanical flow of libidinal energy that is withdrawn from the object and redirected but remains essentially constant. Chasseguet-Smirgel (1985) has pointed out that falling in love is not a matter of directing narcissistic libido toward an object and thus reducing the narcissistic investment, but that both object-invested libido and self-invested libido increase at the same time. I propose that, similarly, the reaffirmation of investment of love for the lost object that is part of the normal mourning process, or rather, the full liberation of love for the lost object previously dampened or obscured by the daily process of living together, facilitates the increase of love toward a new object. At this point, the understanding and tolerance of the new love object of the mourning partner's attachment to the lost object may enrich their relationship and facilitate further the growth of a new love.

Mourning interminably may become part of the increased capability for love and appreciation of life. In contrast to Freud's (1917) assumption that the pleasure with one's own being alive compensates for the loss of the beloved one in the overcoming of mourning, the pleasure of being alive is enriched by the moral responsibilities derived from the integration of the internal mandate proceeding from the person who has been lost.

The activation of the depressive position is reflected in the resurgence of the mourning process regarding earlier losses. In the case of the loss of a spouse or child, the typical reactivated experiences involve parental figures which then tend to become transformed and more fully mourned by virtue of the current grief. Here the highly individualized nature of the relationship to earlier life experiences involving fully developed or avoided mourning reactions makes generalization difficult. The most important feature of those experiences, however, is the deepening of the understanding and of the internal relationship to a lost parent. Under optimal circumstances, that internal relationship may help to mitigate the pain and bring with it a sense of consolation to the new mourning experience. But, at times, the sense of loss of a love object reinforces the feelings of abandonment by the previously lost parental object.

The denial of the disappearance of the loved one, the emotional conviction that the soul of the lost other continues existing in a virtual world, an article of faith held by major religions, is beautifully illustrated in its intensity and as a central aspect of the mourning process in C. S. Lewis's book *A Grief Observed* (1961) and in Joan Didion's book *The Year of Magical Thinking* (2005). While these, of course, are not psychoanalytic studies, the profound introspection of these authors merits psychoanalytic reflection. Both authors clearly describe their difficulty in tolerating the discrepancy between the overwhelming internal presence of the lost object and the external reality of their absence. The ardent wish for a re-encounter in that dark world of the unknown may take many forms and is a major source of the suicidal ideation and suicidal attempts that follow the death of a beloved one. Here the wish for one's own death is the hope for the re-encounter. Also, that wish and the profound experience of the permanence of the lost object is a profound source of religious feelings.

The function of gravestones, memorial monuments, pictures and photographs and works of art symbolically representing the lost person derive their consoling function from the assurance that the dead person is still out there, somewhere, in the external world. Burial sites further serve as 'points of contact', gathering places where the soul of the departed, now in a different and mysterious world, can renew contact with the mourning person. This may function normally as painful yet reassuring symbols of the re-encounter with the lost object. This normal process, however, may evolve into pathological idealization of such memorial places, or their symbolic equivalents, constituting 'linking objects' (Volkan, 1972) that acquire an almost delusional function in the life of the mourner. The religious function of such symbols is a major source of communion with the deity: the presence of the host in a church or a chapel with the image of the Virgin thus becomes places of solace, of reassuring closeness to the deity.

The profound emotional conviction about the continued existence, in another realm of reality, of the soul or the spirit of the person who has died – of the immortality of the soul, in short – is an essential component of the mourning process. It dovetails with religious assumptions of resurrection of the soul and of the body, and of re-encounter with the love object as an aspect of the final encounter with God. C. S. Lewis has movingly described this psychological process in its interaction with religious conviction. It raises numerous questions that involve theological and scientific issues, but also, predominantly, psychological ones. This emotional conviction of the continued presence of the lost object points to an important psychological root of the religious impulse as a basic aspect of the human psyche.

Martin Bergmann (personal communication) has suggested that religion, in this regard, affirming the survival of the soul, protects the mourner from hallucination and delusion – and hallucinary experiences of being in touch with the lost object are, indeed, quite prevalent. But, by the same token, religious convictions also raise the question of what relationship might emerge in a world of the souls, with old and new lost objects simultaneously present. C. S. Lewis, again, proposed the reunion of all love objects in the context of the reunion with God. Different Western religions formulate alternative hypotheses about this puzzle, but what matters is the power of the emotional reality reflected in this aspect of the mourning process. In short, there is a setting up of a permanent internalized relation with the lost object that becomes, in the words of Sara Zac de Filc (personal communication), an 'absent presence'.

From this need also derives the therapeutic function of the capacity to share the internal presence of the lost person with others who share a loving past with the lost person, and, of course, to share them with the analyst who becomes the external depository of this internal world. I believe I had missed the important transferential function, in the case of the patient I referred to initially, of the recreation of the image of his dead wife in the sessions with me, recreating her again and again in the transitional space of our relationship. And again, in these painful yet so desired re-encounters in fantasy, the earlier-mentioned aspects of the mourning process are reactivated: the regret for opportunities missed, the sense of a mandate to be fulfilled in a virtual continuation of the relationship with the deceased, and the pain over the always premature disruption of the life plan of the other are essential aspects of the communicatively shared internal relationship with the lost one. The irresistible urge for reunion, the fantasy and concern over life after death, and the expanding moral universe related to the mandate all combine in the expression of powerful religious impulses, whether they take the form of adherence to an established religious belief system or are constructed individually as a painful yet indispensable aspect of spiritual existence and survival.

Mourning, of course, always implies a traumatic loss. When the trauma is compounded by violence, such as for loved ones killed in the Holocaust, assassinated by ordinary criminals, terrorists, or the repressive machinery of a totalitarian state, intense hostility mingles with the pain of mourning. Pathological mourning, on the other hand, may involve the search for culprits to project unconscious aggression toward the ambivalently loved lost object. Relatives of patients who have committed suicide often look for culprits in the mental health system, particularly in the context of a family member's chronically bad relationship with the suicidal patient.

In cases where the loss is the result of violence, paranoid and aggressive reactions color the mourning process and may temporarily – or over a long time – overshadow it, protecting the mourner from the full impact of the grief. Collective mourning over the death of a beloved leader may take the form of unmitigated grief, without paranoid reactions, thus acquiring an intensively painful yet mature form of mourning – as, for example, the national mourning process over the death of John F. Kennedy. Collective mourning over the victims of the Holocaust also usually takes the characteristics of a normal mourning process. Or else, paranoid features may predominate, such as in the collective memory of the disastrous battle of Kosovo, a 600-year-old Serbian trauma reactivated, as Vamik Volkan (2007) has described, within a regressive large group mourning process in which the paranoid elements predisposed the large group psychology to sadistic revenge on present-day real and imagined enemies. Here the persistence of the mourning process throughout generations clearly carries with it pathological, paranoid–schizoid features within the group identity, paralleling paranoid–schizoid features in the intolerance of the depressive position of the individual. In this regard, in contrast, the permanent features of the normal mourning process described carry important reparative features without terminating the mourning process itself.

Some general conclusions

Perhaps the most impressive aspect of the mourning process is the previously mentioned moral or ethical injunction to carry on the aspirations of the now deceased person. It is as if the most effective way to deal with the pain of loss were the commitment to carry out that mandate, a commitment that has an ethical quality. The achievement of this mandate reinforces the moral values and moral strength of the surviving person as well as being a source of positive, loving, and creative gestures that affect others as well. Here the ethical component, the strengthening of advanced superego functions, transcends the reparative function of re-establishing the internal object of the depressive position. From a religious perspective, Rabbi Moshe Berger (personal communication) has formulated this development, stating that all human love relations are finite, while the absence that necessarily follows the death of one of a couple is infinite. The paradox, he goes on, is that only at the time of infinite absence can the time of finite presence be fully appreciated in all its potential luminosity, and it is absolutely unavoidable that, in that light, feelings of regret and sadness over lost opportunities color the memory of the relationship. Those regrets, whether or not they take the form of guilt feelings, cannot be compensated; there is no repair and no forgiveness, because the person to whom reparation would be directed is irretrievably gone. Here is where the sense of the mandate emerging from the lost person becomes part of one's moral guidance system, and carrying out this mandate evolves the creation of moral values. Rabbi Berger links this development with the fundamental religious demand of *Tikun Olam* (to improve the world), implying a moral mandate to try to improve and bring happiness, as much as we can, within the circle of one's daily life. In this regard, the desperate desire for an existence beyond death, the longing for and faith in such a spiritual world on the one hand, and the adherence to an internalized set of transcendental principles in fulfilling a moral mandate combine to increase the religious aspect of psychological functioning. Objectively, this may be reflected in more maturity, in a more loving and concerned relation to others that, in turn, may elicit growth processes in others, such as the children of a person in mourning. This may be one of the sources of moral growth and development that, in the long run, may have broader impact at a social community level, counteracting the powerful regressive group processes that operate in an opposite direction.

From the perspective of contemporary object relations theory, the persistence of the internal relation with the lost object is a significant confirmation of the power of the world of internalized object relations, and of the dyadic nature of identification processes. Freud (1917) described identification in his classical essay on *Mourning and Melancholia*, and Edith Jacobson's *The Self and the Object World* (1964), as mentioned before, defined identification as the modification of the self-representation under the impact of the corresponding object representation. We may now conclude that identification is a complex process that includes, at least, the internalization of a relationship with the significant other, the modification of the self-representation as influenced by the object representation, and the maintenance of that internalized object relation. The latter implies a potential for its reactivation in a direct form – the search for an object similar or replacing the one that has been lost – or a reactivation with role reversal, in the sense of recreating the relationship while identifying with the object representation and projecting the self-representation on somebody else. Freud (1914) describes this latter relationship in some cases of male homosexuality, but it is probably a much more generally valid process. In short, the persistence of the internal relationship in the process of mourning, with the combined presence of the representation of the other in relation to the self, the incorporation of the corresponding value systems into the ego ideal, and the identification of the self with the lost object constitute complementary processes in the identification with a lost object.

Adult mourning processes after the loss of a beloved other of many years of life together not only reactivate the infantile depressive position, but also constitute a psychological experience that triggers specific mechanisms of grieving and compensation that foster new structural development. It may be that, at this point, the internalized world of object relations, under the impact of the mourning process generates the experience of a world of ethical values, of what may be considered a spiritual realm that has general human validity, that is, a transcendental value system. Similar transformations may occur in the realm of the relation to art, erotic love, and in the religious experience. An intrapsychic, consistent, silent dialogue with the lost object represents the subjective side of this structural development in the case of mourning.

References

Akhtar, S. (2000). From mental pain through manic defense to mourning. In: Akhtar S, editor. *Three faces of mourning: Melancholy, manic defense and moving on*, 95–115. Northvale, NJ: Aronson.

Chasseguet-Smirgel, J. (1985). *The ego ideal: A psychoanalytic essay on the malady of the ideal*. New York, NY: Norton.

Coyne, J. C., editor (1985). *Essential papers on depression*. New York, NY: New York UP.

Didion, J. (2005). *The year of magical thinking*. New York, NY: Knopf.

Fiorini, L. G., editor (2007). *On Freud's 'Mourning and melancholia'*. London: IPA.

Frankiel, R. V., editor (1994). *Essential papers on object loss*. New York, NY: New York UP.

Freud, S. (1914). On narcissism. *Standard Edition, Vol. 14*, 69–102.

Freud, S. (1917). Mourning and melancholia. *Standard Edition, Vol. 14*, 243–58.

Freud, S. (1960[1929]). Letter to Binswanger. Letter 239. In: Freud EL, editor. *The letters of Sigmund Freud*. New York, NY: Basic Books.

Gaines, R. (1997). Detachment and continuity: The two tasks of mourning. *Contemp. Psychoanal.*, 33: 549–71.

Goethe, J. W. (1972[1809]). *Die Wahlverwandtschaften*. München: Winkler.

Grinberg, L. (1992). *Guilt and depression*. London, New York, NY: Karnac.

Jacobson, E. (1964). *The self and the object world*. New York, NY: International UP.

Jacobson, E. (1971). *Depression*. New York, NY: International UP.

Klein, M. (1940). Mourning and its relation to manic-depressive states. *Contributions to psychoanalysis, 1921–1945*, 311–33. New York, NY: McGraw-Hill, 1967.

Kogan, I. (2007). *The struggle against mourning*. New York, NY: Aronson.

Lewis, C. S. (1961). *A grief observed*. San Francisco, CA: HarperCollins.

Pollock, G. (1975). On mourning, immortality and Utopia. *J. Am. Psychoanal. Assn.*, 23: 334–62.

Volkan, V. D. (1972). The 'linking object' of pathological mourners. *Arch Gen Psychiatry*, 27: 215–21.

Volkan, V. D. (2007). Not letting go: From individual perennial mourners to societies with entitlement ideologies. In: Fiorini LG, editor. *On Freud's 'Mourning and melancholia'*, 99–109. London: IPA.

Chapter 11

Out of the analytic shadow

On the dynamics of commemorative ritual (2011)

Joyce Slochower

Editor's note: In this essay Joyce Slochower explores the importance of rituals of memorialization in our lifelong efforts to give meaning to death (thus reaffirming life) and maintain continuity and connection to the people we have lost. She argues against the standard model of mourning and its insistence that health demands relinquishment and decathexis. As she states in the closing paragraph of this very personal and eloquent paper, "It is time for us to reject once and for all the psychoanalytic idealization of renunciation and separation, to embrace our (conflicted) desire and capacity for connection."

This paper was published in 2011 by Joyce Slochower as "Out of the Analytic Shadows: On the Dynamics of Commemorative Ritual" in Psychoanalytic Dialogues, *Volume 21.*

This paper explores the dynamics of commemorative ritual as it is embodied and enacted outside the consulting room. While the function of lifelong acts of memorial in marking traumatic loss has been well documented, psychoanalysis has given short shrift to the value of these ongoing commemorative rituals in instances of "ordinary" (i.e., less traumatic) loss. Historical and sociological writers have explored their functions, but commemorative rituals have tended to evoke resistance within psychoanalysis, perhaps because of their collision with the termination ideal and the value of relinquishment. Here, I build on previous essays concerning Jewish mourning ritual (*shiva*) by addressing the function of several acts of commemoration including that of *Yizkor* (Jewish memorial ritual). Enacted across the lifespan, commemorative rituals serve multiple functions. They allow us to mark absence and create "presence" as we access and sometimes reshape personal memory. Such rituals can create a sense of linkage to "like mourners." At their best, these acts – in their multiple incarnations – mimic aspects of psychoanalytic work by helping us deepen emotional connectedness and facilitating integrated remembering in a way that enriches and frees rather than binds us.

Traumatic loss is sometimes writ small. Orphanhood came to me in middle age and so I am among the fortunate. I escaped the extraordinary suffering of those who lose loved ones in childhood, horrific accidents, disease, war, acts of terrorism. My parents had lived full lives and I was an adult when they died. But we do not experience death comparatively. It had been an especially difficult year, punctuated by my mother's increasing vulnerability and frequent middle-of-the-night calls for help. She did not live alone but might as well have; it was always I whom she called. And that night, she phoned at 2 a.m. I went once again, did what needed to be done. But then I left. And so the morning call announcing her death was especially traumatic. Had I stayed, I might have gotten help, saved her. Her soft face, her stillness in death, evoked a depth of longing for her that had been disavowed. Shock, grief, love unexpressed overtook me. If only.

My father's death a decade earlier had also been unexpected and in this sense, traumatic.[1] I had not felt implicated, but I was not prepared. His death disrupted, indeed dismantled my own illusions – of timelessness, of my going on being his child forever. Now I sat *shiva*, once again, worked over the grief and regret with which I struggled, was comforted by my family and friends. Gradually, I emerged and got on with life. My mother's death faded as my father's had. But the insulation created by time was never thick. The first bar mitzvah without him could pierce it, the first child's wedding without even one grandparent. In each instance, the acute awareness of a hole returned: I was now the oldest generation. The porous nature of that insulation fueled my wish, more intermittent than chronic, to formally remember and honor my parents. I was in a good treatment during some of those years and had help working through these losses. But I wanted, needed something more, and found it in memorial ritual. Struck by ritual's emotional power, I found myself thinking about its role and dynamic functions. Here I turn a psychoanalytic lens on these processes.

Traumatic loss and memorial ritual

Although the value of bereavement rituals in the immediate aftermath of loss is widely recognized, psychoanalysts have long assumed that as acute mourning is resolved, the need for acts of memorial would fade as well. It was thought working through should follow mourning and decathexis rather than sustained, affect-laden remembering (Freud, 1914).

Classical writers primarily view repetitive remembering as evidence of unresolved conflict and pathological mourning (Akhtar & Smolan, 1998). But Loewald (1962, 1976) moved our thinking away from the goal of decathexis by underscoring the mourner's need to internalize rather than relinquish the object tie. From this perspective, the capacity to sustain an inner attachment to deceased loved ones is less pathological than integrative (e.g., Gaines, 1997; Klass, 1988; Lobban, 2007; Rubin, 1985; Shabad, 2001). Yet despite this shift and the privileged place psychoanalytic theories accord memory and grief, we rarely explore the dynamic function of commemorative ritual. Indeed, like religion (Freud, 1927), ongoing acts of memorial are traditionally viewed as a sign of psychopathology, as regressive rather than integrative. For while we expect that our patients will dip in and out of the past across time, we also anticipate a progressive diminution in the intensity of that process. We tend to hear repetitive remembering as evidence of massive trauma, unresolved loss, intense conflict, or guilt that must be worked through rather than enacted and from which the patient will ultimately emerge. We aim for separation, hoping to help release our patients from the weight of pathological mourning processes, to free them (and ourselves) from the binding encumbrances of early, conflicted ties. We valorize, indeed idealize, "moving on" and "letting go." We believe in our capacity to leave the past behind.

The ideal of separation and the affects with which it is associated collide rather directly with those embodied in acts of memorialization. For commemorative rituals are aimed *not* at decathexis and not at moving on, but instead at countering the absence created by death by re-evoking loss and attendant, affect-laden memories.

The few psychoanalytic papers on memorialization explore its function for victims of massive trauma. Jeanne Wolff Bernstein (2000) used Shimon Attie's 1991 to 1993 photographic creation *The Writing on the Wall*, an open-air exhibition held in Berlin's former Jewish quarter, to describe the function of the memorial act. Attie superimposed past on present by projecting photographs of the lives of Berlin's pre-holocaust Jews onto the city buildings where they once lived. As the citizens of contemporary Berlin confronted shards of an earlier time, a complex memory space was constructed. The exhibition captured the destruction of an entire culture, the culpability of parents, grandparents, indeed, the nation. A not-so-subtle reminder of national and personal responsibility, the exhibition countered a culturally embedded need to forget, stimulating nostalgia, guilt, memory, perhaps even a desire to make reparation. Like much post-holocaust artistic expression (Ornstein, 2006), the exhibition offered viewers an antidote to the experience of absence.

Attie's memorial was as transient as it was powerful, for the lights of the projector opened and then permanently closed down the exhibit. It is more common for acts of commemoration to be regularly ritualized across time. Annual memorial rituals, almost always a response to the trauma of war, terrorism and/or genocide, typically take place at the site of physical memorials like the Vietnam Memorial Wall in Washington, DC, *Yad Vashem* in Israel, and similar memorials worldwide (see Homans & Jonte-Pace, 2005). These sites have the potential to function as symbolic grave markers, "missing tombstones" (Ornstein, 2008) or what Volkan (2007) described as "shared linking objects" (p. 53).[2]

Donna Bassin's (2008) film *Leave No Soldier* depicts a memorial ritual in movement. She follows the activities of a group of American Vietnam War veterans as they participate in an annual parade that ends at the Vietnam Memorial in Washington, DC. That parade embodies, even reenacts, the trauma to which the veterans were exposed: Decades after the end of that war, the vets continue to mark, remember, and grieve their losses.[3,4] A similar response to national loss may be found in the annual Israeli observance of *Yom Hazikaron* (Israel Remembrance Day). On that day, a 1-minute siren stops the country's Jewish population in its tracks. Highways halt; stores become still; banks freeze in the midst of transactions; people stand silently next to their cars, offices, and shops. Absence is concretized, and for a moment, Israel becomes a country of mourners who simultaneously share and witness each other's losses. Then the minute ends and life goes on.

Socially and nationally constructed acts of memorial are, of course, variously experienced, shaped both by one's connection to the cultural/political context within which memory is honored and by the quality and intensity of the particular losses being marked. For some, the memorial moment establishes or reinforces a sense of community while for others it functions mainly as an opportunity to honor and grieve personal losses.[5]

When effective, commemorative ritual has an additional impact. By creating a space of linkage, of "like subjects" (Benjamin, 1995), indeed, "like mourners," it facilitates the construction of group memory. Although psychoanalysis has given such experiences little attention, there are rich sociological and historical literatures on collective memory, particularly among scholars of Jewish history. In *Zakhor: Jewish History, Jewish Memory*, historian Josef Yerushalmi (1982) invoked the term "collective memory" to describe the functions of memorial ritual. Arguing that memory flows "above all, through two channels: ritual and recital" (p. 11), Yerushalmi underscored the Jewish injunction to remember history as a religious imperative. He suggested that commemorative ritual reactualizes memory by fusing past and present (see Myers, 2007, for a review of Yerushalmi's contribution). Yerushalmi's work was followed by a proliferation of sociological (e.g., Halbwachs, 1992) and historical writings on collective (traumatic) memory. In *Les Lieux de Mémoire* (*The Sites of Memory*), Nora (1984–1992) explored the location of cultural memory in both physical space and commemorative acts. He noted that sites of memory act to "to stop time, to block the work of forgetting" (Nora, 1989: Vol. 19, p. 7). Describing how ritual narrative shaped, even rewrote, the Israeli national tradition, Zerubavel (1995) detailed the interplay of remembrance and forgetting, continuity and change. She suggested that both secular and religious memorial acts in the Jewish holiday cycle commemorate the past while separating it from aspects of history and chronology.

Sensitive to the interplay and simultaneity of past and present in shaping posttraumatic narrative, these writers identify the core place of memorialization in cultural, religious, and national identity rather than in individual experience. What remains to be explored is the intrapsychic impact of commemorative ritual and the role of such ritual in instances of "ordinary" rather than collective, traumatic loss. Perhaps we psychoanalysts have tended to be suspicious of commemorative ritual because it is largely embedded within cultural and religious practices that have their own strong – and often alien – ideologies (see Hagman's, 1995, critique). Yet we're hardly averse to ritual itself; on the contrary, analytic work uses more than a few rituals of its own. Quiet more than flamboyant, our psychoanalytic rituals (Hoffman, 1998) are lodged in the predictable, organized practices that shape therapeutic time, place, physical position, how we begin and end the session, and so on. As analysts, we act as recognizing witnesses to our patient's remembering, and in this sense the dyad co-creates a memorial space within therapeutic walls.

But this kind of memorialization is a by-product of analytic process, for we do not structure our sessions with commemoration as a goal. Acts of "doing" have a very small place in psychoanalytic work; we abhor that which is prescribed, including the deliberate evocation of particular affect states and memories or explicit attempts to stimulate intragroup connectedness. Instead, analytic ritual is constructed in ways that minimize externally generated evocation in order to make possible maximal access to interior experience, whatever its particulars. And while as witnessing analysts we sometimes participate in our patient's remembering, therapeutic process tilts us toward the former function; it is our patient – not protocol – who shapes the session's content and the process of remembrance. If there is an element of commemorative action embedded within psychoanalytic process, then, it is more often implicit than performative.

Essentialized, the very notion of commemorative ritual collides with the psychoanalytic relationship to time. For although we work within a treatment space buffered by an illusion of timelessness (Hoffman, 1998; Slochower, 2006b), we also assume – and rely on – the existence of a constructed ending. Indeed, termination is both the fate and goal of psychoanalytic process. The considerable literature on termination (see Bergmann, 1985, 1988, 1997; Pedder, 1988; Rubin, 2010) focuses largely on what facilitates (or impedes) the relinquishment and internalization of the analytic relationship. From this perspective, commemorative ritual reflects an underlying (problematic) resistance to facing loss, a resistance to be analyzed rather than enacted.

Do acts of memorialization evoke a core psychoanalytic anxiety – that we never *do* lose our need for the other or our need to rework old connections – that we cannot fully separate, cannot fully terminate (see Bonovitz, 2007; Buechler, 2000; Slochower, 2011)? Have we yet to fully encompass this impossibility and its implications?

It's my belief that at their best, acts of commemoratives – in their multiple incarnations – mimic aspects of psychoanalytic work by helping us deepen emotional connectedness and facilitating integrated remembering in a way that enriches and frees rather than binds us. In what follows, I explore the dynamic functions of memorial rituals, using both my own experience with Jewish memorial ritual and some clinical vignettes to illustrate the variegated impact of such practices. I begin with a brief discussion of rituals associated with death.

Death and memory

Rituals that represent a response to the immediate shock of loss are ubiquitous across time and culture. Formalized in a myriad of burial rites and cultural/religious practices, these traditions make plenty of space for grief and remembrance. In previous essays (Slochower, 1993, 1995, 1996, 2006a, 2010) I explored the therapeutic function of Jewish mourning rituals, using my experience with *shiva* and post-*shiva* rituals to illustrate.

Shiva is a tradition characterized by a rather extraordinary set of social rules that together create a setting reminiscent of the therapeutic holding environment (Winnicott, 1964/1989). *Shiva* ritual establishes barriers against superficial social interchange; it both prescribes and proscribes behaviors that simultaneously express *and* contains the mourner's state of grief. That state is concretized in a range of ways: the mourner sits on a lowered chair (to symbolize her lower emotional state and closeness to the dead); she is served by others (like a sick or vulnerable person); she wears a torn garment or black ribbon throughout the week of *shiva*. Perhaps most powerful is the custom that the caller should wait for the mourner to initiate conversation; if the mourner remains silent, the caller does as well. Like the patient who has the freedom to begin each analytic session in her own way, this custom creates a protected space for the mourner who can grieve when she needs to and disengage affectively when she needs not to. The community of visitors supports the mourner's holding experience by allowing her to be the single subject in the mourning context, to use the other without regard for her needs (i.e., ruthlessly).[6] Within this "container for absence" (Becker & Shalgi, 2005), the mourner is not expected to shift out of her own frame, to engage in mutuality (Aron, 2001; Benjamin, 1995; Winnicott, 1958/1965, 1971).[7]

Like most mourning rituals, *shiva* is relatively brief, lasting less than a full week.[8] Although *Kaddish* continues to be recited for the next 3 months (or in the case of a parent's death, for 11 months), it too comes to an end. But feelings of absence, of course, do not, and many are pulled to find other ways to honor personal losses across the lifetime. A range of socially and religiously constructed commemorative practices create these opportunities. Mexicans observe the yearly Day of the Dead; Roman Catholics celebrate Mass; Muslims read a portion of the Koran; Jews observe *yahrzeit,* and say *Kaddish* and *Yizkor*. Others engage in regular personal acts of remembrance: a periodic visit to a cemetery; an afternoon spent with the photographs, books, letters and songs of earlier years. Performed decades after the phase of acute mourning has passed, these acts come to shape the individual's memories of – and inner relationship to – the deceased by at once countering *and* reevoking the absence created by death.

The Jewish memorial tradition of *Yizkor* offers an interesting frame within which to explore the function and dynamics of commemorative ritual. *Yizkor* is observed as part of a synagogue service that takes place on four major annual holidays including *Yom Kippur* (Day of Atonement). While it is not surprising that Orthodox Jews observe *Yizkor*, it is notable that this tradition is followed in some form by a full 60% of non-Orthodox American Jews.[9] In fact, many secular Jews make a point of attending only this portion of the synagogue service when it takes place.[10]

Yizkor literally means "he will remember," but more colloquially is understood as remembering or remembrance. Although anyone can recite *Yizkor* in memory of those whose losses leave no family, it is ordinarily said for one's parents, siblings, spouse, or child. There is no end point to *Yizkor* ritual; it is recited for the first time a year following a death and then across the mourner's lifetime. Notably, this is a commemorative ritual that is *not* uniquely linked to traumatic loss; it represents instead an "ordinary" way of memorializing both "ordinary" and traumatic loss.

Yizkor falls about halfway through the service, at which point many synagogues become unusually packed with congregants. It is notable that whereas most of the service unfolds fluidly, *Yizkor* is always announced; this gives people who have not lost a close relative an opportunity to leave the room, to (somewhat superstitiously) underscore their distance from those who have losses to mourn. There is a powerful enactment here, for in reaffirming the "real" relationship with living loved ones is embodied a simultaneous denial and acknowledgment of death. We (and our loved ones) are alive – for now.[11]

The particulars of the brief *Yizkor* service vary rather widely as a function of culture and Jewish denomination; my own experience is primarily within American conservative synagogues. Non-Orthodox American Jewish practice has embellished the liturgy by introducing "modern" innovations that elevate the place and emotional power of the memorial service.

Although in many synagogues, the bulk of the service is accompanied by some degree of chatting among congregants, the announcement of *Yizkor* seems to evaporate the desire for social contact and the congregation quiets. In many communities, the *Yizkor* service begins immediately; in some (including mine) it is sometimes introduced with a short talk by a synagogue member, usually a brief personal meditation about a lost loved one. While these talks vary in affective quality and content, they tend to create a reflective mood. After a psalm is chanted aloud, the congregation silently reads memorial prayers for loved ones; the name of each lost relative is inserted quietly into a separate version of the prayer.[12] Next, one or more communal memorial prayers are either chanted or said aloud in unison. Prayers are sometimes included that honor the memory of holocaust survivors (those with no one to say *Kaddish* for them, whose names remain unknown) or Israeli soldiers lost in war. In some synagogues, the names of all deceased members of the congregation are read aloud. In my community, *Kaddish* is then recited in unison by nearly everyone present and a concluding psalm is sung communally.

Until need and loss brought me into this communal space, the affective power of *Yizkor* remained somewhat elusive, its texts sounding stilted and formulaic. Personal loss changed that. While participating in this ritual occasionally feels like an obligation, I more often experience a kind of urgency that pulls me to attend it.

On *Yom Kippur* (the first *Yizkor* service in the year following my mother's death), I found myself caught up short when it was announced. I somehow wasn't expecting it, and the prospect of acknowledging her loss came upon me like an unexpected shock. Feeling suddenly and utterly alone in the crowded room, I did not so much read the requisite words as fall into an intensely private affective space. My loss was fresh and raw; this was the hole of traumatic loss and there was no relief in memorializing her. But unlike the acute and often prolonged period of grief that follows a death (or that which can be evoked within the analytic setting), here memory and grief are touched very briefly – for literally moments later, pulled along by the sound of turning pages and the awareness that I also wanted to say *Yizkor* for my father, I left my mother, moved away from the acuteness of a recent death and entered a quieter place, colored by softer affect, nostalgia and a flood of memories. My father is gone for nearly two decades. He missed the bar and bat mitzvahs, the weddings, he so longed to attend. He died before I could fully appreciate his brilliance or the intellectual exchanges we could have had.

Remote to my middle-aged self, my father suddenly became alive, filling empty memory spaces as I contemplated what might have been. All of this in less than 10 minutes!

My first experience saying *Yizkor* for both parents did not serve as a blueprint for future enactments of the ritual, however. That experience has shifted with time, mood, and other factors. At the risk of telescoping and to some degree flattening what has been a complex journey, I identify two dominant paths: reexperiencing and reworking of core affect states associated with loss, and rediscovering and reshaping emotional memory.

Some years ago on *Yom Kippur*, I found myself pulled into memories of my eldest son's wedding which had recently taken place at the country home my father built in the late 1930s, the place where I spent the summers of infancy and childhood. Evoking a visual memory of the wedding ceremony, I suddenly realized that we had been standing on the very patch of lawn where, as a very small child, I had watched my father clear the trees. For just a moment I could hear his voice, imagined him and my mother (also already deceased) dancing at their grandson's wedding. As I turned to the memorial prayer I always read for my maternal grandmother (the only grandparent I knew), my thoughts lingered over that space and I recalled a very worn black-and-white photo of her sitting in a lounge chair on that same lawn, holding me as an infant. I had forgotten about that chair, and for the first time contacted a body memory of its soft canvas warmed by the sun, an echo of my grandmother's warm arms around me. Her palpable joy in the photo became her joy at witnessing her great-grandson's wedding. A wistful sadness overtook me as I remembered the tenderness with which she held my eldest son in his earliest days.

Yizkor had opened and shifted memory space, allowing me to recapture the past and connect disparate events as a new emotional narrative coalesced – a personal story of my relationship to place and person. That narrative helped me link my grandmother to my father, my mother, me, and to my children, who barely knew her. And with that linkage (Loewald, 1976) came a sense of restoration, as if I had invited my grandmother into her great-grandson's wedding, back into my life. Absence was filled with presence, with a reconstructed image of old object ties. For a moment I undid all the separations that come with living and losing.

Perhaps because I am not ordinarily immersed in the past, *Yizkor* provides me an opportunity to go where I rarely do, to recontact memories and associated self states, to bridge the very distant past by imbuing it with aliveness. I want to emphasize how this new narrative facilitated the restoration and reworking of affect states within a protected, transitional memory space. This is a space that makes room for both connection and separateness, for merger and isolation (Winnicott, 1951). For we do not challenge the "reality" of our loved one's simultaneous absence and presence (Bassin, 2003) just as we do not challenge the actuality of the analytic relationship. During *Yizkor* I surrender to my parents' absence, and in that moment of surrender I re-create and reenliven our relationships. The trajectory of this new memory space is softer and more nostalgic, but it is no less imbued with emotional content. Now I mostly remember the youthful parents of my childhood and less their aging selves or the shock of their deaths. There is pain and loss in remembering, but there is also richness and a comforting sense of continuity.

From the interior toward the intersubjective

Mourning rituals like *shiva* provide a protected space within which to mourn. They limit the press of the other's subjectivity so that the mourner becomes – temporarily – the single subject in relational space. But after *shiva* we return to our lives and away from traumatic loss, reentering the arena of mutuality. This trajectory from object relating toward usage (Slochower, 1996; Winnicott, 1971) is reflected in the shift from rituals of mourning to commemorative acts like *Yizkor* that increasingly reflect an intersubjective element. Unlike the traditions of acute mourning, commemorative ritual does not privilege individual experience but instead creates a context for shared remembrance. It invites reflectivity while moving us into a complexly organized space that facilitates acts of mutual witnessing, for we stand together even as we remember our individual losses. In so doing we affirm our communal bond and relocate personal grief within a wider social context.

This shift, symbolized in the movement from *shiva* to *Yizkor*, is also embodied – indeed, enacted – *within Yizkor* itself. The service begins with a psalm read aloud, a collective call to remembrance that underscores the tension between the communal experience of loss and the utter isolation that death inevitably evokes. We are a community in temporary mourning, yet during this brief service we rarely make explicit contact or move to comfort one another. Alone and together, the service enacts both sides of this tension, moving between group and individual prayers. We silently read prayers for those we've lost, touching personal memories, joys, and pains, remembering our own dead. But only briefly, for moments later we explicitly turn to the collective, whether to read prayers for those who died in the holocaust or war, or (as in my synagogue) to say *Kaddish* in unison.[13] A prayer for the dead said for 11 months following a death and on its anniversary (*yahrzeit*), *Kaddish* can be recited only in a communal context.

Except at *Yizkor*, *individual mourners say Kaddish* only during the formal mourning period following a death or on the anniversary of that death. But during *Yizkor*, we are all mourners: We *all* say a prayer for *all* our dead. In so doing, we symbolically underscore the experience of shared loss and shared witnessing.

In some synagogues, *Yizkor* concludes with a psalm (Psalm 23: "The Lord is my shepherd") that is sung communally. It is less the text of this psalm than the music that is evocative; its haunting, familiar melody touches and opens affect, triggering and assuaging individual grief while creating a group context that contains and holds (Orfanos, 1997, 1999; Solomon, 1995). As we sing together, we co-create a group of like mourners who function for one another as holding objects, witnesses, and, of course, participants (Hagman, 1996, 2001). There are years when singing this psalm makes me weep; at other times I enter a space dominated by nostalgic remembering; at still other times I am a bit disconnected from myself and far more aware of those for whom *Yizkor* has triggered intense grief than of the losses in my own life. But whatever its particular shape, the act of communal singing creates a sense of linkage; my awareness is of being one in a temporary community of mourners, and that awareness holds me and holds us.

The inherent collision between holding on and letting go is embodied in memorial rituals like *Yizkor*. We begin by evoking (and thus re-creating) the lost object and reaffirming our lasting connection to it. Only moments later, though, we leave that object and turn to remembering another, symbolically reenacting and normalizing the death of the first. And then we return to the quotidian, to our "separate" life, freed perhaps to do so by virtue of our capacity to remember.

Memorials outside commemorative space

Acts of memorialization take many forms, some of which are lodged well outside ritual space. We speak of absent loved ones at weddings and other celebrations; we name our children after them; we dedicate objects large and small and give charity in their memory. Autobiographies and memoirs can represent another kind of explicit, though nonritualized attempt to revisit the past and, potentially, to honor lost loved ones.

Which brings me back to the consulting room. For there's almost always loss inherent in an analytic relationship. While these connections are as intimate as any in our lives, they ordinarily end artificially rather than with actual death. Certainly the process of termination helps us say goodbye, but once our goodbyes are said, neither analyst nor patient has easy ways of marking, no matter memorializing, their relationship. Do these endings, sometimes quite stark and final, require their own memorial acts? I wonder whether professional writing and speaking function (on a more procedural than conscious level) in part as symbolic acts of memorial. By writing about our patient (or analyst), we evoke and rework that relationship, and, to some extent, memorialize it. I illustrate this process with a clinical experience that cast a long shadow over my professional life.

It's been over 20 years since I've seen Robin, but she remains alive in my mind's eye, a good treatment that ended violently. Robin came to me in extraordinary distress, suicidal, almost self-less, palpably helpless. I can still see her tall frame, straight brown hair, and the Laura Ashley dresses that embodied the disavowed childlike self state she mostly inhabited. In this, one of the first analyses I did, Robin re-found her past and in that process contacted and reworked memories of neglect and abuse so excruciating that we sometimes cried together. She began to articulate desire, left a sadistic husband, found a kindly man for herself, connected with professional ambitions, began a good career, came alive. A great deal changed, but our work was far from over; Robin remained emotionally fragile, unable to experience anger, in some ways, still masochistically attached. And then, about 7 years into the treatment, a family member went into a precipitous decline and Robin went home to care for him until his death. We kept in touch by phone as she struggled with his loss, her mother's vulnerability, and the traumatic memories triggered by that homecoming.

And then, abruptly, everything changed. On our first session following this visit, Robin entered my office transformed, her face etched in a grimace of hate. Without sitting down, she coldly informed me that our work was over; I had been helpful to a point but that point had passed. She was unwilling to discuss what had happened, what I had done or not done, and abruptly left in the middle of the session. Shocked, angry, and hurt, I tried to get Robin to come back, to tell me what had happened. Eventually she did, but Robin remained furiously adamant, unwilling to talk about her experience with me, no matter return to treatment. Our connection destroyed, Robin vitiated memories of intimacy between us, rejected even the idea of expressing, mourning, or working through her disappointment and anger at me.

Without an apparent interpersonal trigger, Robin had ejected our mutual attachment. Her rageful negation of the work and our relationship felt shattering. Robin had changed in so many ways; how had this suddenly collapsed? Not inclined to blame her, I searched my memory for how I had failed. Could I have done more to access her anger? Could I have gotten her to work it through rather than leaving precipitously?

I wrote about this rupture in my last book (Slochower, 2006b), using it to illustrate the complex dynamics underlying joint idealizations and their vulnerability to rupture. But what I did not say, what I was not fully aware of, was that my essay was also a response to the destruction of relational memory. Unable to understand or talk through with Robin how I had failed and become toxic to her, I had been left in a state of solitary grief until I turned to my own words in an attempt to recapture the more complex dimensionality of our relationship. In so doing, I symbolically repaired a damaged treatment (and damaged analyst), re-found, revitalized memories of Robin, and facilitated a newly shaped therapeutic narrative that helped me make sense of the treatment, her leaving and my (partial) failure. Of course, that narrative also represented a communication to Robin, a symbolic attempt to restore a relationship interrupted.

Robin and I never met again, although I still think of her when I pass the block where she works, or used to work – for I don't know where she is or how she is. I have struggled to encompass the abrupt destruction of a rich relationship and used writing about Robin to move out of solitary grief into a memorial space that is private yet also has a communal element, one shared by the potential reader.

Memory, transience, and memorialization

As we write about our patients and our analysts, we enact the ritual of remembering; we retell the story of a lost relationship to ourselves and in the process we reconstruct and perhaps repair it. If we can and if we dare.

In his brief 1915 essay "On Transience," Freud described how the evanescent nature of beauty and love could block pleasure, linking that difficulty to a "revolt in their minds against mourning" (p. 306). Freud noted that the price to be paid for avoiding the pain of loss is, paradoxically, a diminution of pleasure. It is as if the person says, "I won't love what I can't have, what won't last forever. If I love I'll have to lose. So I won't."

Our phobic response to death has become, to some extent, culturally embedded. We avoid acts of commemorative ritual in order to let sleeping dogs (people) lie, to keep an emotional lid on distress. This dynamic emerges noisily in work around the theme of schizoid detachment but can infiltrate, even dominate, our response to traumatic loss. These losses (especially early losses) are not always remembered, no matter fully mourned, because dissociation shuts down affect and forecloses engagement with memory.

My great-grandfather's sudden death in 1929 was a trauma that the family could not encompass. My grandmother sent the children away for some weeks without saying a word about why; they only learned about their father's death from a neighbor's son. My mother was not allowed to attend her father's funeral, no one sat *shiva*; indeed, in an effort to get on with life, his name was never again mentioned. And so the family went on with a loss neither mourned nor communally remembered, carrying grief silently, suffering physically but never speaking of their psychic pains. There were no family stories about Grandpa Louis, no reminiscences.

When my maternal grandmother died many decades later, this avoidant dynamic resurfaced: My mother, terrified of entering the arena of loss, begged the rabbi to conduct the funeral without requiring that she go to the cemetery. Determined to remain upbeat and solid, she could not grieve and could not remember. And so, in my own life, I have carried the desire to remember for us both. Indeed, in writing the present paper I have enacted my own wish to honor the memory of my parents and grandmother.

For my mother's family, acts of memorial threatened to disrupt a fragile overlay that covered traumatic loss. But sometimes these acts have no emotional impact because they are dissociated from the losses they memorialize. Tamar regularly engages in memorial ritual to honor the memory of her orthodox mother who died suddenly when Tamar was 6. Tamar has few memories of her mother but does remember her engagement with Jewish observance. Tamar enacts this connection by saying *Yizkor*, carrying her mother with her in her own active Jewish identification. But although she feels compelled to say *Yizkor*, Tamar finds this experience neither enriching nor emotionally meaningful. She cannot use the memorial service to access remembrance, grief, or nostalgia and feels more inadequacy (about her failure to remember) than longing or loss during the service. For although Tamar is a vital young woman with an engaging sense of humor and plenty of warmth, trauma has so emptied memory space that there's nothing there with which to memorialize, and commemorative ritual feels prescribed and contentless rather than therapeutic. It remains to be seen whether, in time, Tamar will become able to access memories of this early loss and connect to them, within or outside ritual memorial spaces.

The inability/refusal to remember, to participate in acts of memorial, some-times emerges as part of a wider picture of emotional difficulty. Susan, now 68, has a history of early trauma and dislocation; she has struggled with dissociative symptoms all her life. Susan is phobic about illness and death and cannot sustain any emotional connection to her parents (long deceased). When her mother died (Susan was in her late 20s), Susan threw out everything belonging to her; her sister Bonnie saved everything. When, many years later, Susan's son married, she refused to permit her parents' names to be included on a ceremonial wedding booklet that named and memorialized three other sets of deceased grandparents (the bride's and her husband's). Bonnie's yearly reminder to Susan about their mother's *yahrzeit* is met with hostile indifference. "I don't need to light a *yahrzeit* candle," she irritably declares. Susan reacts to Bonnie's easy shift in and out of their shared history with a mix of derision and anxiety, mocking Bonnie's partici-pation in commemorative ritual, clearly made uneasy by it. Refusing to visit their parents' grave with Bonnie or even to talk about their parents, Susan maintains some degree of emotional equilibrium by sealing off memory space.

But this inability to engage in acts of commemoration also infiltrates the pres-ent. Susan's adult sons wonder about the complete absence of any family stories; they have grown up as a solitary generation. And even more problematic, Susan cannot be empathic when her friends are ill, cannot tolerate anxiety or loss even at a distance. She denies all evidence of illness; at times this has put family members in some danger. Thus, a small grandchild's acute injury was met with impenetrable denial: "She's fine, she doesn't need to go to the emergency room." For Susan, both death and vulnerability are unbearable and disorganizing; denial dominates her experience, bleaching her own life of a sense of connectedness and emotional richness. Susan's desperate effort to avoid affective flooding and disintegration shows itself in multiple ways that undermine the present in addition to cordoning off the past.

There is, of course, an obverse, equally problematic edge to this dynamic: addiction to loss and memorial ritual. When we remain absolutely embedded, "un-separated" from lost love objects, remembrance of things past interferes with our ability to embrace the present; this melancholic position is what stimulated the psychoanalytic emphasis on decathexis and working through. When Fran's father died some years ago, she was bereft; neither her husband nor children could offer her much comfort. Fran's grief and involvement with remembering her father felt understandable to the family for some time. But now, 5 years later, it is less so. Fran's friends and family helplessly watch as she continues to visit her father's grave weekly. She "camps out" there, talks to her father, reads books, unable to leave despite the pulls of everyday life. Both grief and nostalgic idealization remain frozen and overwhelming, blocking her reentry into her life and attachments; Fran's family cannot reach her and she cannot connect to them. She is unable to locate her loss in a transitional realm that would help her to move in and out of the experience of absence; Fran is as stuck in mourning as Susan is in denial.

It's unsurprising that so many flee from the kind of experience in which Fran is submerged. We need to believe in the future, to embrace hope, and history can feel like a counterweight to that sense of optimism. But at its best, memorial rituals allow us to access *both* the desire for connection and for separateness, creating a liminal space within which these experiences can be touched without permanently overpowering us.

Whatever their particular shape, the dynamics of deep attachments are layered and complex. Our personal memorial stories exist at some distance from "truth," representing a more cohesive, emotionally meaningful, and consistent vision of our love objects and our ongoing relationship to and separateness from them. Over time, we may continue to memorialize, but this process is not static; the emotional point of entrée for commemorative ritual is altered by new losses, a growing awareness of our mortality and our shifting dynamics. Since I began saying *Yizkor*, I've confronted my own aging, experienced other losses and other joys. I've become more able to imagine my way into my parents' responses to me and find it easier to identify with aspects of their own experience. Yet at the same time, my parents have become far more remote than in earlier years. I rarely think or speak about the world of my childhood; I have left that part of life, along with analysis, behind. But when a major family event takes place, when (as last year) I lost a dear friend, earlier losses reemerge, reminding me that I am at once connected to and separate from my parents. *Yizkor* offers me a fixed door through which to remember, to find what is lost but not forgotten. Unlike the transitional objects that are remembered but are no longer imbued with emotional meaning, we remain, for better and worse, deeply attached to those we lose even as we struggle (and sometimes long) to detach.

Our need for an illusion of separateness has led to a psychoanalytic idealization organized around renunciation and working through. It contradicts our need to shape and reshape a personal, historical narrative of our connections to lost loved ones. That narrative does more than counter the illusion of separateness or our need to sidestep the grief, pain, fear, guilt, or anger that death creates; it allows us to appropriate our own history and preserves the continuity of experience that coexists with a sense of ourselves apart from our losses (Levi-Strauss, 1985). As Bassin (2002) noted, acts of memorialization imbue the concrete with symbolic meaning (see also Grand, 2000). They invite us to confront our nonpathological concerns about the meaning of life and death, helping us face our losses and affirming their aliveness within us so that we can live more fully in the space created by death. It is time for us to reject once and for all the psychoanalytic idealization of renunciation and separation, to embrace our (conflicted) desire and capacity for connection.

I am grateful to Lew Aron, Steven Cooper, Sue Grand, Bethamie Horowitz, Margery Kalb, Rabbi Jeremy Kalmanofsky, David Kraemer, Barbara Pizer, my son Jesse Rodin, Beverly Schneider, Nancy Sinkoff, and Leora Trub for their thoughtful input, and Minyan M'at for providing a context in which memory is marked, held, and honored.

Dedication

In memory of my parents, Muriel Zimmerman and Harry Slochower, and my maternal grandmother, Belle Zimmerman.

Notes

1 Based on a presentation given at the 2009 annual conference of IARPP, Tel Aviv, Israel.
2 While memorial sites can usefully evoke loss, they can also block the process of remembering. Bassin (2002) and Volkan (2007) underscored how easily memorial edifices become "dead" monuments. The physical place closes off, rather than opening up, the past by doing the remembering for us.
3 The name of their organization, Rolling Thunder, Inc., refers to the thunderous bombing campaign against North Vietnam in which many of them participated.
4 The ride is also a political act, an attempt to draw attention to the plight of those missing in action or prisoners of war, a protest against marginalization.
5 And of course, for subgroups that are dis-identified with the mainstream, communal acts of remembrance are more likely to create a sense of alienation or bitterness than connectedness.
6 See Lamm (1988, 2004) for a thorough review of Jewish mourning ritual.
7 Despite the heavy emphasis on the mourner's need within the *shiva* context, Jewish tradition introduces the needs of the community into the mourning space in small ways. Indeed, there is an intrinsic tension between the mourner's need to mark her loss and the community's need to get on with life and to celebrate it, and aspects of that tension are embodied in the structure and calendar of *shiva*. Thus, there are times when community ritual collides with the mourner's need to mourn (e.g., Shabbat), and *shiva* is interrupted or even cancelled in deference to religious laws concerning the observance of these holidays. Here, the community's need to celebrate overrides the mourner's need to mourn.
8 The precise timing of death in relation to major holidays determines whether *shiva* is observed in a truncated fashion, or not at all.
9 B. Horowitz, Ph.D., personal communication (9/15/10). She analyzed the United Jewish Community's National Jewish Population Survey 2000–2001 data set.
10 On *Yom Kippur* and the festivals of Sukkot, Passover, and Shavuot. Attendance at *Yizkor* is especially common when the parents themselves were religious (Rabbi J. Kalmanofsky, personal communication [9/30/10]).
11 The oldest reference to this practice of "recalling souls" dates to R. Mordechai ben Hillel, *c.* 1240–1298 (D. Kraemer, personal communication [10/1/2010]). It's important to note that other rituals beside *Yizkor* commemorate the anniversary of a death (*yahrzeit*) in Jewish tradition. It is common, for example, to visit the graveside and light a special (*yahrzeit*) candle that burns for 25 hours. Some fast, study, or give to charity to mark this anniversary. Observant Jews say a memorial prayer (*El Moleh*) for the deceased on the preceding *Shabbat*. They may sponsor *kiddush* (a celebratory meal following services) or lead services. On the actual *yahrzeit*, the mourner recites *Kaddish* in synagogue. In some synagogues, the names of those observing *yahrzeit* are publicly announced and a memorial prayer is read aloud. And many name a baby after a deceased relative, thereby linking the dead to the living (in Sephardic communities, children are named after living relatives as well; this is considered to be a way of honoring them).
12 Part of this prayer includes a promise to "perform acts of charity and goodness" in the name of the deceased. That pledge honors the dead and, perhaps, represents a concrete attempt at expiation on the part of the mourner, a "giving back" to the lost object who is no longer there to receive love or remorse in symbolic form.

13 This tradition is a new one; the recitation of *Kaddish* is traditionally reserved for those in mourning or on the anniversary of the deceased's death.

References

Akhtar, S. & Smolan, A. (1998). Visiting the father's grave. *Psychoanalytic Quarterly*, 67: 474–483.

Aron, L. (2001). *A Meeting of Minds: Mutuality in Psychoanalysis*. Hillsdale, NJ: The Analytic Press.

Bassin, D. (2002). In memoriam: "Memorialization" and the working through of mourning *Paper presented at the Doris Bernstein Memorial Lecture, Institute for Psychoanalytic Training and Research, and the American Psychoanalytic Association Meeting*, New York, NY.

Bassin, D. (2003). A not-so-temporary occupation inside Ground Zero. *9/11: Trauma at home*, ed. Greenberg, J. Lincoln, NE: University of Nebraska Press. 195–203.

Bassin, D. Producer and Director. (2008). *Leave No Soldier*. [Motion picture documentary] ShrinkWrap Productions.

Becker, M. & Shalgi, B. (2005). Sameness, difference, play and fear in the I-you encounter. *Psychoanalytic Review*, 92: 747–757.

Benjamin, J. (1995). *Like Subjects, Love Objects*. New Haven, CT: Yale University Press.

Bergmann, M. S. (1985). Reflections on the psychological and social function of remembering the Holocaust. *Psychoanalytic Inquiry*, 5: 9–20.

Bergmann, M. S. (1988). On the fate of the intrapsychic image of the psychoanalyst after termination. *Psychoanalytic Study of the Child*, 43: 137–153.

Bergmann, M. S. (1997). Termination: The Achilles heel of psychoanalytic technique. *Psychoanalytic Psychology*, 14: 163–174.

Bernstein, J. W. (2000). Making a memorial place. *Psychoanalytic Dialogues*, 10: 347–370.

Bonovitz, C. (2007). Termination never ends: The inevitable incompleteness of psychoanalysis. *Contemporary Psychoanalysis*, 43: 229–246.

Buechler, S. (2000). Necessary and unnecessary losses: The analyst's mourning. *Contemporary Psychoanalysis*, 36: 77–90.

Freud, S. (1914). Remembering, repeating and working through. *Standard Edition* 12. 147–156.

Freud, S. (1915). On transience. *Standard Edition* 14. 305–307.

Freud, S. (1927). The future of an illusion. *Standard Edition* 21. 5–56.

Gaines, R. (1997). Detachment and continuity. *Contemporary Psychoanalysis*, 33: 549–570.

Grand, S. (2000). *The Reproduction of Evil*. Hillsdale, NJ: The Analytic Press.

Hagman, G. (1995). Death of a selfobject: Toward a self psychology of the mourning process. *The impact of new ideas: Progress in self psychology*, ed. Goldberg, A. Hillsdale, NJ: The Analytic Press. 189–205.

Hagman, G. (1996). The role of the other in mourning. *Psychoanalytic Quarterly*, 65: 327–352.

Hagman, G. (2001). Beyond decathexis: Towards a new psychoanalytic understanding and treatment of mourning. *Traumatic loss and the reconstruction of meaning*, ed. Neimeyer, R. Washington, DC: American Psychological Association. 13–32.

Halbwachs, M. (1992). *On Collective Memory*. Chicago, IL: University of Chicago Press.

Hoffman, I. Z. (1998). *Ritual and Spontaneity in the Psychoanalytic Process*. Hillsdale, NJ: The Analytic Press.

Homans, P. & Jonte-Pace, D. (2005). Tracking the emotion in the stone: An essay on psychoanalysis and architecture. *Annual of Psychoanalysis*, 33: 261–284.

Klass, D. (1988). *Parental Grief: Solace & Resolution*. New York, NY: Springer.

Lamm, M. (1988). *The Jewish Way in Death and Mourning*. New York, NY: Jonathan David.

Lamm, M. (2004). *Consolation*. Philadelphia, PA: Jewish Publication Society.

Levi-Strauss, C. (1985). *A View from Afar*. New York, NY: Basic Books.

Lobban, G. (2007). Reclaiming the relationship with the lost parent following parental death during adolescence. *On deaths and endings*, eds. Willock, B., Bohm, L. C. & Curtic, R. C. London: Routledge. 131–145.

Loewald, H. (1962). Internalization, separation, mourning and the superego. *Psychoanalytic Quarterly*, 31: 483–504.

Loewald, H. (1976). Perspectives on memory. *Papers on Psychoanalysis*. New Haven, CT: Yale University Press. 148–173.

Myers, D. (2007). Recalling zakhor: A quarter century's perspective. *The Jewish Quarterly Review*, 97: 487–490.

Orfanos, S. D. (1997). Mikis theodorakis: Music, culture, and the creative process. *Journal of Modern Hellenism*, 14: 17–37.

Orfanos, S. D. (1999). The creative boldness of Mikis Theodorakis. *Journal of Modern Hellenism*, 16: 27–39.

Ornstein, A. (2006). Memory, history, autobiography. *Contemporary Psychoanalysis*, 42: 657–669.

Ornstein, A. (2008). Artistic creativity and the healing process. *Psychoanalytic Inquiry*, 26: 386–406.

Pedder, J. R. (1988). Termination reconsidered. *International Journal of Psycho-Analysis*, 69: 495–505.

Rubin, S. (1985). The resolution of bereavement: A clinical focus on the relationship to the deceased. *Psychotherapy: Theory, Research, Training and Practice*, 22: 231–235.

Rubin, S. (2010). *Good Enough Endings*, ed. Salberg, J. New York, NY: Routledge.

Shabad, P. (2001). *Echoes of Mourning in Psychotherapy*. Northvale, NJ: Aronson.

Slochower, J. (1993). Mourning and the holding function of shiva. *Contemporary Psychoanalysis*, 29: 352–367.

Slochower, J. (1995). *The Therapeutic Function of Shiva Wrestling with the Angel*, ed. Reimer, J. New York, NY: Schocken.

Slochower, J. (1996). The holding function in mourning. *Holding and psychoanalysis: A relational perspective*. Hillsdale, NJ: The Analytic Press. 125–138.

Slochower, J. (2006a). Beyond the consulting room: Ritual, mourning and memory. *On deaths and endings*, ed. Curtis, R. New York, NY: Routledge. 84–99.

Slochower, J. (2006b). *Psychoanalytic Collisions*. Hillsdale, NJ: The Analytic Press.

Slochower, J. (2010). Jewish ritual through a psychoanalytic lens. *Answering a question with a question*, eds. Aron, L. & Henik, L. Brighton, MA: Academic Studies Press. 105–128.

Slochower, J. (2011). Unnecessary losses. *Paper presented at the 2010 Annual IARPP meeting*, San Francisco, CA.

Solomon, M. (1995). *Mozart*. New York, NY: Harper Collins.

Volkan, V. (2007). Individuals and societies as "perennial mourners" their linking objects and public memorials. *On deaths and endings*, eds. Willock, B., Bohm, L. & Curtis, R. New York, NY: Routledge. 42–59.

Winnicott, D. W. (1951). Transitional objects and transitional phenomenon. *Through pediatrics to psychoanalysis*. New York, NY: Basic Books. 229–242.

Winnicott, D. W. (1965). The capacity to be alone. *The maturational processes and the facilitating environment*. New York, NY: International Universities Press. 29–36. (Original work published 1958).

Winnicott, D. W. (1971). *Playing and Reality*. London: Tavistock.

Winnicott, D. W. (1989). The importance of the setting in meeting regression in psychoanalysis. *Psychoanalytic explorations*. Cambridge, MA: Harvard University Press. 96–102. (Original work published 1964).

Yerushalmi, Y. H. (1982). *Zakhor: Jewish History and Jewish Memory*. Washington, DC: University of Washington Press.

Zerubavel, Y. (1995). *Recovered Roots: Collective Memory and the Making of Israeli National Tradition*. Chicago, IL: University of Chicago Press.

Chapter 12

New mourning

A new psychoanalytic understanding and treatment of mourning

George Hagman

Editor's note: This is a revised version of a chapter I contributed to the volume Meaning Reconstruction and the Experience of Loss *which was edited by Robert Neimeyer and published by the American Psychological Association in 2001. The original title was 'Beyond Decathexis: Towards a New Psychoanalytic Understand and Treatment of Mourning' and was an overview of recent developments in the psychoanalytic literature at that point in time. I have updated it for this volume. In 2001 I did not as yet appreciate that a new model of mourning had in fact already been articulated in the analytic literature, and that the basic framework of the New Mourning Model was confirmed by researchers and clinicians outside of psychoanalysis. Hence we were no longer moving towards a new understanding; rather, we had begun to already live within it and use it in our work.*

This is an updated version of a paper published in 2001 by George Hagman as 'Beyond Decathexis: Towards a New Psychoanalytic Understanding and Treatment of Mourning' as a chapter in the volume Meaning Reconstruction and the Experience of Loss *edited by Robert Neimeyer, the American Psychological Association.*

As I noted in the preface, this volume contains a selection of papers which reflect the psychoanalytic contribution to the sea change that has occurred in our culture's view of bereavement and mourning. Given that psychoanalysis has played a central role in the development of modern mourning theory (Parkes, 1981; Jacobs, 1993; Rando, 1993), I believed a review of the current status of analytic thinking in this area was called for. This chapter will discuss recent developments in the psychoanalytic theory and treatment of bereavement, mourning and grief that are represented by the papers included in this volume. Because I was unable to include many important papers that have been published over the past 20 years I will extend my range in this chapter and reference a number of analysts not included in this volume, but who I believe have contributed to what I have come to call the New Mourning Model. I will begin with a brief overview of the standard psychoanalytic model of mourning, which was based primarily on Freud's early metapsychological theories, and more specifically, on his paper *Mourning and*

Melancholia of 1917. Following this, I will discuss the critiques made by myself and fellow contributors of the standard model as well as some proposals we have made for its revision. As we have seen, these critiques target the asocial, intrapsychic nature of the standard model and its failure to address the full complexity of mourning reactions. I will then elaborate the outline of the new psychoanalytic model of mourning that has emerged from the current debate. In closing, I will return to the case report by Dr. Rynearson to see the implications of the new model of mourning for clinical practice.

Literature review

For purpose of review, this section will examine the major writings that have contributed significantly to what has been referred to as the standard psychoanalytic model of mourning. (See Hagman, chapter 1, this volume for a more extended discussion of the origin and nature of the Standard Model.) First, I do not believe that the analytic mourning literature is homogenous and without valuable deviations from the norm. However, what seems to be the case is that there has been a model that has dominated psychoanalytic thinking and practice since Freud originally outlined the basic components of his mourning theory in 1917. We will be concerned with the origin and development of that standard model.

Freud's writings about mourning are few in number, as well as extremely brief, which is surprising when one considers the importance of the subject. They consist of several scattered references most of which are notes included in papers devoted to other subjects. Freud's most sustained discussion of mourning was in his 1917 paper *Mourning and Melancholia*. It was there that Freud first delineated the framework of what would become the standard model of mourning. However, that is not to say that Freud intended to promulgate a standard model. Erna Furman (1974) argued that Freud's only purpose might have been to set up a model situation to explore the dynamics of narcissism and melancholia. Furman claimed that it was misleading to assume that Freud intended to portray 'actual mourning processes in their full clinical complexity' (pp. 241–242). Nevertheless, analysts after Freud would grant truth status to Freud's speculations on mourning. Hence, the following quote became one of Freud's best-known and most influential writings:

> Now in what consists the work which mourning performs? The testing of reality, having shown that the loved object no longer exists, requires forthwith that the libido shall be withdrawn from its attachment to the object. Against this demand a struggle of course arises – it may be universally observed that man never willingly abandons a libido-position, not even when a substitute is already beckoning to him. . . . The normal outcome is that deference for reality gains the day, Nevertheless its behest cannot be at once obeyed. The task is carried through bit by bit, under great expense of time and cathectic energy, while all the time the existence of the lost object is continued in the

mind. Each single one of the memories and hopes which bound the libido to the object is brought up and hyper-cathected, and the detachment of the libido from it is accomplished. . . . When the work of mourning is completed the ego becomes free and uninhibited again.

(1917, pp. 244–245)

In this passage Freud describes a normal, even universal, intrapsychic process the main function of which is the incremental divestment of libido (decathexis) from memories of the lost object. It is by means of this painful process that psychological equilibrium is restored and motivation to love is renewed. With the successful completion of the work of mourning all ties to the lost object are relinquished and pre-morbid functioning restored.

In later writings, Freud continued to view mourning in terms of the economy of psychic energy. For example in his monograph *Inhibitions, Symptoms, and Anxiety* of 1926, he reconsidered an as yet unexplained characteristic of mourning – its extreme painfulness. His answer was basically a matter of hydraulics. He asserted that separation *should* be painful in view of 'the high and unsatisfiable cathexis of longing which is concentrated on the object by the bereaved person during reproduction of the situations in which he must undo the ties that bind him' (p. 172). In other words, energy (libido) that had been discharged through interactions with an object cannot be released because the object is gone. This energy, still pressing for satisfaction, builds up in the mind, resulting in emotional pain. Recovery, according to this view, follows the redirection of libido from the memory of the lost person to available survivors with whom discharge can occur (recathexis), thereby removing the cause of the pain and renewing opportunities for pleasure in life.

A later addition to the developing standard model was the role of identification with the lost object. Although not discussed in his 1917 paper, Freud made significant, but once again brief, comments in later works that would influence the writings of major psychoanalytic thinkers such as Karl Abraham and others (Klein, 1940; Fenichel, 1945). For example in *The Ego and the Id* (1923) Freud stated: 'It may be that this identification is the sole condition under which the Id can give up its objects'. Abraham would develop this idea further, commenting that the bereaved person affects 'a temporary introjection of the loved person. Its main purpose is to preserve the person's relation with the lost object' (Abraham, 1924, p. 435). This notion of identification following object loss would become a central component of object relations theory and the typology of ego defenses. However, despite its importance, identification with the lost object would play only a peripheral role in the developing standard model. Analysts continued to emphasize decathexis over continuity while identification was viewed as at best an indication of unresolved mourning, or at worst, a symptom of depression (Gaines, 1997).

Regarding the affective component of mourning, Helene Deutsch (1937) wrote a short paper that has had an enduring impact. Titled *Absence of Grief*, the paper

argued that the absence of the expression of the affect of grief was indicative and/
or predictive of psychopathological mourning. Deutsch stated:

> Every unresolved grief is given expression in some form or other . . . the
> process of mourning, as a reaction to the real loss of a loved person must be
> carried out to completion. As long as the early libidinal or aggressive attach-
> ment persists, the painful affect continued to flourish, and vice versa, the
> attachments are unresolved as long as the affective process of mourning has
> not been accomplished.
>
> (pp. 234–235)

Influenced by Deutsch's paper, analysts and non-analysts alike have come to
view the expression of grief as an essential component of successful mourning.
In fact the absence of grief-expression in a bereaved person became for many the
diagnostic hallmark of pathological mourning; and to this day, in order to be considered normal from the point of view of mourning theory, bereaved persons must
endure the additional stress of *having* to express sadness and grief. Many popular
forms of bereavement counseling, influenced by analytic thinking (Volkan, 1981),
prescribe that the therapist challenge bereaved patients' 'resistance' to mourning,
compelling them to express sadness, in the belief that the abreaction of suppressed
affect is at the core of successful treatment.

In 1961, there was another important addition to the standard model: the idea
that the mourning process, by then accepted as an indubitable reality, was a biologically based process characterized by specific, identifiable stages (Bowlby,
1961; Pollock, 1961; Parkes, 1981; Volkan, 1981). For years, the central concern
of bereavement theorists became the identification of the nature and quantity of
these stages. Once again this idea was enormously influential. With the advent of
Kubler Ross's work on death and dying, the idea that mourning unfolded in prede-
termined phases became accepted as nothing short of the truth. No one seemed to
raise a dissenting voice as the stage model began to dominate the Western cultural
perspective on bereavement.

Components of the standard model

There are a number of component assumptions that comprise the standard model,
which I would like to identify and discuss. These assumptions have been tremendously influential in psychoanalytic circles as well as modern Western perspectives on grief more generally. In fact several of these assumptions may appear so
familiar and basic to us that they are beyond question. Therefore, to contrast new
developments in psychoanalytic mourning theory we will start with a discussion
of the essential components of the traditional model of mourning.

1   There is an identifiable, normal psychological mourning process: Before
    Freud bereavement was understood as a commonplace experience, viewed

primarily in social/behavioral rather than psychological terms. Freud was the first to articulate a perspective on mourning as a private, interior psychological process having specific characteristics and dynamics. This is perhaps Freud's most significant contribution to bereavement studies: the intrapsychic process model of mourning.

2   The function of mourning is a conservative and restorative one, rather than transformative: Rather than leading towards change, the psychoanalytic model is a conservative process. Restoration of psychic equilibrium and the return to pre-morbid conditions are the goals of mourning. The notion of mourning as a creative and transformative process has been articulated by psychoanalyst George Pollock (1989), but without having had a major impact on the standard model.

3   Mourning is a private, intrapsychic process, rather than social and relational: The model of the mind, upon which the standard model was based, was of a closed psychological system with its own inherent tendencies towards organization and conflict. Freud's model was constructed to explain the economics of energy distribution within the mind. Some analysts have argued that the mourning process is part of the mind's biologically grounded adaptive responses, having developed over time to insure optimal survivability in the face of inevitable separations and losses (Pollock, 1989). This view of the mind as isolated and intrapsychic did not allow for the role of relationships and social factors in mourning (Hagman, chapter 6, this volume for a discussion of the role of the other in mourning). Other recent authors have given some consideration to the social environment as playing an essential role in supporting what had traditionally been seen as the private, individual work of mourning (Slochower, 1996, 2011, chapters 7 and 11, this volume).

4   The affect of grief arises spontaneously from within the individual, and denial or suppression of grief leads to pathological states: In classical psychoanalysis, affects were viewed as derivatives of the drives, possessing a powerful motivational role. Thus they were seen as arising from the depths of the person's unconscious, the most private and primitive part of the mind. As noted above, Helene Deutsch was the clearest proponent of this viewpoint (Deutsch, 1937). To Deutsch, grief was an internally arising force, which was undeniable, and the suppression of grief would lead to psychological illness. Thus in the standard model, grief has no communicative or relational function. Grief in the standard model is primarily a physical aspect of mourning, closer to a bodily function than to thought or language.

5   Mourning has normal, standardized characteristics, rather than being unique and personal: Freud's speculations lead almost ineluctably to the normalization of mourning in the stage models of Bowlby and Pollock. From that point on, mourning became increasingly regimented and standardized. Despite attempts by many stage-model theorists to argue for a flexible application of the model, in practice the more personal idiosyncratic reactions to loss became de-emphasized. According to the standard model, health and normalcy are determined by successful progression through a specific sequence of stages

within which the bereaved person was expected to complete certain tasks. Some recent authors (Walter, 1994; Neimeyer, 1998; Foote and Frank, 1999) have argued that these expectations have been granted an almost dogmatic status as the personal and different is viewed as resistance and/or pathology.

6   Mourning is painful and sad, rather than involving a range of affects: The standard model, following Freud, limits the consideration of affect to painful grieving and despondency. This has also led to the expectation that the expression of pain and grief is indicative of successful mourning. Other affects such as humor, pleasure, even joy are viewed as aberrations and/or resistances to normal mourning.

7   The central task of mourning is detachment (decathexis), rather than continuity: This is perhaps the central component of the standard model. The primary function of mourning is to relinquish one's attachment to the dead person. Even those who included identification as a component of the standard model saw identification as a strategy to give up the object, rather than maintain continuity in a meaningful, vital sense. Given this, a continuing passionate attachment to the dead is almost invariably viewed as pathological. To experience the dead as a living presence, with which one maintains a dialogue, would be viewed as maladaptive from the perspective of the standard model.

8   The vicissitudes of psychic energy is the basis of the standard psychoanalytic model; the meanings associated with the loss are not emphasized: The standard model stresses accommodation and the internal vicissitudes of psychic energy. The meanings of the mourning process are only important to the extent to which they assist or impede the work of mourning, but the notion of meaning does not in and of itself have a motivating function in the standard model.

9   The normal mourning process leads to a point of full resolution, rather than being open and evolving: Following Freud, the standard model postulates that normal mourning leads to resolution; after all, there must be a point at which all energy is withdrawn and reinvested. The attachment to the dead is given up; painful mourning remits and the bereaved person joyfully and productively invests themselves in new relationships. In addition, since normal mourning is viewed as having a typical and time-limited course, there is the additional expectation that the resolution of mourning occur within a certain time frame. For years this was reflected in the DSM criteria that indicated duration of mourning as diagnostic. Those persons who continue to be sad, or who continue to maintain a sense of relatedness to the dead, are viewed as suffering from unresolved mourning, or worse, pathologic grief.

Critiques of the standard model: Creating a new psychoanalytic mourning theory

Contemporary psychoanalysts, particularly those whose theory base is Object Relations, Self Psychology and Relational Psychoanalysis, have largely abandoned Freud's psychological model of instinctual energy and isolated, closed system mental functioning. There has been a growing acceptance that psychological life is fundamentally motivated towards and embedded in relationships and relationally based meaning (Mitchell, 1993). Analysts, once empiricists studying the universal principles of psychodynamics, now view themselves as interpreters (perhaps even co-authors) of complex and ambiguous organizations of meaning and personal narratives. This realization that psychological life is neither so private nor so predictable has led to a reconsideration of many long-held beliefs (Stolorow and Atwood, 1992). Recently, in keeping with this 'paradigm shift', a number of psychoanalytic writers have begun to question the standard model of mourning and some of its characteristics cited above (Shane and Shane, chapter 2; Hagman, chapters 1 and 3; Shelby, chapter 5; and Gaines, chapter 9, all this volume; and Kaplan, 1995; Shapiro, 1996). In the following review I will structure the discussion thematically, roughly following the components of the standard model discussed in the last section:

1   Freud's original depiction of mourning was not valid as a general model: The source of Freud's model of mourning, as delineated in *Mourning and Melancholia*, is unclear. Rhetorically, Freud delineated the 'normal' mourning process as a baseline for his discussion of the psychodynamics of melancholia. However, the emphatic quality of his writing is striking. The mourning process is 'universally observed'. There is a clear and unquestioning presentation of the work of mourning. Freud seems to believe that the description offered is proven and obvious. However, prior to the publication of *Mourning and Melancholia* there had never been a systematic study of mourning and little if any serious writing on the subject had been done. Mourning had not as yet become an object of medical or psychiatric study – this would not happen for another 30 years. Hence, it remains unclear on what empirical basis Freud founded his model of mourning. Furman's argument mentioned earlier, that Freud was not making an empirical assertion, seems weak when one considers the assertive language and tone of Freud's essay. This *is* how people mourn, he is obviously claiming.

In chapter 1 of this volume, 'Mourning: A Review and Reconsideration' (Hagman), I argue that Freud's model of mourning was based on views of mourning which were prevalent in Western society during his lifetime – specifically, that mourning is a state that is distinct and exceptional; that the bereaved is withdrawn and preoccupied with the lost person; that grief is extremely painful and that despondency is characteristic. I cite the historical analyses of Aries (1974, 1981) and Schor (1994), who both discuss the ostentatious and extreme behaviors of mourners during the nineteenth century in Europe. Aries calls this reaction 'hysterical mourning' and Schor refers to the 'deep mourning' characterized by ostentatious displays of prolonged grief. I claim that it appears that Freud's model, which became the basis for contemporary psychoanalytic mourning theory and has influenced virtually all other models as well as general social attitudes, may have been descriptive of a new type of dramatic and passionate mourning that developed in nineteenth-century Europe, thus limiting its usefulness as a general model of human bereavement. (The psychoanalyst Charles Brenner [1974] believed that Freud drew the wrong conclusion from his observations and mistook defensive reactions for normal mourning.)

2   Several contributors to this volume note that a model of isolated mourning does not recognize the important role of others in mourning (Shane and Shane, chapter 2, Shelby, chapter 5, and Hagman, chapter 6, all this volume): The standard model of mourning was developed within a theoretical paradigm that is currently under revision. The notion that the mind is a private, closed system that primarily functions to regulate its own inner world of energies and defenses is essentially defunct (Stolorow and Atwood, 1992; Mitchell, 1993). Modern psychoanalysis has recognized that human psychological life is profoundly relational. In addition, interest in the importance of meaningful self-experience within the context of relatedness to others has been driving psychoanalytic thinking towards how our psychological life is socially embedded. A central feature of virtually all of the recent critiques of the standard model is that the intrapsychic focus does not convey the role of other people and the social milieu in facilitating or impeding recovery from bereavement (see Shane and Shane, chapter 2, Shelby, chapter 5, and Hagman, chapters 6 and 8, all this volume).

3   We must look beyond decathexis and relinquishment to the central goal of continuity in mourning: In 'Detachment and continuity: The two tasks of mourning' (chapter 9, this volume), Robert Gaines states: 'Emphasis on the need to detach from the lost object has obscured another aspect of the work of mourning, which is to repair the disruption to the inner self-other relationship caused by the actual loss. . . . This is the task I call "creating continuity" (p. 549). Several of the new mourning theorists echo Gaines's critique. Baker (2001), Hagman (chapter 1, this volume), Kaplan (1995), and Shapiro (1996) each argue that the emphasis on relinquishment has so dominated the psychoanalytic perspective that normal processes of preservation and continuity have been neglected if not pathologized. Shapiro states: 'Grief is resolved through the creation of a loving, growing relationship with the dead that recognizes the new psychological or spiritual (rather than corporeal) dimensions of the relationship' (p. 552). John Baker (2001) concludes in his study of mourning and the transformation of object relationships that mourning involves 'not the breaking of an object tie, but the transformation of the attachment into a sustaining internal presence' (p. 55). A fundamental argument of the new psychoanalytic model of mourning is the need to preserve attachment to the lost person, and the importance of securing a sense of meaningful relationship, which transcends loss. Anton Kris (1992) points out that the painful process of alternation between wishing to hold onto the lost relationship and wishing to live on in the present and into the future cannot be resolved by choosing one or the other. Kaplan (1995) describes the

importance of the continuing dialogue with the dead. Gaines (chapter 9, this volume) stresses the work of 'creating continuity'. Shapiro (1994) underscores the social factors in preserving the object tie, and Hagman (chapters 1 and 8, this volume) and Kernberg (chapter 10, this volume) emphasize the transformation and internal restructuralization of the attachment to the deceased. Finally, Gilbert Rose (1999) stresses the importance of acknowledgement of loss in the context of continuity.

4   The psychic energy model is too concrete: Meaning and dialogue are at the heart of mourning. Robert Stolorow and his associates in their recent work have made powerful arguments against the classical psychoanalytic model of the 'isolated mind'. A central part of their critique is the notion that our standard metapsychology concretizes subjectivity, as if human experience could be reduced to things, which can then be described and studied. The standard model of mourning is such a concretization and to that extent it reduces meaningful human experience to a mechanistic process. The new psychoanalytic mourning theory stresses the view of mourning as a crisis of meaning (see Neimeyer's introduction to this volume where he discusses mourning as 'the attempt to reaffirm or reconstruct a world of meaning that has been challenged by loss'). In the chapter 'Self experience in mourning' (chapter 8, this volume), I describe how 'the network of cognitive-affective schemata (self-organizing fantasies) sustained by and within the selfobject tie is traumatized, broken down, reworked and gradually transformed to maintain the integrity of self-experience and restore self-cohesion and vitality'. Louise Kaplan approaches the problem more interpersonally; she states: 'The human experience of loss is about our ongoing and everlasting dialogue with the dead' (1995, p. 16). Mourning dialogue is the means by which human beings maintain the vital meaning of the lost relationship in psychological and social life. The new model views mourning as most importantly a crisis of meaning both on an intra-psychic level through the transformation of psychological structure as well as the maintenance of meaningful human connections in reality and fantasy (see Neimeyer, 'Introduction', where he discusses *imaginal dialogue* in which the bereaved person is encouraged to imagine a restored interaction with the deceased).

5   The classical view of pathological mourning does not capture the positive function of the attempt to preserve meaning in the face of disruption: The conceptualizations of pathological mourning associated with the standard model take several forms. Freud emphasized conflicts in the drives, specifically the vicissitudes of aggressive feelings towards the lost person and the redirection of aggression inwardly. Deutsch emphasized the denial of affect. Pollock and Bowlby sought to identify the specific phase of mourning in which the bereaved found them fixated. The most common way of viewing pathology given the predominance of the process (stage) model has been the notion of an inhibited or derailed mourning process. Refusal to give oneself over to the inevitable mourning process has been viewed as the single biggest cause of

pathological bereavements. Recently some have questioned this perspective that they see as inaccurate and perhaps harmful. With the growing recognition that mourning is intersubjective, meaningful and concerned with continuity of the tie with the deceased, our assessments of pathologic mourning must now consider, among many factors, the following: 1) whether there has been a failure of the social surround to assist with mourning (Hagman, chapter 3, this volume), 2) how the patient is attempting to maintain meaningful life-experience in the face of loss (all authors, this volume), and 3) how the patient is attempting to hold onto the tie to the deceased, thus preserving a threatened relationship (Hagman, chapter 8, Gaines, chapter 9, and Kernberg, chapter 10, all this volume).

6   The standard model's perspective on grief as private does not capture the complexity and fundamentally communicative function of grief affects: Freudian psychological theory held that affects, such as grief, could be explained as arising from the somatic abreaction of instinctual drives which are denied their normal avenues of discharge. In the case of bereavement, the absence of the object of love results in the experience of psychological pain and the eruption of despondent longings and grief. On the other hand, depression follows from the loss of an object of ambivalence, as aggression is turned inward taking the self as its object. Recent analytic models have revised this endogenously based model of grief, and affects in general, and replaced it with a view of affect as relational and intersubjective. Beginning in the 1960s, John Bowlby (1961, 1980) argued that the expression of grief was not simply a private response to loss but an effort on the part of the bereaved to reestablish connection with the lost object and/or obtain comfort from other survivors. More recently, analysts (Stolorow and Atwood, 1992) have stressed the importance of affect attunement and responsiveness in psychological development, the resolution of trauma, and the integrity of self-experience. As a consequence of this relational approach to affects, grief is viewed as communicative and meaningful, its primary function being the preservation and/or restoration of interpersonal connection. Clinically this means that the analyst's attunement to the bereaved's expression of grief and responsiveness to the need for comfort and protection is now viewed as of central importance to the facilitation of mourning (see Shane and Shane, chapter 2, and Shelby, chapter 5, both this volume).

7   The stage model of mourning does not recognize the complexity and uniqueness of each mourning experience: In chapter 1 I argue that normal mourning processes should be judged within a broad context that includes multiple variables and acceptable outcomes. Gaines (chapter 9, this volume) states explicitly that 'mourning is not something that can be finished' (p. 568). Once we move beyond decathexis, it becomes clear that there is no need to declare an expectable endpoint to mourning. From this new perspective a person may mourn for a lifetime. Most importantly, the new perspective links mourning with developmental stages and crises. An example is when a childhood loss is

revitalized in middle age, and when, during periods of new loss, old bereavements are revitalized. Rather than being resolved, the significance of a loss may be elaborated throughout life; most importantly it is the unconscious meanings which we attach to bereavement and the dynamic function of the internal relationship with the dead that account for the ongoing open-ended work of mourning (see Kernberg, chapter 10, this volume, for a discussion of the elaboration of mourning over time).

New mourning: A definition

Let me offer a definition of this new psychoanalytic model of mourning, or new mourning, as I have come to call it. Although I am wary of any definition which might lock us into some fixed notion of what is a protean and fundamentally personal experience, I think it is worthwhile attempting to bring together into a brief statement the changes proposed by recent analytic writers with the understanding that a definition should be held lightly and be open to change at a moment's notice when clinical reality demands it of us. In this spirit, I offer the following definition:

Mourning refers to a varied and diverse psychological response to the loss of an important other. Mourning involves the transformation or reconstruction of the meanings and affects associated with one's relationship to the lost person, the goal of which is to permit one's survival without the other while at the same time insuring a continuing experience of continuity despite loss (often involving a residual relationship with the deceased). The work of mourning is rarely done in isolation and commonly involves active engagement with fellow mourners and other survivors. Individual mourning processes are always culturally embedded and influenced by societal beliefs and rituals. An important aspect of mourning is the experience of disruption in self-organization due to the loss of the function of the relationship with the other in sustaining self-experience. Thus mourning involves a reorganization of the survivor's sense of self, and self-in-relation, as a key function of the process.

The treatment of pathological mourning

There are a number of implications for changes in clinical practice, which arise from the emerging psychoanalytic model of mourning. These changes are in striking contrast to the closed system, isolated, step-wise model of treatment that arises from the standard model. To my mind the following are just several aspects of this new clinical perspective:

1   Each person's response to bereavement is unique, and what is normal and what is pathological must be considered in the context of the patient's specific personality, relationship to the deceased and familial/cultural background.

Openness to psychological individuality and a willingness to explore the unique bereavement response of the patient are crucial.

2   What we call pathological responses may be unsuccessful strategies to maintain meaning and preserve the attachment to the lost object. Treatment does not require relinquishment but an exploration of the continuing value of the attachment for the survivor, and a consequent reconstruction of the meaning of that person in the context of the survivor's ongoing life.

3   Bereavement results in a crisis in the meanings by which a person's life is given structure and substance. Therefore, pathologic grief is meaningful, however disturbed and painful it appears.

4   Grief affects are not the external manifestations of private processes but efforts to communicate. Given this, pathologic mourning, traditionally viewed as regressive and asocial, must be assessed for its often hidden communicative motive. No matter how withdrawn into grief a person appears to be, they are struggling to maintain relatedness, whether to the internal representation of the dead or to the social surround.

5   Mourning is fundamentally an intersubjective process and many problems arising from bereavement are due to the failure of other survivors to engage with the bereaved in mourning together.

In concluding this chapter, I would like to illustrate the clinical implications of a new psychoanalytic model. To do this I would like to return to the paper by E. K. Rynearson, which I discussed in chapter 8, in which he illustrates how his work changed with a particular patient when he began to question some of the standard assumptions of traditional mourning theory. What I find valuable in this paper is the way in which a therapist who approaches his patient with openness and a willingness to jettison unhelpful and constricting assumptions can become better able to understand the underlying meanings and strengths of so-called pathological states. Unfortunately, space constraints will not allow a full summary of the paper, but I will present enough to illustrate some significant clinical points.

In 'Psychotherapy of Pathologic Grief: Revisions and Limitations', Rynearson (1987) described the treatment of a woman who suffered from a refractory, pathological bereavement subsequent to the death of her teenage son. He pointed out how every effort to encourage the final resolution of mourning failed. In spite of years of therapy and a generally good treatment relationship, the woman remained despondent and deeply attached to the memory of her dead son. The patient would even say how she found the treatment 'helpful enough', but 'it will never bring my son back', she would add despairingly. Despite all efforts, the patient remained determined to continue her vigil. 'I began to wonder aloud', Rynearson wrote, 'how her dying son might help in reviving our therapy'. He ' the patient to compose a letter from her son. He noted, 'It did not feel con- 'nnatural to seek some caring and strength from an internalized "pres- ` needed so much from us'. The patient composed a series of moving and beautiful letters as if from her son, an admiring and supportive tribute to her as a mother. In one of these she wrote:

Dear Mom and Dr. Rynearson:

I will try to help you. Mom you know I don't want you to stay so sad and hopeless and I don't think it's good for you to visit my grave so often. You've got to start living more for you and the family and start taking better care of yourself.

Don't give up on my mom, Dr. Rynearson, she's real stubborn and she won't give up, so don't you.

Rynearson concluded,

We now look to David (the son) as a part of her that is increasingly able to help us by becoming more alive and nurturant. David remains an obsession, but he also advises and guides as a mother would a child. I cannot say precisely what is changing in this dissociated, highly traumatized and tangled attachment, but my patient and I, and now David, are all working together.

(p. 497)

It is curious that Rynearson offers few comments regarding such a radical change in technique. He seems surprised by his changed vision and strategy. I would like to suggest that Rynearson's new approach is quite consistent with recent thinking in psychoanalysis and is a fine illustration of the technical changes that follow from the new model of mourning. From this perspective let me conclude with some comments regarding Rynearson's case report.

1   Rather than being simply a refusal to give up the attachment to the lost object, Rynearson looks for the positive function served by the continuing relationship. He recognizes that his active encouragement of relinquishment of her attachment to the son is at best ineffective, at worst traumatic. His sudden insight into the positive function of the attachment to the son allows him to become more empathic regarding the woman's experience and especially of the positive meaning associated with the relationship to David. While understanding the meaning of David is important to the treatment, in terms of technique, Rynearson's willingness to ask the question is even more crucial.

2   Mourning is viewed as varied and unique. Most of the treatment of the bereaved woman is based on assumptions derived from the standard model of mourning. The idea that the woman must be encouraged to engage in a normal process, which is expected to lead to relinquishment, is the basis of his clinical assessment and treatment strategy. The application of these standards essentially misses the point and may even be said to violate the woman's primary need for continuity. Once Rynearson is willing to accept

the woman on her own terms (i.e. as needing an ongoing relationship with her dead son in order to recover) and recognize and appreciate the uniqueness of her grief, he is able to join her from within rather than outside her subjective experience.

3   Rather than viewing the therapist as a catalyst of the mourning process, the therapist plays an active, even central role in facilitating mourning. At first, Rynearson takes a position external to his patient's experience. He acts upon her, challenging her to give up her lost son and 'go on with living'. The conceptualization of grief as an internal, private process driven by universal psychological principles leads to an approach to the bereaved which is characterized by estrangement and in the worst case intersubjective disjunction (Stolorow and Atwood, 1992).

4   The affects of mourning extend beyond grief and include positive affects such as joy and pride. The assumption that mourning is primarily a painful and sad experience is basic to the standard model derived from Freud. Rynearson also focuses at first on the woman's grief in terms of her distress and this results in a failure to elaborate and explore other affective features of her grief. Eventually, his openness to the woman's experience leads to the expression of tremendously important positive affects such as pride and even joy associated with her relationship with her dead son. From the perspective of the standard model these affects would have been viewed as defensive, if not pathological, but Rynearson eventually welcomes these feelings and, rather than discouraging her positive affects in deference to painful grieving, he welcomes their full expression and exploration.

5   The therapist is interested in the meaning of the relationship to the deceased. The standard model emphasis on relinquishment leads inevitably to a suspicion of the continuing meanings of the relationship to the deceased. In fact, one of the effects of the standard model has been a fear on the part of therapists that the exploration of the positive meaning of the relationship will get in the way of relinquishment. One of the most important aspects of Rynearson's revised approach is his final question about what it all means in terms of the woman's continuing internalized relationship with her son. He has moved beyond assumptions about mourning and has placed the question of meaning and the continuity of relatedness at the center of his clinical approach. But most importantly, he has included himself in the equation. It is no longer just a matter of what David means to the bereaved woman; it is what the meaning is of this new relationship configuration of which Rynearson is now a central part. Rynearson has moved into a clinical realm where meanings and subjectivities are no longer private and isolated, but social and intersubjectively based.

6   A key aspect of the experience of bereavement is the impact of the loss on the self-organization of the bereaved. Another of Rynearson's insights is the function that the relationship to David plays in the woman's self-experience.

David is part of her self, and it is the nature of the selfobject function of David that Rynearson begins to emphasize. In chapter 8, 'Self experience in mourning', I wrote the following about Rynearson's work with David's mother:

> He became aware of the 'function' of the selfobject (David), as he explored with the patient the positive, self-sustaining, self-repairing, and self-regulating nature of the woman's 'moribund' attachment to her son. Once he ceased to promote decathexis and began to explore the functions of the selfobject in the areas of affirmation, mirroring, and merger needs, he noted a change in the ambiance of the treatment and a revitalization of the treatment relationship.

In other words, it was Rynearson's recognition of the powerful role that the relationship to David played in his patient's self-experience which permitted the expanded exploration of the meanings of his patient's mourning. This leads to my next point:

7   In terms of technique, rather than confronting the patient's resistance to mourning, the therapist's empathy and support creates an opportunity for self-reorganization – the therapy being a holding environment. The standard model of mourning leads to a clinical approach, which can be coercive and unempathic. At worst, the frequent use of confrontation to challenge resistance and provoke mourning results in further trauma and defense, which may masquerade as improvement. New mourning emphasizes the importance of empathy and security. Slochower (chapter 7, this volume) showed us just how important the maintenance of a secure holding environment is to the mourning process. In her discussion of the holding function of the Jewish ritual of 'sitting shiva' she wrote, regarding her own grief experience:

> How did shiva help? It seems to me that shiva facilitates mourning by establishing an emotionally protective setting – one reminiscent of the analytic holding environment. In shiva the caller, like the analyst, brackets her subjectivity in order to provide a large emotional space for the mourner.
>
> (1996, p. 132)

In his brief but evocative case report, Rynearson showed us how he created a facilitative context for his patient's mourning in which she could securely engage with him in the exploration and elaboration of the continuing meaning of her relationship with her dead son. What the ultimate outcome of the treatment was I do not know. However, the case report shows how, whatever the outcome, it is clear that moving towards a more open and intersubjective approach can liberate both our patients and us from the restrictions and distortions of traditional models of grief.

References

ABRAHAM, K. (1924). A short history of the development of the libido. In *Selected Papers of Karl Abraham*. New York: Brunner Mazel.

ARIES, P. (1974). *Western Attitudes Towards Death*. Baltimore: John Hopkins University Press.

ARIES, P. (1981). *The Hour of Our Death*. New York: Alfred Knopf.

BAKER, J. E. (2001). Mourning and the transformation of object relationships: Evidence for the persistence of internal attachments. *Psychoanalytic Psychology*, Vol. 18: 55–73.

BOWLBY, J. (1961). The processes of mourning. *Int. J. Psychoanal.*, Vol. 42: 317–340.

BOWLBY, J. (1980). *Loss: Sadness and Depression (Attachment and Loss, Vol. 3)*. New York: Basic Books.

BRENNER, C. (1974). Some observations on depression, on nosology, on affects, and on mourning. *J. Geriatric Psych.*, Vol. 7: 6–20.

DEUTSCH, H. (1937). Absence of grief. *Psychoanal. Q.*, Vol. 6: 12–22.

FENICHEL, O. (1945). *The Psychoanalytic Theory of Neurosis*. New York: Norton.

FOOTE, C. and FRANK, A. (1999). Foucault and therapy: The disciplining of grief. In *Reading Foucault for Social Work*, (ed.) A. Chambon. New York: Columbia University Press.

FREUD, S. (1917). Mourning and melancholia. In *Standard Edition, Vol. 14*.

FREUD, S. (1923). The ego and the id. In *Standard Edition, Vol. 19*.

FREUD, S. (1926). Inhibition, symptom, and anxiety. In *Standard Edition, Vol. 20*.

FURMAN, E. (1974). *A Child's Parent Dies: Studies in Childhood Bereavement*. New Haven, CT: Yale University Press.

GAINES, R. (1997). Detachment and continuity: The two tasks of mourning. *Contemporary Psychoanalysis*. Vol. 33(4): 549–571.

JACOBS, S. (1993). *Pathologic Grief: Maladaptation to Loss*. Washington DC: American Psychiatric Press.

KAPLAN, L. (1995). *No Voice If Wholly Lost*. New York: Simon and Schuster.

KLEIN, M. (1940). Mourning and its relation to manic-depressive states. *Internal. J. Psycho-Anal.*, Vol. 21: 125–153.

KRIS, A. (1992). Interpretation and the method of free association. *Psychoanal. Inquiry*, Vol. 12: 208–224.

MITCHELL, S. (1993). *Hope and Dread in Psychoanalysis*. New York: Basic Books.

NEIMEYER, R. A. (1998). *Lessons of Loss: A Guide to Coping*. Raleigh, NC: McGraw Hill.

PARKES, C. (1981). *Bereavement: Studies of Grief in Adult Life*. Madison, CT: Int. U. Press.

POLLOCK, G. (1961). Mourning and adaptation. *Internal. J. Psycho-Anal.*, Vol. 42: 341–361.

POLLOCK, G. (1989). *The Mourning-Liberation Process*. Madison, CT: Int. U. Press.

RANDO, T. (1993). *Treatment of Complicated Mourning*. Chaplain, IL: Research Press.

ROSE, G. (1999). Discussion of Donna Bassin's paper 'Rituals/Memorials/Mourning'. Institute for Psychoanalytic Training and Research, New York.

RYNEARSON, E. K. (1987). Psychotherapy of pathologic grief: Revisions and limitations. *Psych. Clinics of N. America*, Vol. 10(3): 487–500.

SCHOR, E. (1994). *Bearing the Dead: The British Culture of Mourning from the Enlightenment to Victoria*. Princeton: Princeton University Press.

SHAPIRO, E. (1994). *Grief as a Family Process: A Developmental Approach to Clinical Practice*. New York: Guilford Press.

SHAPIRO, E. (1996). Grief in Freud's Life: Reconceptualizing bereavement in psychoanalytic theory. *Psychoanl. Psychology*, Vol. 13(4): 547–566.

SLOCHOWER, J. (1996). *Holding and Psychoanalysis*. Hillsdale, NJ: Analytic Press.

SLOCHOWER, J. (2011). Out of the analytic shadow: On the dynamics of commemorative ritual. *Psychoanalytic Dialogues*, Vol. 21(6): 676–690.

STOLOROW, R. and ATWOOD, G. (1992). *Contexts of Being: The Intersubjective Foundations of Psychological Life*. Hillsdale, NJ: Analytic Press.

VOLKAN, V. (1981). *Linking Objects and Linking Phenomena*. New York: International University Press.

WALTER, T. (1994). *The Revival of Death*. New York: Routledge.

Index